For Reference

Not to be taken from the

PIONEER AVIATORS OF THE WORLD

A Biographical Dictionary of the First Pilots of 100 Countries

HART MATTHEWS

McFarland & Company, Inc., Publishers

Jefferson, North Carolina, and London

The present work is a reprint of the illustrated casebound edition of Pioneer Aviators of the World, *first published in 2003 by McFarland.*

This book was conceived and supported by William J. Kealy

LIBRARY OF CONGRESS CATALOGUING-IN-PUBLICATION DATA

Matthews, Hart 1967–
Pioneer aviators of the world : a biographical dictionary
of the first pilots of 100 countries / Hart Matthews.
p.   cm.
Includes bibliographical references and index

ISBN 978-0-7864-3880-8
softcover : 50# alkaline paper ∞

1. Air pilots—Biography.   I. Title.
TL539.M3235 2008   629.13'092'2—dc21   2003003689

British Library cataloguing data are available

On the cover: Henry Farman in 1908 winning the Grand Prix d'Aviation
in France (Art Today); sky background ©2008 PhotoSpin

Manufactured in the United States of America

*McFarland & Company, Inc., Publishers
Box 611, Jefferson, North Carolina 28640
www.mcfarlandpub.com*

Acknowledgments

Credit for this book must go first and foremost to William J. Kealy, the president of Icarus International and a resident of Manhattan and the Outer Banks of North Carolina. In the course of planning an Icarus art show eight years ago, Bill Kealy found that this information had never been published, and he set out to remedy that. Through several researchers and a dozen or more translators, through archives in Washington, London and Paris, through setbacks and delays, he never lost sight of what he wanted to accomplish: a vast tribute to the invention of flight, to the brothers who accomplished it and the pioneer fliers who came after. Bill is a retired partner in Goldman Sachs & Co., a chartered financial analyst, a trustee of the Woods Hole Oceanographic Institution, a director of the North Carolina Aquarium Society, a director of the North Carolina Community Foundations, a member of the Board of Visitors of the North Carolina School of the Arts, a member of the Dean's Council at Harvard University's Kennedy School of Government, and an Adjunct Professor at the Columbia University Graduate School of Business.

I would like to thank all the scholars, librarians, diplomats and descendants around the world who helped document the lives of the first fliers. At the top of that list belongs the present and former staff of the National Air & Space Museum archives in Washington, D.C., including Dr. Tom Crouch, Dr. Dan Hagedorn, Dr. Peter Jakab, Melissa Keiser, Kate Igoe and countless others who answered questions, recommended sources and tracked down obscure documents when they would rather have been doing their own research. I would like to thank their counterparts at the Royal Air Force Museum in Hendon, and at the Musée de l'Air et de l'Espace at Le Bourget, Paris.

Research help also came from Drs. Russell Naughton and Keith Meggs at Monash University in Australia, Sergio Calderara in Rome, Tim Sandberg and Nick Floyer in Canada, Dr. Jan Sykora at the Letecké Muzeum Historického Ústavu ACR in Prague, Dr. Jitka Zamrzlova at the Narodni Technicki Muzeum in Prague, Henri Kaper and Thijs Postma in the Netherlands, the staff of the Grozdenski Dzjarzhavnyj Gistoryka-Arxealagichny Muzej in Belarus, the staff of the Azerbaijan History Museum in Baku, Dr. Bojidar Dimitrov of the Nacionalen Istoricecki Muzej in Sofia, Dr. Toivo Kitvel at the Tallin Technical University in Estonia, Germinal Sarasqueta of Panama, Les Brook of the U.K., Dr. Albano Fernandes at the Museo do Ar in Lisbon, Major

Farhad Nassirkhani of the Imperial Iranian Air Force Association, the staff of the Danish Embassy to the United States, Turkish Defense and Air Attaché to the United States Brigadier Salih Getinkaya, Venezuelan Air Attaché Lt. Col. Roberto Castro, Group Capt. S. Muzaffar Ali of the Pakistani Embassy to the United States, the staff of the Musée Royal de l'Armée et d'Histoire Militaire in Belgium, Buica Tiberiu in Bucharest and N. I. Kapustina of the Dnepropetrovsk Historical Museum in Ukraine.

Finally, I'd like to thank the many translators and research assistants who sifted through materials, put them in a useful form, and periodically dropped everything to help with an urgent piece of correspondence: Amy Chambless, MA, Ioanna Chatzidimitriou, MA, Dr. Kim Jastremski, Dr. Kathy Johnson, Dr. Hossein Navab, M.D., Jordan Schwarz, Emily Spencer, Thomas Spencer, MA, Marco G. Silva, MA, and Dr. Andreas Weber. Special thanks to our all-purpose Czech, Russian and all-things-Cyrillic translator, Anne Keown, MA, and to research assistant, proofreader and German translator Dr. Karin Breuer.

—Hart Matthews
April 2003

Table of Contents

Introduction

…I have not the smallest molecule of faith in aerial navigation other than ballooning.

Lord Kelvin, 1896[1]

At the turn of the 20th century, everyone knew that only a crackpot or a fool would try to fly a machine. If you had enough money for a gas-filled balloon, you could float around with the wind currents. But fly? Like a bird? Nonsense. Even the world's most respected intellects weren't immune to this prejudice, and government scientists with five-figure grants were just as likely to find themselves the subject of ridicule as the backyard inventors with no high school diplomas. When their experiments went well, the skepticism was thick as a humid summer day. When they failed, derision poured from the skies.

Into this atmosphere stepped two of the most practical-minded men in the history of invention. In 1899, a pair of backwater bicycle builders set out to construct a flying machine. Their neighbors in Dayton, Ohio, must have winked at each other. Neither of these mechanics had any college or formal scientific training. What made them any more qualified than the famous names who had failed, who had died, trying to fly machines? Yet the untrained brothers distinguished themselves, even from their degreed competition, by

rigorous, methodical experimentation and adherence to the basic principles of science. That fall, the elder brother developed the first practical mechanism for control in banking turns. After some preliminary gliding, they added a vertical rudder. The younger brother built one of the earliest wind tunnels and tested different air foils using bicycle spokes and bent hacksaw blades. With those results, they redefined the accepted coefficient of air pressure and built their own tables of lift and drag. They made more than a thousand test glides. They reinvented the propeller. Finally, the brothers designed and tooled their own engine when no manufacturer would make one light enough.

Little more than four years after beginning, at 10:35 A.M. on December 17, 1903, Orville Wright took their fledgling machine into the air against a twenty-knot wind for 12 seconds and 120 feet. By the end of the day, his older brother Wilbur had flown 852 feet and stayed in the air nearly a minute, covering, with the headwind, the equivalent of one half of a mile. These were the first manned, sustained heavier-than-air flights in the history of

1

the world, and the 1903 *Flyer* would develop over the next two years into the world's first practical airplane. The public, even the aeronautical community, would discount their claim for five years. When he heard that the Wrights had flown, a Dayton newspaper editor reportedly said, "Man will never fly, and if he does, he will not come from Dayton."

This book was conceived in anticipation of the 100th anniversary of the Wright brothers' success. Recognizing December 17, 1903, as the date of the world's first sustained flights, we in a sense consecrate the book to the achievements of Wilbur and Orville Wright, since no matter what sort of accolades we heap on other inventors, we reserve the hallowed "first" label for the Wright brothers. To do so, however, requires some definition, and it should be noted that despite the virtual hegemony the Wrights enjoy in the English-speaking world, other aviators are honored for first flight elsewhere.

What seems clear to most reasonable historians is that the Wrights were the first successful aviators, that is, that they piloted the first sustained heavier-than-air flights, and that the brothers later developed the world's first practical airplane. The preceding qualifiers should alert the reader to several things: First, that men had been flying lighter-than-air craft (balloons, airships, dirigibles) for some time; second, that the Wrights followed on the heels of a long line of inventors who flew models, glided, and even made manned, powered take-offs; third, that there is still much controversy over who "flew" first. Much of South America discounts the early Wright flights and honors the Brazilian Alberto Santos-Dumont, who flew the world's second successful plane in 1906. Some in France credit their countryman, Clement Ader, for covering 50 meters in his steam-powered machine, *Eole*, in 1890. According to the definition we'll apply to

flight, Ader achieved only a "hop," or an unsustained flight, though it was unquestionably the world's first-ever manned, heavier-than-air take-off from a level surface.

All of this is only meant to inform the American reader that there are other perspectives and plenty of interesting discussions on the subject if one is inclined to look further. Practically speaking, no one can strip the Wrights of their place in aviation history. Before anyone else could get off the ground for 100 meters, they had flown 24 miles. Before anyone else could make a safe turn in an airplane, they could bank corners, fly in heavy wind and carry a passenger. Theirs was not only the first fully controllable plane, it was the first airplane design that was able to improve its performance with further development.

Terminology

In choosing first pilots from various countries, we have used the elements mentioned above to define successful flight. A heavier-than-air machine must be capable of taking off from level ground carrying a pilot, who controls to some degree the ascent, descent and path of the machine. To be called "flight," it must be sustained past the point to which the machine's take-off momentum would normally carry it through the air. Obviously, different pioneer flying machines achieved differing degrees of control, and we have had to exercise some judgment in naming first fliers.

The term "hop" will be used, as it historically has, to mean a take-off or "flight" that was unsustained. Ader's early take-off has been labeled a hop, for example, because the pilot had no effective means of steering in the air and therefore no control over when or for how long the craft left the ground. The momentum it built up on the runway and the upward thrust of its wings carried *Eole* into the air, but once airborne, it began to lose speed and equilibrium until it slipped to the ground again. Conventional definition says that a flight must also be "controlled" and "free" (that is, not tethered). The term "sustained" will be adequate for our purposes, since it seems contradictory to say that a pilot "sustained" a flight if he had no control over the machine's direction or ability to compensate for air currents, or if his craft were tied to a pole, which in this case would do a large proportion of the sustaining. In the case of later fliers, many of whom would have been trying for a pilot's license, a qualifying flight must also be solo. Flights with an instructor, who could have intervened to help a floundering student, do not count.

Sir Charles Harvard Gibbs-Smith, English aviation historian. National Air and Space Museum, Smithsonian Institution (SI Neg. No. 2001-6613).

For the sake of consistency and because the words became interchangeable 70 years ago, flying machines will be called "airplanes" rather than "aeroplanes." Many authors have used both terms, or have used "aeroplane" to refer to early machines, since the modern American term, "airplane," didn't gain wide use until long after the pioneer years. "Aeroplane," coined in 1809 by the Father of Aviation, Sir George Cayley, originally referred to what we would now call a "wing," the planar surface that lifts the machine into the air. Although in Britain Cayley's is still the word used to describe the entire machine, a single term will suffice here.

During the pioneer years, flying machines were often modified daily, so that it became difficult to know where one model ended and the next began. To make matters worse, some inventors did not name their planes, or had them manufactured by several different companies with slightly different features, or called all models by one name. In the interest of remaining consistent with earlier histories, very early flying machines (pre–1910) will be called by those titles English historian Sir Charles H. Gibbs-Smith designated in his 1966 catalogue, *A Directory and Nomenclature of the First Aeroplanes, 1809 to 1909.* This will apply only to planes flown by a particular pilot in a biography of that pilot. Since this is not an overarching aviation history, other airplanes are mentioned in general terms. A "Wright *Flyer*" or a "Voisin biplane," for example, might be mentioned in a biography where those planes are merely noticed but not soloed first by the pilot in question. That said, the Gibbs-Smith designation "mod." (for a design that was "modified") will not be appended unless necessary to distinguish that plane from one already mentioned. After 1910 a number of standard types emerged, and designers began to keep better track of their different models.

Nationality

On the ever-changing political map of the world, it can be extraordinarily difficult to decide to which nationality a flier belongs. Based on political boundaries alone, a pilot born in the northern part of what is today Yugoslavia would have been classified Hungarian or Yugoslav or Serbian during various periods of the twentieth century. Besides birthplace, nationality is also defined, in different cultures, by factors like language, parentage and religion. To continue with the Balkan example, many in Serbia would say the first Serb pilot, regardless of place of birth, must also speak the language and worship in the Greek Orthodox tradition. A Catholic pilot would not qualify as a Serb aviator, even if he spoke Serbian and had been born there. An Orthodox pilot of Serbian descent, on the other hand, would qualify even if he were born in Croatia or Bosnia.

These are the arguments of ethnic nationalists, to be sure, but they illustrate the challenges involved. Political boundaries all over the world have shifted since the turn of the twentieth century. In the Balkans many smaller countries, based on ethnic and religious background, have sprung up where there were large, multicultural empires. Many ethnic groups, like the Native American Indian, the Oaxaca of Mexico or the Montenegrin of Yugoslavia, do not have their own recognized governments. For most of our pilots, birthplace will be the deciding factor. There will be

Blériot XI competing at the first Reims aviation week, the Grande Semaine d'Aviation de la Champagne, August, 1909. National Air and Space Museum, Smithsonian Institution (SI Neg. No. 80-15345).

exceptions, most often in the case of those born away from a country with which they obviously identified, but we will adhere as much as possible to a flier's place of birth within modern political boundaries and skirt the quagmire of ethnic identity.

We will not identify aviators by the political maps of 1900 or 1910 or 1915, partly because those were, as always, in flux and would complicate questions of first flight before and after whatever random date we chose for our world map. This book is designed so that modern readers, on the centennial of heavier-than-air flight, can easily identify their countrymen who first took to the air. Although the names of now-defunct empires will be listed in parentheses, pilots will be classified by the names of the countries that succeeded those empires.

First Aviators

This a history of first pilots. Like the Wrights, some of our fliers will also be inventors, innovators or scientists, but many others are noblemen, showmen, soldiers and wealthy businessmen. Most of the time, they are those who had the time and the money to pursue flying. This is precisely the situation that moved Sir Gibbs-Smith, England's foremost historian of aviation, to write on the fallacy of defining history by "firsts." Obviously, the citizen of a particular country who happens to fly first is not necessarily the one who contributes the most to the science or to that country's aviation history. What particularly galled Gibbs-Smith about the familiar litany of "first" inventors and pilots was the injustice that approach perpetrates on those whose greatest contributions were theoretical rather than practical. The Frenchman, Alphonse Pénaud, for example, never flew anything in the standard sense of piloting a craft. But with his models—his "child's toys," a contemporary may have sneered—Pénaud demonstrated in 1871 an elegant solution to fore-aft equilibrium in a flying machine. He also seems to have stumbled on the fact that narrower (high aspect-ratio) wings, relatively speaking, give more lift than deeper (low aspect-ratio) wings, an important discovery for the eventual achievement of heavier-than-air flight. Likewise, Sir George Cayley remains an obscure historical figure even though he was the first to realize, a hundred years before the Wrights, that human flight would require a set of fixed wings and a separate power plant rather than flapping wings.

However, this book is not a history of the technology or science of aviation. We do not attempt to recount the invention and development of the airplane, as done hundreds of times by Gibbs-Smith and others. This is, foremost, a history of people. Accordingly, our purpose is not to argue that these collected fliers deserve primary or exclusive recognition, but that in many cases they deserve to be known in addition to their more influential peers. We do not set out to define the greatest contributors but to examine a widely varied cross-section of humanity that felt the allure of flight and pursued it, whether at great financial and physical risk, or with relative ease.

AFGHANISTAN

Date: 1931
Location: Reading, England

Shah

Shah is the first Afghan name to appear, in mid–1931, in the Western aviation literature. No first name is given, no flight date, no age or birthplace. Just this in the English periodical *Flight*: "Mr. Shah ... is the first Afghan to obtain his "A" pilot's license in this country and did so at the Phillips and Powis School at Reading."[2]

Considering Britain's repeated attempts to colonize or control Afghanistan in the century prior to 1931, England would probably be low on the list of places an Afghan would seek his license. Accordingly, there may have been earlier Afghan fliers who obtained their training elsewhere. It appears that a party of soldiers traveled from Afghanistan to the Soviet Union almost a decade earlier for pilot training, but it is unclear whether they were Afghans or mercenaries, whether they earned their brevets or even whether they returned to Afghanistan.

Prior to 1920, flights in Afghanistan seem to have been made only by foreigners.

ALBANIA

Ali Husein

Ali Husein served in the Serbian air force in 1917, on the front at Salonika. We know only that he was the first non–Kosovar Albanian to fly, so he may not, in fact, be the first true Albanian pilot. This information comes from correspondence with a Serb historian, and we know nothing else of Husein's life.

ALGERIA (FRANCE)

Date: May 2, 1910
Location: Pau, France
Plane: Blériot XI monoplane

Lieutenant Paul Victor Acquaviva (1883–1944)

The world's first African pilot was the child of European colonials. Paul Acquaviva was born in Bône (now Annaba), near Tunisia, to parents of French descent. It should come as no surprise that early pilots from most of Africa, as well as from other undeveloped areas, turn out to be European colonials. By the First World War, every African country but one had been colonized to some extent by a European power. Some colonies had been around for centuries, some had been more recently acquired. But while colonial administrators, traders and missionaries were quick to export religion and market economics, they weren't so prompt to improve their new subjects' standards of living. Even 80 years after the colonization of Algeria, most native Africans continued to trade in livestock, produce, handmade goods and services. While barter can have certain advantages over currency, livestock and handmade goods were hardly sufficient to trade in technologies like aviation.

Although born in Algeria, Paul Acquaviva spent a good portion of his childhood on the French island of Corsica and, being a bright student, studied at the École Polytechnique in Paris. He served several years with the French army, which in 1910 sent the young lieutenant to the Blériot flying school at Pau. Acquaviva learned under Alfred Leblanc, a long-time collaborator of pioneer aviator and inventor Louis Blériot. Acquaviva earned French pilot's brevet No. 68 on the 2nd of May, 1910, flying a Blériot XI monoplane.

In two months' time, Acquaviva was winning competitions at a Normandy air meet in Caen and was also flying Henry Farman biplanes. He took part in very early military maneuvers in the Picardie region and experimented with aerial communications by wireless telegraph. The city of Paris awarded him a medaille d'or, apparently for his aerial exploits, though we have no exact details. Although he was obviously a gifted pilot, aviation histories offer little informa-

Lt. Paul Acquaviva, c. 1910, at the Blériot school in Pau, France. Technical Reports & Standards Unit, Library of Congress, L'Aérophile Collection.

ANGOLA (PORTUGAL)

Date: June 2, 1916
Location: Hendon, England

Major Óscar Monteiro Torres (1889–1917)

Óscar Monteiro Torres made such a name for himself in military flying school during World War I that within months the Allies' most successful ace recruited him for the famous Cigognes (Storks), the most storied of France's fighter squadrons. It was on the terrace of the Café de la Paix in Paris, where Monteiro Torres had stopped for a drink with Portu-guese aviator Norberto Guimarães, that he met the fighter pilot Georges Guynemer. Instructors at the fighter school in Pau were still talking about a student of Portuguese descent who they said had "beaucoup, beaucoup de cran!," meaning he would take on anything. Guynemer, not knowing what Monteiro Torres looked like, walked over from a nearby table to ask Captain Guimarães about this notorious pilot. Guimarães replied that he was in luck and introduced the two. They shook hands, and Guynemer invited Monteiro Torres to join the Cigognes.

One can hardly imagine a bigger compliment for a new fighter pilot. Georges Guynemer had been an ace and the darling of France for more than a year. He was unafraid of enemy gunners and in his search for kills was known to fly as many as five missions a day. In all, he would earn 53 confirmed kills and be wounded seven

tion about his life after 1910. According to several sources, he received a decoration from the Tsar of Bulgaria that same year at Mourmelon. The Bulgarian sovereign was reputedly the first head of state to fly, but we do not know whether the 27-year-old Lieutenant Acquaviva may have taken the Tsar for a passenger flight or given him lessons.

Acquaviva began flying many years before planes were used in battle. It seems logical he would have flown in World War I, but we have found no evidence that he did. We do know that he eventually became a provincial director of public works and that he ended his days in the Bas-Pyrenees, in Oloron, a year before the end of World War II.

times. The press called him the "Ace of aces." When Monteiro Torres met Guynemer at the Café de la Paix, it was already 1917, and within months both men would be dead.

Óscar Monteiro Torres was born to Portuguese parents in Luanda, Angola's capital city, on March 26, 1889. He set a straight course for glory in arms. Monteiro Torres went to military school at the age of 11 and straight from there to Portugal's Army Academy. He graduated in 1909 and served an uneventful six years before the unfolding European conflict convinced him that aviation was the path to military and public honors. When he made the decision to pursue aviation, Monteiro Torres said he felt he was acting in the chivalrous spirit of Camelot and the Knights of the Round Table.

At the time, however, Portugal had not entered World War I and had no active air wing. It took the young lieutenant nearly six months to get permission, with two of his friends from the cavalry, to attend the Royal Flying Corps school in Hendon, England. He finished his full military certification on June 2, 1916, and returned to Portugal to teach cadets at the army's new flying school. When Portugal entered the war on the Allied side, Monteiro Torres garnered an appointment to the Portuguese squadron that was to serve in France. But the unit had no planes, so he was allowed to join an English reconnaissance squadron instead. With No. 10 Squadron he flew missions northwest of Paris, near Rouen.

Sometime in 1917, the Portuguese squadron seems to have regrouped, and Monteiro Torres attended fighter-pilot school in Pau, France, where he earned his reputation as a gutsy flier. It's unclear exactly when he met Guynemer and joined the Cigognes, but his career as a fighter pilot wouldn't last long. One source claims the two met in November of 1917, but by then Guynemer had been

Major Óscar Montiero Torres, June 2, 1916. Royal Air Force Museum, Hendon London; Royal Aero Club of the United Kingdom certificates, Rac 3013.

dead for two months. Monteiro Torres would fly his last mission on November 19. He went on patrol that day with a captain of the Cigognes in northern France near Laon, only a few kilometers from the birthplace of international aviation, Reims. The Allies had been successful that year, and the front had moved steadily east from where Monteiro Torres had flown reconnaissance with the English squadron.

When the two-plane patrol reached altitude, they spotted a couple of German reconnaissance planes having shooting practice near Laon. What they didn't see were three more Fokker fighters in the air keeping an eye on their comrades. The French Spads broke up the target practice but quickly found themselves under fire from behind. Captain Lamy, a more experienced fighter pilot than Monteiro Torres, made an aerobatic maneuver that got him clear of the Germans and away toward French lines. Perhaps not seeing his pursuers or not noticing

they had killed before being killed themselves. Accordingly, the Germans buried Monteiro Torres in the Laon cemetery with full military honors. Nearly 13 years later, on June 22, 1930, a French squadron flew his remains to Portugal for a national funeral and reburial in Lisbon. Oscar Monteiro Torres received French and Portuguese crosses of war, was inducted into the Légion d'Honneur, and was promoted posthumously to major.

ANTIGUA & BARBUDA (GREAT BRITAIN)

Date: December 20, 1915
Location: Shoreham, England
Plane: Maurice Farman biplane

2nd Lieutenant Richard Malcolm Sisnett Shepherd (1895–?)

Richard Shepherd earned his British pilot's license at the military school in Shoreham, England, on December 20, 1915, at the age of twenty. At the time he served as a second lieutenant in the 4th Royal Irish Regiment. We have not been able to learn with which squadron he flew during the war, but happily his name is not listed in the postwar casualty rolls.

2nd Lt. Richard Malcolm Sisnett Shepherd, December 20, 1915. Royal Air Force Museum, Hendon, London, Royal Aero Club of the United Kingdom certificates, Rac 2208.

that Lamy had pulled out, Monteiro Torres dove over a grove of trees after the German observers. He downed both reconnaissance planes but in the process was hit by the pursuing Fokkers and went down behind enemy lines. Monteiro Torres died of his wounds the next day, November 20, 1917. It was his sixth wedding anniversary.

In a war in which technology put an end to chivalric notions of honor on the battlefield, the romantics of the various air corps went out of their way to preserve for as long as possible honor among combatants. As a rule, pilots received not only proper burials, but also military honors, many times from the comrades of aviators

ARGENTINA

Date: June 10, 1910
Location: Buenos Aires

Jorge Alejandro Newbery (1875–1914)

Few men have been as widely loved and idolized as the pioneer aviators of South America. Though most of the world accepts the Wright brothers as the first pilots of heavier-than-air craft, Latin America almost universally recognizes the first Brazilian, Alberto Santos-Dumont. And one of the most familiar names from early aviation is the first Peruvian flier, Jorge Chavez Dartnell, known as Georges Chavez, who despite his enduring fame flew for less than a year before his death.

Jorge Newbery has been so widely acclaimed in Argentina that it has become difficult to discern whether he did in fact fly before any other Argentine. He was a founding member of the Aero Club Argentino and its president for five years, had a strong hand in establishing a national aeronautics station and the country's first piloting school, repeatedly set Latin American records for ballooning, and beat the world record for altitude as a heavier-than-air pilot.

As with Santos-Dumont in Brazil or Chavez in Peru, it is simply without question that Newbery was foremost in Argentina. Whether he was the first to leave the ground is beside the point to his countrymen. We do know that Newbery received his license on the first day that Aero Club Argentino awarded licenses—June 10, 1910. We also know he started lessons shortly after his first passenger flight with Italian Alfredo Valleton three months earlier. On licensing day, Newbery apparently went to the field with a group of Aero Club friends to get their brevets all at once. We cannot determine who was first to fly that day, nor whether Newbery was the first of his compatriots to fly a plane before that day. He may well have been the first, and no one seems to make a first flight claim for the other fliers who got their licenses that day.

Jorge Newbery traced his lineage back four centuries to Renaissance France and England. His grandmother was said to have descended from France's King Charles VIII and England's 9th Baron of Lochmore. Jorge's father, Ralph Newbery, was born in New York City in 1848. As a young dentist, Ralph Newbery signed on for a trip around the world that left him stranded in Montevideo, Uruguay. He eventually settled a few miles to the west in Buenos Aires, and his first son, Jorge, was born May 29, 1875. Young Jorge occasionally spent time in New York City with his grandparents, and when it was time for college, traveled to the United States again to attend Cornell. He later transferred to Drexel Institute in Philadelphia, where he obtained his electrical engineering degree with honors in 1895. Newbery returned to Buenos Aires to take a supervisory position with a power company, La Compañía Luz y Tracción del Río de la Plata. Two years later, he went to work for the Argentine navy as Chief Electrical Inspector, in charge of purchasing electrical materials.

Newbery made his final career move in 1900 when he accepted a position as the Buenos Aires Director of Public Lighting. He split his time working for the city, teaching at the national industrial college and participating in his many sporting pursuits, among them boxing, fencing, wrestling, rowing, sailing and auto racing.

It was no surprise that such an active gentleman, having already won titles in boxing, crew, regatta and knife throwing, should take up ballooning as soon as a hot-air balloon made its appearance in Argentina. In fact, within a fortnight of Newbery's first ascent in his friend Aaron de Anchorena's new balloon, he had helped to found the Aero Club Argentino. The club was chartered on January 13, 1908, with Anchorena as president, Newbery as secretary. But that arrangement lasted only the first year, after which Newbery was elected president every year until his death.

From 1908 onward, the city's lighting director seems to have spent his sporting time almost exclusively in aeronautics. After the founding of the aero club, Newbery and his colleagues began working to establish Argentine aeronautics and began raising money for a national airfield. But a tragedy almost stopped the budding effort cold. On October 17, 1908, in the same balloon Anchorena had brought from Paris the year before, Jorge's brother, Eduardo Newbery, disappeared over the Atlantic ocean with his flying partner, Sergeant Eduardo Romero. The loss of the two young men shook the sporting community to its roots. Many abandoned aeronautics.

Although he had lost his brother, Jorge

Jorge Alejandro Newbery, right, at the Gordon Bennett Cup in Chicago, September, 1912. Technical Reports & Standards Unit, Library of Congress, L'Aérophile Collection.

Buenos Aires with a load of instruments and a notebook to study air currents at different altitudes. When he finally came down, 13 hours later, Newbery had crossed the whole of Uruguay and landed in the Brazilian town of Bague. He had covered 541 kilometers (336 mi.) and set the South American records for both distance and duration. The residents of Bague were apparently not used to strangers dropping out of the sky into their town square. The police escorted Newbery and his equipment to the station for questioning but released him when they determined no harm was intended.

Newbery studied the air currents well and became expert at taking his lighter-than-air craft exactly where he wanted them to go. A couple of years later, he wowed the Argentine military by taking off from Buenos Aires in a stiff east wind and, using different winds at different altitudes, landing at a parade ground north of town where exercises were under way. The Argentine sportsman set his last ballooning record in the summer of 1911 when he rose to 5,100 meters (16,732 feet), a South American record for altitude.

Newbery remained loyal to his new pursuit. He made personal visits to the members of the club, asking for their continued support, and, six months and one day later, he made the nation's first balloon ascent since the accident. Thus it was Newbery who was credited with increasing the aero club's membership and reviving the nation's interest in air travel after the crisis.

Later that year, in the southern summer of 1909, Newbery set his first continental record in ballooning. He had gone up from

Meanwhile, Newbery had already earned his pilot's license the year before on a Blériot monoplane. His aviation career was delayed a couple of years, however, until Newbery hit on a project large enough to distract him from ballooning. That project was an army school of aviation. In 1912, Newbery pitched the idea to the Argentine Minister of War.

He was told there weren't sufficient funds to buy the planes, so Newbery organized a fund drive with a film festival and a specially designed stamp. On June 19 of that year, he announced that the Aero Club had raised the money to donate a "flotilla" of planes to the military and found an aviation school. It was inaugurated September 8, 1912.

Newbery had long dreamed of flying over the Andes. He had puzzled for years over how to accomplish the flight in a balloon but had finally given up the balloon as an impractical means. Late in 1912, he turned his attention to heavier-than-air flight in the hopes that an airplane might get him over the spine of South America. Newbery began to fly regularly from the new army school. A French aviator had been hired as instructor, but Newbery and another Aero Club member took over the teaching after only three months. In his earliest flights that spring, Newbery began stretching his altitude mark, starting with a continental record of 2,323 meters (7,621 ft.) on October 16. Before long he had nearly doubled that height with a flight to 4,400 meters (14,435 ft.).

Newbery had planned his Andes crossing for the summer of 1913. He had purchased a new plane, the same model Morane-Saulnier in which Frenchman Roland Garros had set the world altitude record the previous spring. But an automobile mishap put Newbery's arm in a cast and postponed his big flight until favorable winds could be had the next summer. That winter, the restless pilot traveled to Europe, where he could consult with pilots and engineers and enjoy flying during the northern summer. He was disappointed with the machine he had ordered and hoped to improve its performance at altitude with a better propeller. The motor manufacturer, Le Rhône, also designed and built him a new engine that would run better at high altitudes. The trip from Mendoza, Argentina, to Santiago, Chile, would require Newbery to cross the pass at Las Cueva, 3,998 meters (13,117 ft.) high. Based on his study of the winds at the pass, Newbery felt he must be able to fly comfortably at 4,500 meters (14,764 ft.). A Chilean pilot made an attempt that year to cross the Andes in the other direction,

giving fits to the expectant Argentines, but his plane could not make the altitude.

In January 1914, Newbery returned to Argentina to prepare for the crossing. He installed the new Le Rhône engine and a new propeller. On February 5, quickly approaching the window of good weather during which he hoped to make his flight, the engine suffered a malfunction and required three days to repair. On the 10th, Newbery took the plane up for a test flight to 4,500 meters. The plane reached that altitude with such ease that he decided to try another 500 meters. The engine ran faster, but everything was otherwise well at the higher altitude. After he reached 5,500 meters (18,045 feet), Newbery began to feel the effects of altitude sickness. Since he had not expected to be flying so high, he had not carried his oxygen tank on this trip. He couldn't breathe, his ears buzzed, his hands became numb. The cold was unbearable. The front gas tank began leaking on Newbery's left foot, causing his toes to freeze. When he could take it no longer, Newbery shut off his engine and descended. The world altitude record, set a month and a half previous by Georges Legagneux, was 6,150 meters. According to his altimeter, Newbery had reached 6,225 meters (20,423 ft.). In order to set a new world mark, the old record had to be beaten by at least 150 meters. Newbery had stopped 75 meters short of an official world record.

After his successful altitude test, Newbery took his equipment west to Mendoza to prepare for his attempt at the Andes. By March 1, everything was in place, and Newbery had set his flight for later that week. He was preparing to return to Buenos Aires with fellow aviators Giminez Lastra and Teodoro Fels when a friend's daughter asked that he make a demonstration flight for her. Newbery initially turned her down, since his own plane was being taken down, but on the woman's insistence, he took Lastra up in Fels's plane for some quick aerobatics. He began having trouble with the plane almost immediately and had to abort three attempts to loop the machine. Newbery began descending to the airfield, when suddenly, at about 100 meters altitude, the plane took a sudden and inexplicable dive to the left. According to Lastra, who survived the crash, Newbery tried to straighten the machine and restart the engine, but they were already too close to the ground.

Jorge Newbery was killed on impact. His fame was such that his funeral in Buenos Aires was attended by 200,000 mourners.

ARMENIA
(RUSSIAN EMPIRE)

Date: September 6, 1912
Plane: Blériot monoplane

Y. Nazarian (1886–?)

The earliest mention of an Armenian pilot occurs in a 1914 list of licensed fliers. The *Aero-Manuel* mentions a Y. Nazarian, nationality Armenian, who earned French brevet number 1,014 on September 6, 1912, in a Blériot monoplane.[3] Although his license declares Nazarian's citizenship, it also mentions his birthplace: Toul, in the northeast of France. Nazarian represents Armenia here because our search has not turned up a pilot actually born in Armenia.

The next appearance of an "Armenian" pilot in the license rolls occurs in late 1920, a Yenovk Dickran Papzian. Papzian, however, was born in Turkey.

AUSTRALIA
(GREAT BRITAIN)

Date: October 7, 1910
Location: Mia Mia, Victoria
Plane: *Duigan I* biplane
Length of flight: 196 meters (637 ft.)

Captain John Robertson Duigan (1882–1951)

When John Duigan began his first aviation experiments with a large kite near Melbourne in 1908, there wasn't much competition to be the first to fly in Australia. As in most colonial outposts, there had been no motorized flights up to that time. Until late the next year, aviation would be confined, for the most part, to France and the United States. As 1910 approached, factory-built machines became available abroad, and aviators from Paris began to travel the world making exhibition flights. This heated up the Australian competition long before Duigan had a chance to finish his first airplane.

In an article he wrote for an English journal, the Victoria native described his first experiment of 1908 as "a large pair of wings with no balancing arrangements of any kind."[4] He went on to say that this kite took him less than a day to build and was not successful, in fact, that it ended its career in smoke, for it was "used to light the fire with." In 1909 Duigan moved on to a glider built from photographs of an early Wright machine. His father's "Spring Plains" farm in

Captain John Robertson Duigan, 1918. Duigan Family Archives.

Mia Mia had no hills steep enough to launch a glider, but Duigan was able to anchor the glider with a long roll of fencing wire and get it off the ground in a steady breeze. When the wind really scoured the Victorian plains, the glider was able to lift both Duigan and his brother, though the ride was jerky and hard to control.

That spring the Aerial League of Australia was founded to further the cause of national aviation. Its first task was to convince the government to lend its financial support to would-be Australian inventors. To that end, the dominion's military offered in September 1909 a £5,000 prize (roughly $450,000 today) for the first Australian-built airplane that could stay aloft for five hours, something no plane in the world could do at that time.

Whether or not the military prize was an inducement, or whether he was simply following the logical progression of flying machines from kite to glider to airplane, Duigan and his brother, Reginald, got to work that fall on their first motorized flying machine. The same remoteness that had kept their aeronautical competition to a minimum now worked against the timely construction of a new machine. Aircraft hardware was not easy to come by in Mia Mia, 130 dirt kilometers north of Melbourne. Duigan ordered a four-cylinder engine and a propeller and set about making the rest of a pusher biplane with materials he had at hand.

Although it was built from magazine descriptions and photos of a Henry Farman machine, Duigan's design most closely resembled a Curtiss plane.[5] It had an elevator located in front of the pilot, a single stabilizing tailplane with rudder, ailerons located between the wings, a fair bit of dihedral to its wingplanes, and bicycle wheels for landing gear. Duigan added a nice touch with two air-dampened shock absorbers on each wheel, a necessity when trying to take off or land on ungroomed Australian plains. Everything but the engine, the propeller, the wingcloth, "and part of the wheel gear," Duigan told *The Aero* proudly, was manufactured by himself.

While all this exacting work was going on, however, a couple of factory-built planes had made their way into Australia. The first was a Wright machine owned by Colin Defries, an Englishman allied with a Sydney theatre interest. Defries said he had learned to fly in France, and tickets went like hotcakes to a "Flying Fortnight" of exhibitions at the Victoria Park Racecourse in Sydney.[6] The fortnight was to begin December 4. It may well have been worth two and a half shillings to watch Defries that night as he tied his Wright *Flyer* to the back of an automobile and attempted to tow himself into the air. At that time, the Wright machines had no wheels, only landing skids, so spectators were treated to the sight of Defries sledding his way round the horse track, trying to gain enough speed to lift off. It's unclear what the pilot intended to do if he took off and then had to negotiate a corner while tethered to a speeding automobile. Defries had an immediate collision with a fence, repaired the damage, and tried two more times, but the towing and dragging damaged the machine's undercarriage, and Defries had to give up for the night.

He tried again on December 9, this time managing to get the *Flyer* off the ground before it was damaged and stay in the air for a straight tow of 105 meters. The crowd was so excited by this performance that Defries was off the hook for the evening, which was probably a relief for the pilot. By January it was in the English newspapers that he had been airborne for a mile. Defries's mechanic, a Melbourne garage owner named Ralph Banks, salvaged the *Flyer*. In March, Banks brought the machine to a mano-a-mano contest against none other than escapologist Harry Houdini, the first Hungarian pilot. Houdini had started flying the previous fall as a gimmick to promote his beer hall shows in France and Germany. The Aerial League of Australia had asked that he bring his Voisin biplane along with him on his Australian tour. The idea was to pit Houdini against all comers for the title of first to fly in Australia. Banks was, unfortunately, the only comer, and he knocked himself out of the running on the first day of the contest when a gust of wind turned his *Flyer* on its nose while taxiing.

John Duigan in the 1910 biplane at Spring Plains farm in Mia Mia, Victoria. The pilot is using the ailerons to make a strong lateral correction. Duigan Family Archives.

Houdini's mechanic refused to let him fly until the weather was perfect, which kept him on the ground for nearly three weeks. Meanwhile, near Adelaide, an Australian businessman named F. H. Jones had imported a *Blériot XI* from France. His own mechanic, Englishman Fred Custance, reportedly took off from his employer's land on March 17 in his first-ever flight attempt and flew three 1-mile loops around the property for five and a half minutes. If this sounds farfetched, that's because it probably is. The "witnesses" to the flight, Jones and some of his neighbors, supposedly watched the plane fly 4.8 kilometers at five A.M. In the dark, no less. The Blériot monoplane, along with the Wright biplanes, incidentally, was one of the most difficult planes to fly and would have been almost impossible for a beginner pilot to control in a straight line, much less in banking turns. When Custance tried for a

daylight flight, at 6:15 A.M., he jerked the machine up too hard, overcorrected, and plowed in nose-first. Had he learned nothing from his previous five kilometers of uninterrupted flying? Chances are the witnesses to the first flight listened to Custance taxi around the property for five minutes in the pre-dawn and testified to this "flight." Custance's fellow mechanic, Bill Wittber, had probably seen more flying time three days before when he caught a sudden wind gust and stayed in the air for 37 meters before he could force the machine safely back to earth. None of this prevented Houdini fretting over his record as Australia's first heavier-than-air pilot. On March 18, the day after Custance's attempt, Houdini succeeded in making a series of flights at Digger's Rest, not far from where Duigan was still assembling his airplane in Mia Mia. Houdini's longest flight was three and a half minutes and earned him the Aerial League trophy as the first conqueror of Australia's airspace. Concerned about newspaper reports from Adelaide, however, Houdini continued to fly for several days, eventually stretching his time to seven and a half minutes, and made public exhibitions at a racetrack in Sydney. Houdini's Aerial League trophy is inscribed "March 16, 1910," two days before his flights and, more importantly, one day before Custance's attempt. No one knows whether the Aerial League made the inscription or whether Houdini had it added later.

Despite all this activity by Englishmen and Hungarians, an Australian citizen still had not made it into the air, nor had an Australian airplane. It wouldn't be until July that John Duigan had finished hand-crafting his own flying machine. The engine had given him quite a bit of trouble until he installed a different carburetor, and the homemade wheel shocks needed a lot of adjustment. On July 16, 1910, Duigan made his first trials in a "rough ploughed paddock" on the Spring Plains farm.[7] The field was nearly 1,200 meters (¾ mi.) long, but only 91 meters wide, so there was no room for airborne turns. The ground made it difficult to reach the 40 kilometers per hour (25 m.p.h.) needed to lift off, as anyone who's ever ridden a bicycle across a cow pasture will understand. The machine was made of ash and red pine, wire from an old piano and steel bands normally used to bale wool. The rattling alone must have terrified the livestock. To make things even more interesting, Duigan's workshop was located across two streams and up a steep embankment. It took three men just to haul the airplane to its testing ground. Once everything was in place, however, the novice pilot found he could get into the air periodically for hops of 15 or 20 feet. At this point, Duigan contacted the government about the £5,000 Commonwealth Prize that had been offered the previous fall.

Concluding that the four-cylinder engine and propeller hadn't enough thrust to keep him in the air, Duigan began tweaking the machine for more power. He ordered a larger propeller with a greater pitch, he drilled out the engine's exhaust valves and

machined new piston rings. His belt-drive kept slipping, so he substituted a chain drive and promptly bent the propeller shaft. He rebuilt the landing wheels with heavier-gauge spokes, turned a new propeller shaft and built a cradle to support the shaft under stress. In September, he was ready to go again.

The first run was uphill (the "rough ploughed paddock" was also not flat), and though the machine had more acceleration, he couldn't do well enough uphill to get into the air. The downhill run was quite a bit more exciting. After about 40 meters and without any command from the pilot, the plane leapt off the ground at a steep angle and twisted hard to the left. Duigan was able to correct, but the machine had lost so much speed that it crushed a wheel and the leading edge of its left wing in its fall back to earth.

Duigan had the habits of an inventor. He worked methodically, slowly altering pieces of the machine he thought would make it more air worthy. After this last trial, he continued pushing the engine for more power, adding a water jacket for cooling and boring out the cylinders. He modified the plane's balance to keep it from taking off so suddenly and to correct for the torque of the propeller which had made the machine turn on its side so quickly. He replaced the between-wing flaps with bona fide ailerons, making the plane look more like the Farman it had been modeled after. In late September, Duigan stayed in the air for roughly 100 meters and landed without incident.

On October 7, 1910, in front of six witnesses, John Robertson Duigan made the first official heavier-than-air flight in an Australian-built machine, the first flight by an Australian citizen, when he covered 180 meters (591 ft.) at the Spring Plains farm. Duigan definitely flew like an inventor, also. He took his time mastering the new biplane, not pushing himself or his machine too hard. Six months later, he was in full control of his airplane and gave exhibition flights for reporters and crowds of racetrack spectators. The Australian government informed him that he had missed the deadline for the

Commonwealth Prize, but it agreed to a demonstration the next May. Duigan and his brother both flew on May 31 for the defense department, but the £5,000 prize was never awarded.

The next year Duigan returned to England, where he had spent his university days, to earn his official pilot's license and to work with British pioneer A. V. Roe. He came back to Melbourne in 1912 to live with his parents and build a new plane based on Roe's designs. He tested the Avro-type biplane on February 18, 1913, but some sort of wind sheer caught one wing and overturned the machine as it came in for a landing after several minutes of flying. At only 40 or 50 feet, the pilot's corrections weren't enough to save it. The new biplane landed upside down, crushing its upper wings, breaking the fuselage in half and bruising Duigan badly. Although brother Reginald repaired the machine, it was never flown again.

Duigan seems to have taken some time off after this last smash. Just over two years later, six months after the beginning of World War I, John Duigan married Kathleen Rebecca Corney at St. Paul's Church in Caulfield, Victoria, on February 22, 1915. He joined the Royal Australian Flying Corps as a Lieutenant the next year and shipped for England on October 25, 1916. What would become No. 3 Squadron, R.A.F.C., arrived at the South Carlton aerodrome near Lincoln in late December. Most of the next year was taken up with general military training, training on the Bristol R.E.8 reconnaissance plane, and attending the Artillery Observation Course at Brooklands. When the squadron was mobilized to France late in 1917, Duigan was promoted to Captain and commander of one of the squadron's three flights.

The next year would be an eventful one for Captain Duigan. No. 3 Squadron acted as a so-called "Army Cooperation Unit," which meant its pilots flew slower, two-seater planes, made reconnaissance and photo runs of enemy lines, and occasionally carried the mail or dropped bombs by hand. They were constantly harassed by the faster enemy fighter planes and didn't rotate off duty periodically like their fighter-pilot comrades. On April 21, 1918, one of the squadron's planes was harassed by the famous Baron von Richthofen at the head of a group of four German fighters. The Australian observer managed to fight off the Germans. The "Red Baron" disengaged and flew low over the Allied lines, where he was shot down. No. 3 Squadron recovered Richthofen's plane and buried his body with full military honors the next day.

Months earlier, before Duigan had even arrived at the squadron's aerodrome in Baileul, France, No. 3 had lost one of its three flight commanders in a wreck. The month after Richthofen was shot down, the Germans dug in and reconnaissance missions were stepped up. With the increased number of missions, there were many more aerial confrontations with the enemy. In May of 1918, German planes would bring down each of No. 3 squadron's flight commanders. Duigan would be the only flight commander to survive the month.

On May 9, 1917, Duigan led a group of three planes on reconnaissance. Although they picked up a fighter escort, he and his observer, Lt. A. S. Patterson, soon found themselves alone 5 miles inside enemy lines. They had just finished shooting pictures when Duigan spotted four enemy scouts bearing down on them. A burst of fire grazed Duigan's head, smashed the gun and left Patterson unconscious. Duigan dove to pick up speed and for 5 miles tried maneuver after maneuver to evade the chasing scouts. Not long after the observer was hit, Duigan took a bullet in the shoulder. Then another in the back. One shot hit his gas tank, failing to ignite the petrol but dousing the entire machine in flammable liquid. Duigan took another hit in the leg. "After what seemed like months," according to Duigan, they reached French lines and put the Bristol biplane down between shell holes.[8] One wing was burning, and his observer had been shot five times. The biplane had been hit so many times it could not be salvaged. The photographic plates had come through okay, and both pilot and observer recovered at a hospital in England.

Duigan was awarded the Military Cross for this flight and was back in the pilot's seat later that summer, when he and Patterson spotted a tremendous German gun that was being used from a railway car against the city of Amiens at a distance of 25 kilometers. The Australian infantry would later capture that gun, which had a barrel diameter of 28 centimeters. The barrel alone weighed 45 tons.

Hostilities ended November 11, 1918. In the absence of fighting, the indefatigable Aussies carried the mail. They wouldn't make it home until June 16, 1919, when their ship finally docked at Melbourne. John and Rebecca Duigan remained in the Melbourne area for nearly a decade, then moved to Yarrawonga, in northern Victoria, where Duigan started a motor engineering business that lasted 13 years until the beginning of World War II. In 1941, they moved back to Melbourne, where Duigan served with the Royal Australian Air Force Quality Control Branch until the end of the war. Duigan re-

tired to Ringwood, Victoria, where he died on June 6, 1951.

Nine years later, on the fiftieth anniversary of his first flights, a memorial pylon designed by Duigan's nephew was erected outside Mia Mia. In 1970 Victoria Museum completed the restoration of his first biplane, and the government issued a stamp commemorating his work.

AUSTRIA
(AUSTRIA-HUNGARY)

Date: January 15, 1908
Location: Issy-les-Moulineaux, France
Plane: *Vol-au-Vent*, tractor biplane
Length: 80 meters (262 ft.)

Alfred Ritter de Pischof
(1882–1922)

Until the spring of 1908, only Henry Farman had been able to log a flight of more

Alfred Ritter de Pischof in his 1908 biplane. Courtesy of the Library of Congress.

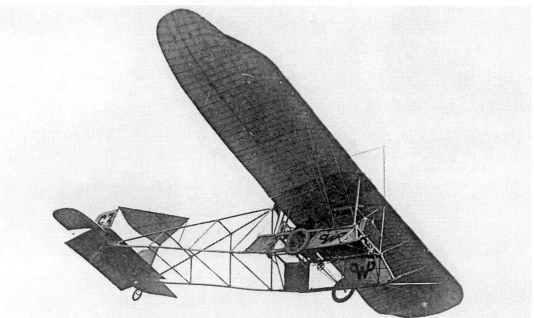

Top: Alfred Ritter de Pischof in the 1910 *Autoplan*, or *Vindobona I.* The clutch lever allowed the pilot to start and warm up the engine without engaging the propeller. Technical Reports & Standards Unit, Library of Congress, L'Aérophile Collection. *Bottom:* The 1910 *Autoplan* in flight. Courtesy of the Library of Congress.

than one minute in Europe. Despite the lack of air time, however, airplane design blossomed in the two years after Santos-Dumont made the first flight in Europe and before Wilbur Wright's visit to France in 1908.[9] Young inventors from all over Europe flocked to a military parade ground in the south–Paris suburb of Issy-les-Moulineaux, where they observed their peers and tried out their own ideas. The first to use the Issy field was Paris lawyer and aviation booster Ernest Archdeacon, who had towed an unmanned glider aloft with a motor car there in 1905. Romanian Trajan Vuia worked on his influential but unsuccessful monoplane at Issy throughout 1906. The field hit the headlines at the beginning of 1908 when Farman flew the first-ever circuit kilometer in Europe just two days before the first Austrian flew.

It may seem paradoxical to claim that aviation progressed during a time when the vast majority of working designs never left the ground at all. But the open-air laboratory of Issy-les-Moulineaux paved the way for Europe to take the lead in aviation once the Wrights had relinquished the key to lateral flight control. For some years still, aviation in North America would follow a single line leading from the original Wright *Flyer*: biplanes with elevators in front and rudders in rear, pusher propellers, and primitive skid or wheeled landing gear. At Issy there were monoplanes, triplanes, "tandems" with wings fore and aft, myriad different engines and propeller designs, "tractor" planes with propellers in front, full canards and modern cruciform tails, shock-absorbing and steerable landing gear, and innovative pilot-control systems. It wouldn't be an exaggeration to say that for a short time Issy-les-Moulineaux and the surrounding suburbs became the modern airplane's incubator.

Austrian Alfred Ritter de Pischof joined the Voisin brothers, Henry Farman and Louis Blériot at Issy in 1907 with a tractor biplane bearing an uncanny resemblance to machines that would evolve three years later. De Pischof was born in Vienna, the historical (and current) capital of Austria, but his parents were of Russian descent and took young

Alfred to Paris, where he grew up and attended school. Vienna was then one of the two capitals of the Habsburg Dual Monarchy, and in France, de Pischof would have been called "Hungarian."

Although almost none of the individual components of his first biplane, *Vol-au-Vent,* can be attributed to de Pischof, he seems to have picked the best aspects of numerous different machines: his cruciform tail assembly from a Chanute-Herring glider, the solid bicycle-wheel undercarriage from a Voisin, the tractor configuration of Sir George Cayley, the light and reliable Anzani 25-horsepower engine in a half-fan, or semi-radial, shape, and the most efficient propeller available in Europe, the laminated wood *Chauvière.* De Pischof was the first of his European contemporaries to move the elevator to the rear of a biplane and to use the *Chauvière,* which was a major technical breakthrough. In fact, de Pischof's entire plane was constructed in Lucien Chauvière's workshop in Paris. The de Pischof touch seems to have been the wings, in semi-biplane form, with the lower wing rather shorter than the upper, looking ahead to the first sesquiplane design of 1910. Although the Austrian aboard his plane at Issy looks to modern eyes like a Cossack riding a winged tricycle, it wasn't a huge step from that open-air, open-frame construction to an enclosed cockpit, the result being a plane not much different in appearance from the biplanes of World War I.

The *Vol-au-Vent* had less success in the air, however, than it had on later drawing tables. Some have credited de Pischof with flights in December of 1907, but evidence is scant and distances cannot be determined. Years later, one periodical even gave him an aerial kilometer in the biplane, which seems unlikely, since the only known kilometer flight in Europe had occurred barely a month before, and de Pischof would have had little or no experience at that early point. Had the Austrian flown a kilometer at Issy in 1907, it would have been headlines that evening. Most historians have instead called all take-offs in *Vol-au-Vent* "hops," opting to give de Pischof more recognition for his 1910 design, *Vindobona I*, a small, stable plane with an unquestionable record. But the Austrian covered 80 meters (260 feet) on January 15, 1908, and it had only been nine months since the 60-meter flight for which we give the Voisins credit. The standard will soon rise, but for now we recognize flights that a year later will seem like child's play. Later in 1908, de Pischof produced a tandem with his partner in design, a man named Jean Paul Koechlin, about whom details are scarce. Although the wing layout on that machine (two smaller wings following behind the first in the same horizontal plane) was highly suspect, the builders later removed the smaller wings and flew it 500 meters as a conventional monoplane.

During his work with Koechlin, de Pischof also collaborated on designs with Blériot and with the Short Brothers firm in England. Probably his biggest commercial success was the pusher monoplane dubbed *Vindobona I* or *Autoplan*, the first flying machine with a clutch. The engine could be started from the cockpit without having to spin the propeller by hand. Once everything was running smoothly, the propeller could be engaged by releasing the clutch. The design even looked a bit like an automobile with wings, but it fit with de Pischof's long emphasis on lightness and stability. For a low center of gravity, the 50-horsepower E.N.V. motor and the pilot hung underneath the wing, and through a trick of supporting shafts and bearings, the propeller was situated in the middle of the fuselage just behind the pilot. The whole apparatus was 9 meters long and 11 meters wide. In this plane de Pischof made the first flight around the famous island castle of Mont St. Michel in August of 1910.

Sometime in 1911, de Pischof sold the rights to *Autoplan* to the Werner-Fleischer firm and went to work as a technical director in the company's aviation subsidiary, Autoplan-Werke, headquartered in Vienna. He returned briefly to France, flew several air meets around Europe, and in 1912 moved to Kiev as the director of a new Russian airplane factory. There, de Pischof worked for several aviation firms, at some point pro-ducing machines for the Tsar's army, and served in the Russian military during World War I. After World War I, while the civil war still raged in Russia, de Pischof returned to France and produced his last airplane. The *Avionette* was an even smaller plane, and de Pischof dubbed it his "flying motorcycle." At 5.2 meters across and 3.5 meters long, it was less than half the size of *Autoplan* and weighed barely 102 kilograms (225 lbs.). *Avionette* could take off in a mere fifty meters with its tiny, 16-horsepower Clerget engine, not much more powerful than the motor on a 1903 Wright *Flyer*. The bi-plane, which did indeed have a motorcycle seat, could land and come to a stop in 25 meters.

On August 12, 1922, de Pischof was flying an *Avionette* near d'Orly, outside Paris, when he encountered turbulence. Even after the piloting advances of World War I, aviators still did not understand "air holes," as downdrafts were called. Air pockets of this sort posed a serious threat, especially to small planes. De Pischof's plane dipped so violently that it threw him from his seat at 1,500 feet and to his death. He was 40 years old at the time.

AZERBAIJAN (RUSSIAN EMPIRE)

Ali Samed ogly Verdiev (1891–?)

Ali Verdiev earned a French pilot's brevet just after the start of World War I. An Azeri mechanical engineer and airplane mechanic, Verdiev had been born in Elizavetpol, Azerbaijan, in 1891 and trained at the Zakavkazskaja teachers' seminar. Upon graduation he enrolled in the French Polytechnic Institute in Paris.

During the war, Verdiev served as a test-pilot and instructor, teaching Russian officers to fly French planes. After European hostilities and the Russian civil war had ended, Verdiev returned to Azerbaijan. He worked as a mechanic and served on a delegation that traveled to Lyons to purchase industrial spinning and weaving equipment for the state in 1923.

At some point, Verdiev went to work for the Azerbaijan planning commission. He stayed in this position through World War II and until his retirement in 1957.

BARBADOS (GREAT BRITAIN)

Date: January 29, 1916
Location: Shoreham, England
Plane: Maurice Farman biplane

2nd Lieutenant William Raymond Campbell da Costa

The first mention of a pilot from Barbados appears in the license rolls of World War I England. Second Lieutenant William Raymond Campbell da Costa earned license number 2,395 at the military flying school in Shoreham on January 29, 1916. He was flying a Maurice Farman biplane, probably the famous training machine known as the *Longhorn*, though that particular model was a few years past its prime in 1916. Da Costa is mentioned in a war office dispatch from early September of that year. He and another pilot from 22 Squadron "fired two drums [of ammunition] into the enemy's support line at Haines."[10] He doesn't appear in the British casualty rolls, so it is presumed he lived through the war.

Incidentally, the first exhibition flights on this Windward Island took place in 1912, but no one would fly into Barbados until 1929. The first locally-built plane made its maiden voyage on November 16, 1932. A man named Jack Skinner had spent nearly three years building the single-engine monoplane *Miss Barbados*. On that Tuesday another man named Noel Nicholls took *Miss Barbados* up for ten minutes, flying at about 90 meters (300 ft.), before he wrecked her on landing, tearing off the undercarriage and reducing the cockpit "to matchwood."[11] No one

2nd Lt. William Raymond Campbell da Costa, January 29, 1915. Royal Air Force Museum, Hendon, London; Royal Aero Club of the United Kingdom certificates, Rac 2395.

else would fly in Barbados until 1938 when a group of wealthy young enthusiasts imported a small plane from the United States.

BELARUS (RUSSIAN EMPIRE)

Date: 1915
Location: Gatchina, Russia

Captain Avenir Markovich Kostenchik (1889–1935)

The *Ilya Mouromets* was the giant of early aviation. The creation of 25-year-old

Voisin-Goupy 1908 triplane, very similar to the first machine flown by Baron Pierre de Caters. Courtesy of the Library of Congress.

Igor Ivanovich Sikorsky, in 1914 there was not another plane half its size. This 5-ton wonder had an enclosed cockpit and cabin that were furnished, heated and lighted. Other designers had ventured into dual engines, but only Sikorsky had put four engines on a flying machine. Critics said a plane of this size would weigh too much to take off and that the lopsided power would make it uncontrollable if one of the engines were lost. The critics turned out to be dead wrong. Not only did the larger wings give plenty of lift, but Sikorsky tested his behemoth successfully with only the two motors on one wing, thereby doubling the torque on one side of the plane. Because it could lose three of its 100–140 hp. motors and still fly, the *Ilya Mouromets* turned out to be much safer and more reliable than a single-engined plane. It shattered all records for range and cargo when, on February 12, 1914, it flew for five hours nonstop while carrying 16 passengers and a dog.

The same year that Sikorsky was born in Kiev (1889), Avenir Markovich Kostenchik was born in Grodno in the neighboring imperial Russian province of Belarus. Kosten-

chik's father, a middle-class businessman, wanted his son to be a priest. Avenir chose military school instead. Like Sikorsky, Kostenchik read about the exploits of Louis Blériot and the Wright brothers in 1908. While Sikorsky was trying to get his first design, a helicopter, into the air in 1910, Kostenchik graduated from the Vilenskij military school and joined the 33rd Infantry Eletskij regiment at Poltava. Unhappy in the infantry, Kostenchik applied for a transfer and was accepted into the military aviation school at Gatchina, near St. Petersburg, in 1914. He must have been a talented pilot, for when he graduated the next year, Kostenchik joined the Eskadra Vozdushnykh Korablei bomb wing and began flying the prize machine of the Russian army, the *Ilya Mouromets*.

By now, Sikorsky's airliner had grown even more powerful and been modified for military use. It sported two 200-h.p. and two 135-h.p. Canton-Unné radial engines, some of the largest available (and produced by our first Swedish flier). The *Ilya Mouromets* could carry half a ton of bombs, a crew of seven and fly at an average speed of 60–70 m.p.h. It was also equipped with anywhere from three to seven machine guns to keep enemy fighters at bay. At the peak of its activity, the Russian air corps had only a couple dozen of these aircraft. In the two and a half years the *Ilya Mouromets* was used for bombing raids into Germany and Lithuania, the squadron saw more than 400 runs and lost only two machines.

Kostenchik commanded one of these aircraft, and his story is indicative of the plane's hardiness. Loaded with twenty bombs, aircraft commander Kostenchik and his crew took off one morning to raid a German railway station that had been the target of bombing runs on several days previous. The Germans had fortified the area heavily the day before, and anti-aircraft fire hit Kostenchik's plane front and rear on his first pass over the target. Kostenchik was wounded but decided for another pass to drop the remaining seven bombs. Enemy fire damaged three engines on the second pass. The copilot had to take over when Kostenchik began to lose consciousness, but the machine and its crew made it back to base. Kostenchik survived the incident but was discharged from the service and never fully recovered his health. His aircraft had taken 64 hits.

Kostenchik retired to Stolbtsky, a small village in Belarus where his brother lived. Before the Bolshevik Revolution he was awarded the Order of St. George, and a monument was later erected on his grave in Stolbtsky. Captain Avenir Markovich Kostenchik died December 12, 1935, at the age of 46.

Belgium

Date: October 17, 1908
Location: Brecht, Belgium
Plane: *De Caters No. 1*, tractor triplane
Length of flight: 800 meters (2,625 ft.)

Baron Pierre de Caters
(1875–1944)

In August of 1908, Wilbur Wright stunned Europe when he demonstrated the third version of the *Flyer* at Hunaudières race track east of Paris. His tightly banked, graceful turns surprised a population used to watching planes with rudimentary steering as they crabbed and sideslipped around corners, taking hundreds of yards to perform a simple turn. Wilbur's flying dominated the news in Europe. By autumn, every western European nation felt she ought at least to have a man in the air, and wealthy young men like Baron Pierre de Caters began to heed the call.

De Caters, a prototypical gentlemen playboy, hailed from his ancestral castle of Catershof in 's-Gravenwezel, Belgium, near Brecht. He was 33 and had been racing cars for five years, competing in many early races against English first-flier Henry Farman. De Caters had become known as "King of the Corners" and had set two world speed records, the best at 152.542 kilometers per hour (94.8 m.p.h.) in 1904. He raced speedboats and had set several records on water, also. Having earned an engineering degree from the University of Liège, de Caters lived in the family castle, owned a tremendous amount of land and enjoyed a respectable income. The baron was one of a new breed of flier, a breed we should distinguish from the inventor-pilots who did most of the flying before 1909.

It may seem odd to delineate those who built planes from those who flew them, since today the lines between engineer, manufacturer and pilot are so clearly drawn. In the first five years of aviation, however, successful inventors became fliers out of necessity. They flew their own machines because no one else would, not for prizes or thrills or even because they enjoyed flying. The Wrights were cautious pilots, especially Wilbur, and rarely flew above a couple hundred feet. Of Farman's 13 records, only one was for altitude, at 25 meters (82 ft.) in 1908.[12] Frenchman Gabriel Voisin hardly ever flew. The wreck-prone French inventor, Louis Blériot, had he not stayed low and over safe landing zones, would probably have died long before he got a chance to make history with the first crossing of the English Channel. (He also crashed at the conclusion of his Channel flight.)

Baron Pierre de Caters in his Voisin biplane, April 24, 1910, at an air meet in Nice. Technical Reports & Standards Unit, Library of Congress, L'Aérophile Collection.

But if a wealthy young man wanted to fly in 1908, he no longer had to invent his own airplane. The Voisins, Farman or Blériot could build a plane to order or sell one of their own designs. Hence the rise of the sportsman pilot. After the Wrights' public exhibitions, de Caters traveled to a military parade ground in south Paris, Issy-les-Moulineaux, to acquire an airplane. If one were buying a plane in 1908, the logical place to go would have been Issy, and de Caters wasn't disappointed. He saw Blériot testing a monoplane, Léon Delagrange flying his Voisin biplane and Voisin himself testing triplane designs with a collaborator, Ambroise Goupy.[13] According to de Caters's grandson, who compiled an account for an aviation periodical 70 years later, Baron de Caters chose to purchase a triplane from Voisin because it was the only machine readily available. De Caters claimed to have provided the specifications for the plane himself (the machine is generally referred to as *De Caters No. I*), but

historians have pointed to broad similarities with the other Voisin triplanes of 1908 and questioned de Caters's part in the design. The grandson's account seems credible, since it doesn't make undue claims for the baron's design role and, furthermore, since the triplane wouldn't seem to have been the logical choice at Issy that fall. In fact, the Goupy and Voisin triplanes never got off the ground at Issy for anything but very short hops. Blériot was still working on the monoplane design and making short flights spiced with occasional crashes. Delagrange, on the other hand, had flown his Voisin biplane for nearly half an hour at a time, covering more than 20 kilometers. So it seems likely that, as Guy de Caters later wrote, his grandfather chose a triplane design because that's what could be delivered quickly.

In any case, Baron Pierre de Caters fitted the machine with a 50-horsepower Belgian automobile engine manufactured by Vivinus. Back in Brecht, he enlarged a

Baron Pierre de Caters in a Voisin biplane, probably at his estate near Brecht, c. 1909. Technical Reports & Standards Unit, Library of Congress, L'Aérophile Collection.

field on his estate for testing the triplane. Probably owing to his long experience with speeding vehicles on the edge of control, the novice pilot managed a flight of 800 meters (2,625 ft.) on October 17, probably the best performance ever measured by one of these triplanes. That machine didn't last long, however. De Caters said it handled like jelly, and he traveled to Paris again, this time to purchase a biplane like the one he had seen Delagrange flying. He had it fitted with a 100-horsepower Vivinus that weighed 165 kilograms (364 lbs.), and by early November, de Caters made his first short biplane flights.

With an eye toward the future, de Caters took the triplane to a show in Brussels in January and began negotiating with Belgian authorities to provide pilot training and planes for the military. He also spoke with Henry Farman about distributing *Far-man* planes in Belgium. In anticipation of future work with the military, de Caters enlarged the field at Catershof to eight times the size of the parade ground at Issy, a mile long and nearly a mile wide. But the Belgian military declined his offer that spring, and Henry Farman retained another distributor. Perhaps in an attempt to impress Belgian authorities, de Caters began flying more in public. His third Voisin plane arrived in May of 1909, and he signed a contract to make ten exhibition flights in Frankfurt in August. In July he took his plane to the Belgian shore to practice where he could better be seen. He visited Issy again and then shipped his planes to Frankfurt to fulfill his contract.

His scheduling was unfortunate. While in Germany, de Caters missed the single largest spectacle so far in aviation history, the first Grande Semaine de l'Aviation de la Champagne in Reims, France. Billed as the "first international air meet," the event attracted half a million spectators, half of whom showed up on the final day of the "flying week." The businessmen who made the initial 40,000-franc investment ($144,000 today) in the event saw a profit of twenty times that amount.[14] Despite several days of inclement weather, the twenty-two competitors left the ground a total of 100 times and flew a collective 2,462 kilometers. They broke every record Wilbur Wright had set during his visit the previous year, finally making room for Europe in the aviation record books. Henry Farman was the big winner and took home 60,000 francs ($216,000 today) in prize money. His altitude record of 1908, 25 meters (83 ft.) had been surpassed six-fold by the second-place finisher for the week, Englishman Hubert Latham. None of the pilots had been seriously injured, though Louis Blériot had crashed twice.

De Caters participated in a Berlin meet at the end of September, placing fourth overall after damaging a propeller and motor on the second day. But his name finally made the aviation marquee the next week at the Frankfurt meet, where he beat out Blériot for first place. Both placed in seven different events, but the baron made the meet's longest flight (1:17:25) and spent more overall time in the air. De Caters earned 47,500 German mark ($215,000 today) for this performance.

By the end of 1909, de Caters was one of only 16 pilots worldwide who had stayed in the air for more than an hour. He was awarded the first Belgian pilot's brevet. After his racing successes, de Caters packed up his plane and hit the exhibition circuit. He had

Clive Robert Hays Logan, January 18, 1916. Royal Air Force Museum, Hendon, London; Royal Aero Club of the United Kingdom certificates, Rac 2312.

already made the first flights in Belgium and the first passenger flights in Belgium and Germany. Now he logged first flights in Poland, Turkey, India and Egypt. His Egyptian flights were the first in all of Africa. In Johannisthal the next spring, de Caters again dominated the rolls, taking nine medals, including total time spent in the air. His persistence with the Belgian military paid off, and he began training two cadets in the summer of 1910. His first student, Lt. Montens d'Oosterwijck, gained brevet No. 19 on September 30. But a lack of politicking left de Caters out in the cold. The military signed a long-term contract with someone else, and the baron sold his airfield and workshop to the competing interest that eventually landed the Farman contract for Belgium and Holland. De Caters looked on while another company manufactured the planes he had wanted to build on land that had belonged to him.

Soured on aviation, de Caters returned to automobiles for a while before World War I. When Germany invaded Belgium, he enlisted and was assigned to a motor unit protecting a British Royal Naval Air Service squadron at Leopoldsburg. Early in the war, during the siege of Antwerp, a Belgian plane was forced to land behind enemy lines. Without the room to take off again, the pilot and his observer snuck back to the Belgian line on foot. A couple of days later, when it had been ascertained that the plane was still where they had left it, with a small detachment guarding it, de Caters dashed across the German lines with a couple of armed vehicles and recovered the valuable machine. The next spring, de Caters was asked to establish a flying school at Étampes, outside Paris. The baron began training students in June of 1915, but his love of planes had diminished, and his school suffered. A year later, he was reassigned to a post in Paris where he helped the Allies put together motor brigades for the Russian front.

After the war, Baron Pierre de Caters ceased all competitive sports and retired to Paris permanently, where he apparently lived by selling off his Catershof estate little by little. He died on March 25, 1944.

BELIZE

Date: January 18, 1916
Location: Catterick Bridge, England
Plane: Maurice Farman biplane

Clive Robert Hays Logan (1889–?)

Clive Logan was one of many colonials who traveled from their homes in far-flung corners of the world to fly for the British Empire during World War I. From his pilot's certificate, we know Logan was born February 10, 1889, in what was then British Honduras.

When he reported to flight school at Catterick Bridge, Logan began his lessons on a Maurice Farman biplane, a famously well-behaved machine and a favorite of flying schools. (Maurice Farman was the brother of our first English flier, the renowned Henry Farman.) Students learned to fly the Farman "Longhorn" by sitting close behind the instructor and threading their arms under his armpits and around his chest to reach the control stick. A second pair of pedals on the floor allowed the novice to feel the pilot's lateral adjustments.

Clive Logan earned license No. 2,312 on January 18, 1916, presumably as an officer in the Royal Flying Corps. This is all we know of his life. His name does not appear in British casualty lists, so he probably survived the war.

BOLIVIA

Date: October 1916
Location: Palomar Air Field, Buenos Aires

Captain José Alarcón
(?–1917)

José Alarcón had one of the shortest flying careers of any of our first pilots. Lithuanian Ernst Leman flew for a year and a half before his death. The Peruvian hero, Jorge Chavez Dartnell (Georges Chavez), flew for only eight months before he died crossing the Alps. The saddest story must be that of Norman de Beer of Zimbabwe, who died in an auto wreck at a British flying school only one month after earning his license, most likely before he'd had much chance to fly. The first Bolivian pilot outlasted de Beer by a mere two months.

The Bolivian government decided in 1916 to send three officers to pilot's school in Argentina. Along with his fellows, Second Lieutenant Horacio Vásquez and Captain Renato Parejas, Captain Alarcón made the trip in September to El Palomar, the air field

Alberto Santos-Dumont in the cockpit of a *Demoiselle* monoplane. Archive Photos.

established outside Buenos Aires by our first Argentine pilot, Jorge Newbery.

We don't know when, or if, Alarcón earned a brevet. His first flight was reportedly in October. He died on January 23, 1917, in a crash at El Palomar while flying a Farman trainer.

BRAZIL

Date: October 23, 1906
Location: Bagatelle Park, Paris
Length: 60 meters (197 ft.)
Plane: *14 bis*, canard pusher biplane

Alberto Santos-Dumont
(1873–1932)

The story of the world's second aviation success may seem anticlimactic, especially coming three years after the first. But Alberto Santos-Dumont's 1906 flights in Paris threw the world into a jubilant frenzy. Even then, very few people believed the Wright brothers had really flown, which is how the diminutive son of a Brazilian coffee-grower, already famous for his navigable hot-air balloons, became the world's first aviation hero.

"Le Petit Santos," as he was known in Paris, lifted off from the grounds of Bagatelle Park on October 23 in a canard biplane resembling a giant white goose and traveled an estimated 60 meters. (The judges were too excited to measure exactly.) Twenty days later, after several unsuccessful tries with new flaps installed between the wings, Santos flew the *14-bis* over the heads of his adoring French public for 222 meters (722 ft.). The crowd dragged him from the plane upon landing. Headlines around the world proclaimed his success. Even Santos and his fellow experimenters believed he was the first man in the world to fly. When confronted soon after with a newspaper editorial crediting the Wright brothers, Santos-Dumont summarized the European point of view: "There is absolutely no evidence to support

Alberto Santos-Dumont transporting a *Demoiselle* monoplane, c. 1908. National Air and Space Museum, Smithsonian Institution (SI Neg. No. 2001-6615).

the alleged statements of the Wright brothers. They may have flown, but there is nothing in any report of their proceedings that inspires confidence."[15] Even American newspapers that had already published accounts of the Wrights credited the famous Santos in 1906 with the "first important demonstration" of flight.[16]

Alberto Santos-Dumont grew up on his family's coffee plantation in Cabangu, Brazil, the youngest of seven children. He followed the exploits of Jules Verne's aeronauts and amused the other plantation children with his stubborn insistence that man could fly. His friends would later report that, during games of "Pigeon Flies," whenever the leader said "Man flies!," Alberto was the only player to point skyward in affirmation, invariably causing a ruckus and breaking up the game. He showed a streak of engineer early, and spent much of his time on and around the small locomotive that transported the plantation's coffee beans and supplies.

In the spring of 1891, not long before his 18th birthday, Alberto traveled to Paris for the first time. His father, Henriques, then 59, had suffered a severe concussion in a horseback accident, an injury he hoped European doctors might be able to treat. Spending time with his youngest son during the long Atlantic crossing, the elder Santos noticed Alberto's aptitude for mechanics, and he arranged for his son to return to France later to study engineering. Before leaving Brazil, Henriques had sold the plantation, and when he divided the proceeds between his wife and children, the roughly one-tenth share that went to Alberto left him independently wealthy. (Although the defunct Brazilian contos are difficult to translate to dollars, Alberto received about $571,000, or $11 million today.)[17]

Santos-Dumont distinguished himself quickly in the industrial and cultural center of the Western world. Foiled by an intransigent balloonist in his first attempt at a

Alberto Santos-Dumont in *Demoiselle No. 20*, flying from St. Cyr to Buc, France, c. 1909. Technical Reports & Standards Unit, Library of Congress, L'Aérophile Collection.

lighter-than-air flight, Santos eventually devoted himself to building his own airships so he could fly whenever he liked. He embraced the aeronautical lifestyle, being always careful to keep his weight at 50 kilograms (110 lbs.), and dining at a raised table with chairs taller than barstools. By 1899, Santos had become well-known in France for his navigable balloon, *No. 1*, which used an internal combustion engine and an "air screw" to direct its flight. *No. 1* held 180 cubic meters (6,357 cubic ft.) of gas, at a cost of a franc per cubic meter every time it was filled. Like the rest of his "dirigibles," the soft gas bag was stabilized by a rigid frame, or keel, underneath and a series of connecting tubes and straps. In 1901, Santos-Dumont piloted airship *No. 6* around the Eiffel Tower and back to its starting place at the former royal palace of Saint-Cloud, a trip of 11 kilometers (6.9 mi.) in 30 minutes, to win the coveted Deutsch de la Meurthe prize of 100,000 francs (nearly $400,000 today). Santos split

this massive sum between his loyal builders and the Paris poor, boosting his already well-recognized public image.

The extent of Santos-Dumont's fame at the turn of the twentieth century has been compared to that of Charles Lindbergh 30 years later. A notorious dandy, Santos had a corner table at the most fashionable restaurant in Paris, Maxim's, and called on the European nobility living in the city. He was seen coming and going from his balcony in a tiny dirigible. The stiff, jaw-brushing collars he made popular were called "Santos-Dumonts." Certainly a factor in his fame was Santos's absolute unflappability. During the course of his experiments, he had numerous mishaps, and several literally landed him in uncomfortable spots. His calmness while hanging from, say, the side of a hotel, inspired his rescuers to rise above the dangers or potential embarrassments of the situation.

Santos had particular troubles with air-

Alberto Santos-Dumont in the *14-bis*, autumn of 1906. National Air and Space Museum, Smithsonian Institution (SI Neg. No. 75-7730).

ship *No. 5*, with which he made his first attempts at the Deutsch prize. When *No. 5* crashed into a chestnut tree in the Rothschild's private garden, Santos directed the Rothschild's servants from a branch of the tree as they untangled the explosive hydrogen-filled balloon. The former Imperial Princess Regent of Brazil, Comtesse d'Eu, who happened to live next door, had a picnic lunch sent up the tree on a ladder. The same airship met its demise in the light well of the Trocadero Hotel. Santos saved himself a nasty fall by wedging the keel of his machine against a balcony at one end and an inside corner of the hotel at the other, all while hanging from his belt 40 feet in the air. These are only his two most spectacular mishaps, but none of the accidents seemed to frighten or embarrass the popular Brazilian. So powerful was his yearning for celebrity that, despite his deep aversion to violence, Santos put airship *No. 9* on display at the 1903 Grand Review of the French army and offered his services in case of war. This move garnered him much attention, and in

his book, *Dans l'Air,* published the next year, he speculated on the dirigible's potential military applications, a decision that may have haunted him when aircraft of all sorts became weapons of indiscriminate destruction during and after World War I.

In 1905 Santos-Dumont met Gabriel Voisin, a middle-class builder and test pilot of other people's designs, and became intrigued by the heavier-than-air problem. Santos had already experimented secretly and unsuccessfully with a monoplane, his project *No. 11*. His name had become so linked with airships that his colleagues were shocked when he entered two aviation contests sponsored by the Aéro-Club de France, two contests that he would eventually win with his 1906 flights at Bagatelle. In the fall of 1905, Santos-Dumont began working with Voisin on what would become project number *14-bis*, so-called because Santos tested the plane's controls by "flying" it while suspended from dirigible *No. 14*. The plane could not muster enough speed, tethered to an airship, for its wings to generate lift or for its control surfaces to have any effect on the airstream. Santos also tested the machine's controls while hanging from a guy wire. A mule provided the locomotion. These episodes were probably the closest Santos came to looking ridiculous in the press, and they show how little he actually understood heavier-than-air flight. These testing methods, and the plane itself, remain unique in aviation history.

Although the canard design was not uncommon at the time, the body of *No. 14-bis* was longer than most, accounting for its goose-in-flight look. The sectioned biplane wings, based loosely on the boxkite designs of Australian pioneer Lawrence Hargrave, canted noticeably upward from the body (known as "dihedral") to add lateral stability. In addition to the pair of hand-wheels that operated the elevator and rudder, Santos-Dumont used a chest harness to control the between-wing flaps he had installed before the November flight. The pilot had to steer by spinning hand wheels and leaning side-to-side, and it has been said that only the brave Brazilian could, or would, have flown such a craft. Credit for the plane's outward design probably lies more with Voisin, who had already been flying gliders and working on boxkite wings for some time. The handwheel controls, on the other hand, were similar to those Santos used in his airships. After the fiascoes with airship *No. 14* and the mule, however, Voisin was careful not to associate himself with that plane. An observer of the 1906 flights might have said it was the vast amount of cloth that got *14-bis* off the ground, but credit probably goes instead to one of the most powerful engines available at the time—the eight-cylinder fuel-injected Antoinette that gave 50 horsepower. After November 12, *14-bis* flew only one more time, a hop of fifty meters the next April.

The wildly successful Wright demonstrations in 1908 startled Europe and sent Santos-Dumont into a funk that would last until the success of his final plane, *No. 20* or *Demoiselle*, in 1909. Several designs intervened in the three years between *14-bis* and *No. 20*, but none were very successful, and none as noteworthy as the *Demoiselle*

("young lady" in French). This last design made beautifully efficient use of every strut and cable and was one of the most graceful designs of the pre-war years. This tiny dragonfly had a wingspan of about 5 meters and weighed 143 kilograms (315 lbs.). Even Santos-Dumont had to squeeze into the pilot's seat. The design is remarkably similar to the ultralight planes that wouldn't become popular for several decades.

Always concerned for those less fortunate than himself, Santos-Dumont wanted his work to remain available to the public. He never patented his designs. He dreamed of a day when everyone would be able to build *Demoiselles* in their back yards and enjoy traveling the air as he did. And while the technology and its cost outstripped his dream, it was a great point of pride for the inventor that no one ever died piloting a *Demoiselle*. Indeed, Santos tested all of his designs, and no one died piloting any Santos-Dumont machine.

The happy story of Alberto Santos-Dumont ends here, at the age of 36, though the tale continues into darkness for more than twenty years. The celebrity aviator retired unexpectedly in 1910. At the time it was given out that he had suffered a nervous breakdown, but at least one historian believes that was the year he was initially diagnosed with multiple sclerosis.[18] His sudden loss of coordination must have troubled the man used to piloting a barely steerable airplane or working on a stalled airship motor a thousand feet above the ground. As his condition deteriorated over the decades, Santos watched air machines evolve into instruments of destruction. He felt himself responsible for the death of every person who fell victim to a bomb or a strafing airplane. He was dealt a hard blow in 1927 when, during festivities marking the anniversary of his first flights, a number of Brazilian intellectuals were killed in an airplane crash while Santos looked on. On the 23rd of July, 1932, while warplanes attacked a ship near his seashore home in Guaraja, Brazil, Santos-Dumont committed suicide.

Although during his career he won hundreds of thousands of francs in avia-

1st Officer Simeon Petrov at the Blériot school in Étampes, France, 1912. National Museum of History, Bulgaria.

tion prizes, he gave much of his winnings to charity and always freely shared what he knew with his fellow designers. Alberto Santos-Dumont is considered by his countrymen the Father of Aviation, and a museum has been dedicated to his life in the Brazilian capital of São Paulo. In 1929 he was awarded the highest rank in the French Légion d'Honneur, and the Aéro-Club de France erected a monument to his work in Paris.

BULGARIA

Date: June 1, 1912
Location: Étampes, France
Plane: *Blériot XI*

Porochik Simeon Petrov
(1888–1950)

When the First Balkan War began in October of 1912, Bulgaria had just finished training its first military pilots. The officers who had traveled to Russia, England, Germany and France that spring were some of the first pilots in the world to fly wartime missions. The airplane had been used for reconnaissance against guerrillas in Mexico and by Italian pilots for dropping handheld bombs on Tripoli the year before. Now, pilots from across Europe and the Russian Empire joined their Bulgarian counterparts to fight the crumbling Ottoman Empire. Since planes had not at that time been mounted with guns, the Balkan missions consisted of reconnaissance and dropping small bombs.

Among the Bulgarian officers who began their flight training in 1912, the first to successfully pilot a plane was Simeon Petrov, a First Officer of the 4th Artillery Regiment based in Sofia. On June 1, 1912, Petrov soloed a *Blériot XI* monoplane at the Blériot school at Étampes, near Paris. During his training, Petrov impressed the Parisians with his coolness under pressure.

While flying at 1,400 meters, his engine quit working. Petrov pointed the nose of his machine down and spiraled back to the school's flying field, making a perfect landing. His feat was hailed in the press, and thereafter a landing with a stopped engine, or *vol plané*, became a part of French military pilot training.

Petrov and two of his fellows earned their brevets on July 25, 1912. Porochik ("Flying Officer") Petrov received license number 949; Porochiks Hiesto Toprakov and Nikifor Bogdanov earned licenses 948 and 950, respectively. Nineteen days later, Petrov became the first Bulgarian citizen to fly over his country's soil.

Little more than a week after the start of the First Balkan War, Bulgarian pilots began making raids on Adrianople. Petrov flew reconnaissance in that area and made the world's first night bombing raid there on November 7. Late that winter, he became the first war pilot to fly over the enemy's capital city. Fighting with the Central Powers during the First World War, Petrov flew missions over Greece. He helped design and build the Bojurishte aerodrome, which became Bulgaria's main air force base. At various times he also served as chief of the military aviation school and as chief of the nation's airplane workshops.

When the war ended, the 30-year-old Petrov enrolled in the Historical and Philosophical Studies program at Sofia University and began to broaden his interests. At first, he made a living as a welder and engine mechanic.

Later, Petrov began importing bicycles and gramophone records into the country. He may have competed as a cyclist, for he became the Bulgarian national cycling coach and took a team to the 1936 Olympic Games in Berlin. To round out his experience, Petrov began archiving Bulgarian folk songs with his gramophone. At the time of his death in 1950, he had made some five thousand recordings.

CANADA
(GREAT BRITAIN)

Date: May 17, 1908
Location: Hammondsport, New York, U.S.A.
Plane: *White Wing*, pusher biplane
Length of flight: 285 feet (87 m.)

Frederick W. (Casey) Baldwin
(1882–1948)

The first flight by a Canadian grew from one of the most interesting partnerships in the history of the airplane. The five members of the Aerial Experiment Association included not only the first military officer to fly, but also the inventor of the telephone, the Fastest Man on Earth, a future Canadian legislator and a future Lieutenant Governor of Nova Scotia. This fertile collaboration was born in the middle of 1907 when Mabel Graham Bell, a woman of independent means, offered to finance the aviation experiments of her famous husband, Alexander Graham Bell, and the two young engineers who were assisting him that summer, Frederick W. "Casey" Baldwin and John A. D. McCurdy. McCurdy's father had served for years as Dr. Bell's secretary. John McCurdy had invited Baldwin, his roommate from the University of Toronto, to spend the summer testing man-lifting kites in Baddeck, Nova Scotia. Casey Baldwin was a Toronto native, 25 years old, and the grandson of Canadian Prime Minister, Sir Robert Baldwin.

Dr. Bell accepted his wife's offer of $35,000 and a year-long charter to get a manned machine into the air. Bell invited American engine manufacturer and former motorcycle racer Glenn Hammond Curtiss to join the group as its Director of Experiments, at a respectable salary of $5,000 a year ($90,000 today). Curtiss was a successful manufacturer of motorcycles and had recently begun adapting his light motorcycle engines for dirigibles. He had gained notoriety for a motorcycle ride of 136 m.p.h.

Opposite: Bulgarian flight students in Étampes, 1912. *Left to right:* Hristo Toprakchiev, Krustiu Samsarov, Dimitar Sakelarov, Simeon Petrov, unknown, Stefan Kalinov, Nikola Mankov, Ivan Platnikov, Nikifor Bogdanov. National Museum of History, Bulgaria.

Aerial Experiment Association with Augustus Post, 1908. *Left to right:* Frederick W. "Casey" Baldwin, Thomas E. Selfridge, Glenn H. Curtiss, Alexander Graham Bell, John A. D. McCurdy, Augustus Post. National Air and Space Museum, Smithsonian Institution (SI Neg. No. 2001-6603).

earlier that year, a ride that made him officially the fastest man alive. The United States government asked the Bells to include a military observer, so U.S. Army Lieutenant Thomas E. Selfridge joined the group when it gathered for the first time that autumn. At the Bells' home in Baddeck, the Aerial Experiment Association was officially chartered on October 1, 1907. McCurdy, acting as Treasurer, and Baldwin, as Chief Engineer, drew salaries of $1,000 each.

Dr. Bell, then in his 60s, had already been experimenting with large kites, and the group turned first to testing the *Cygnet*, a flying machine designed after those kites. The *Cygnet*'s "wings" were a large bank of more than 3,000 individual cells that stood upright behind the pilot. The machine was destroyed during its only manned test, when it was towed aloft by a boat over Lake Bras

d'Or in Baddeck. Upon landing, the boat's crew failed to cut the tow line, dragging the expensive machine underwater and forcing the hapless Selfridge to jump for his life.

Each member of the A.E.A. had been challenged to come up with his own design for a flying machine, and the group's headquarters moved to the Curtiss factory in Hammondsport, New York, for the building of the association's first airplane, a Selfridge design. Like most planes at the time, the *Red Wing* had a lot in common with the Wright *Flyer*. Both Curtiss and Selfridge had been in contact with the Wrights, and their new airplane was a pusher biplane with its elevator in front. It had only one propeller, instead of the two on the Wright machine, and it had no wing-warping, ailerons or other form of lateral control. The top wing was 43 feet across, the lower a little shorter, and they

Alexander Graham Bell's tetrahedral kite, *Cygnet*, with John A. D. McCurdy at the controls, c. 1907. National Air and Space Museum, Smithsonian Institution (SI Neg. No. 92-4073).

Aerial Experiment Association's *Red Wing*, or Aerodrome No. 1, on Lake Keuka near Hammondsport, New York, probably after the plane's second crash and last flight, March 18, 1908. National Air and Space Museum, Smithsonian Institution (SI Neg. No. 93-9128).

Frederick W. "Casey" Baldwin in the Aerial Experiment Association's Aerodrome No. 2, *White Wing*. National Air and Space Museum, Smithsonian Institution (SI Neg. No. A-53067).

angled closer to each other as they got further from the plane's body. A Curtiss engine of 40 horsepower provided the thrust. For its first test, the group fitted *Red Wing* with skids and used frozen Lake Keuka as a runway. The A.E.A. members drew straws, and so, by the length of a stick, Casey Baldwin became the first Canadian to make a heavier-than-air take-off. On March 12, 1908, Baldwin took the controls in the kitchen-chair cockpit. According to Curtiss, *Red Wing* "sped over the ice like a scared rabbit for two or three hundred feet, and then, much to our joy, it jumped into the air."[19] *Red Wing* made 319 feet (97 m.) before the right wing dipped and, having no means to correct, Baldwin hit the ice and spun out. Despite the successful take-off, the crash on landing invalidates March 12 as the association's first successful flight.

The brave pilot got the honor of designing the next Aerial Experiment machine, though its groundbreaking feature has been attributed to a group decision to add some "lateral stability," actually lateral control.[20] Baldwin placed ailerons, or flaps, at each end of the upper wings and rigged a shoulder yoke to move them simultaneously as the pilot leaned against a dipping wing. If the right wing dipped, as happened in the *Red Wing* flight, the pilot would naturally lean left. The control wires connected to his shoulder yoke would then lower the right wing flap to increase lift on the right, while it raised the left flap to decreased lift on that side, thereby leveling the plane. Besides its new ailerons and fabric, the *White Wing* also had wheeled landing gear and a steering system similar to that on modern planes, a wheel on a control stick that activated both rudder and elevator. Baldwin became the first Canadian aviator on May 17, 1908, when he piloted *White Wing* 285 feet (87 m.) and put the flying machine down intact. Though it wasn't as long a flight as the *Red Wing* test, it had a successful conclusion. Each of the younger members of the A.E.A. made flights in *White Wing*. Curtiss logged the longest on May 22, flying 1,017 feet (310 m.).

The next A.E.A. project was the Curtiss-designed *June Bug*, named after the clouds of bugs that overran Hammondsport in the spring of 1908. The builders even added a yellow ochre to their turpentine and paraffin air-proofing "dope," giving the plane's fabric a characteristic june bug color. The control surfaces were refined and the whole plane lengthened for stability. On its first flight on June 21, Curtiss took the *June Bug* more than 1,100 feet (335 m.). Two weeks later, Curtiss won the Scientific American Cup (for an officially observed kilometer) on the Fourth of July with a straight-line flight of 5,090 feet (1.5 km). McCurdy later took the *June Bug* on its best flight of 2 miles in three minutes. When Curtiss's kilometer hit the news, the Wright brothers promptly notified him that the association had stepped on their patent for lateral control, which had been written to include wing flaps as well as the wing-warping used by the Wright planes. After this shock and that of seeing the Wrights begin their very successful public demonstrations that summer, tragedy visited the A.E.A. in September when Thomas Selfridge was killed riding as an observer during military trials of the Wright plane. While Orville Wright, with Selfridge as passenger, flew some 100 feet off the ground, a cracked propeller snagged a guy wire, cutting the support for the rudder and allowing it to fall into a nearly horizontal position. When the machine hit the ground, Selfridge struck his head on a wing strut, crushing his skull. Orville broke a thigh and four ribs.

At its one-year anniversary a couple of weeks later, the A.E.A. voted to continue its

Alexander Graham Bell, telephone pioneer, kite experimenter and senior member of the Aerial Experiment Association. National Air and Space Museum, Smithsonian Institution (SI Neg. No. 2001-6622).

partnership for another six months. *June Bug* was given a pair of pontoons, dubbed the *Loon* and tried from the water, but without success. Later that fall, the A.E.A. turned out its last and best plane, McCurdy's *Silver Dart*. The *Silver Dart* flew in Hammondsport and was then taken to Baddeck for the first-ever flight on Canadian soil on February 23, 1909, making McCurdy the first British subject to pilot in the territories. Curtiss surprised the group that spring when he signed a contract to build a plane for the Aero Club of America—without his partners. Unfortunately for Curtiss, the Wright brothers largely focused their patent litigation on his planes. Curtiss had a highly successful tenure as an airplane manufacturer and competitive pilot, but his legacy would be tarnished by the increasingly ugly patent battle and the levels to which he stooped trying to win it, even going so far as to produce a bogus reconstruction of a 1903 Samuel Langley machine in order to prove someone had been capable of flight before the Wrights.[21] In principle the Wrights eventually won the court battles, but counterclaims and new patent issues involving other companies kept the matter from settlement until the U.S. went to war in 1917.

With Curtiss, his engines and his factory gone, the A.E.A. dissolved in the spring of 1909. Baldwin and McCurdy started the Canadian Aerodrome Company with the Bells' backing. They produced two more biplanes, named for the Nova Scotia town where the A.E.A. had got its start and where the new company now set up shop. After persistent political efforts by Dr. Bell, they demonstrated *Baddeck I* and *Silver Dart* for the Canadian military near Ottawa. Unfortunately, the testing ground was soft and very uneven, and the pilots had difficulty getting the machine into the air and back to the ground in one piece. On August 2, the *Silver Dart* met its end when a rough landing pushed the right wingtip into the sand and ripped the entire wing from the fuselage. *Baddeck I* was damaged during landing on August 12, and despite eight good flights the Canadian military called an end to the trials. The government wouldn't purchase its first plane until late 1914.

McCurdy continued to pilot both *Baddeck I* and *Baddeck II* and set a world biplane speed record at Belmont Park, New York, the next spring. In 1910 the partners built and successfully tested a monoplane for a Boston customer and founded the Aero Club of Canada. Also that year McCurdy transmitted the world's first wireless telegraph message from an airplane, and as business faded for the Canadian Aerodrome Company, he went to work as chief test pilot for Curtiss's company. In 1911 McCurdy attempted the first flight from the United States to Cuba, missing the mark by only a mile when his engine suddenly began leaking oil.

After the disappointing military trials, Canada's first pilot gradually quit flying. When the Canadian Aerodrome Company ceased operation, Baldwin continued to work with Alexander Graham Bell on many maritime projects and concentrated much of his energy on developing hydrofoils, a technology that would later benefit Canadian seaplane pilots. McCurdy stopped flying in 1916 when he began to have trouble with his vision, and later became Lieutenant Governor of Nova Scotia. John McCurdy died in Montreal in 1961.

Casey Baldwin was elected to the Nova Scotia legislature in 1933 and headed the Nova Scotia Conservation Association starting in 1937. He died in 1948 and was buried near Dr. Bell in Baddeck, overlooking Lake Bras d'Or.

CHILE

Date: August 25, 1909
Location: Reims, France
Plane: Voisin (Sánchez-Besa), pusher biplane

José Luis Sánchez-Besa
(1879–1955)

José Luis Sánchez-Besa took up his wings when aviation was beginning to attract widespread attention. Frenchman Louis Blériot had crossed the English Channel in late July 1909. A month later, a French syndicate held the first international flying meet on a vast plain northeast of Paris, near a town called Reims. La Grande Semaine de l'Aviation de la Champagne attracted half a million spectators in one week, and it was here that the 30-year-old Santiago native made his first recorded flight, roughly one kilometer on August 25.[22] It has been said that Sánchez-Besa attended a Voisin flying school at Mourmelon the year before, but that particular school didn't open until after the first Reims meet, and we have no record of him flying earlier. All we know for certain is that he had purchased a Voisin biplane built to his specifications (the Voisin Sánchez-Besa) and had some practice with it before the Reims "flying week."

Sánchez-Besa biplane, 1909. National Air and Space Museum, Smithsonian Institution (SI Neg. No. 2001-6611).

The hub of world aviation activity had begun to shift from the suburbs of Paris to the Plain of Châlons earlier that year. It was over this great flat that Henry Farman had made the world's first cross-country flight from Bouy to Reims the previous autumn. After this historic *raid*, as it was called in France, Farman set up his workshop on the plain, near Bouy, at a spot thereafter dubbed "Camp-de-Châlons." This move may have been spurred by the French military, which for a short time in 1908 had denied aviators the use of their ersatz testing ground at Issy-les-Moulineaux, near Paris. Farman may also have wished to distance himself from the Voisin brothers after they had sold his first design to someone else. Or maybe he just preferred the flight-friendly countryside to Issy and its skyline of factories and protruding smokestacks.[23] In any case, Farman started his factory and flying school there in early 1909. He was soon followed by the Voisins, who set up a repair shop and later a flying school, and by the Antoinette firm of Leon Levavasseur.

During all this activity, Sánchez-Besa was probably learning to fly his new biplane. After Reims he competed at the Berlin and Hamburg aviation weeks. Once he had some piloting under his belt, the Chilean moved quickly to secure a place in the blossoming French aircraft industry. On the plain of Bétheny where the Reims meet had been held, he started his own factory and flying school in 1910. At the school, Sánchez-Besa taught the American manufacturer Thomas Benoist and the distinguished Peruvian pilot Juan Bielovucic to fly. Not long afterward, he moved again to Billancourt, a suburb of Paris adjacent to Issy-les-Moulineaux. A picture taken in his office shows the distinguished Santiago native with a pen in one hand and a watch in the other. He appears serious, perhaps a little distracted by business, in his bowler, tie and stiff wing collar.

Sánchez-Besa's early planes were similar to the Voisin on which he had learned, pusher biplanes with wheeled undercarriages, but his wings were more streamlined than the Voisins', and Sánchez-Besa did away with the wasteful side-curtains of the Voisin planes. The pilot-builder competed again at

Above: Sánchez-Besa hydroplane over the Monaco shore, c. March 1912, piloted by Jean Benoist. Technical Reports & Standards Unit, Library of Congress, L'Aérophile Collection. *Below:* José Luis Sánchez-Besa, c. 1943. Technical Reports & Standards Unit, Library of Congress, L'Aérophile Collection.

Lyons and Reims in 1910. Sometime that year, he was flying his Voisin when a wing collapsed and left him with serious injuries. More than a year after his first recorded flights, he earned his French pilot's brevet, No. 155, on August 29 for a flight in one of his own planes.

Earlier that year, Frenchman Henri Fabre had ushered in a new phase of aircraft development when he made the first successful take-off from water in a canard-style biplane with floats for landing gear. Spotting a potential niche, Sánchez-Besa promptly expanded his factory to build hydroplanes and thereby made his fortune. He filled orders for France, Russia and Chile. His planes won hydroplane prizes in Barcelona, Brittany and Belgium, gaining him worldwide recogni-

Chinese Prince Tsai Tao on a diplomatic visit to France, 1910, at Issy-les-Moulineaux with French aviator Louis Blériot. Technical Reports & Standards Unit, Library of Congress, L'Aérophile Collection.

tion. His new monoplane design also won an aerobatic contest in Vienna. The business exploded, and Sánchez-Besa had to hire managers to watch the plant at Issy so he could continue to fly competitions.

When war came in 1914, the French government consolidated a number of aircraft factories and dictated what planes should be built in the remaining firms. Sánchez-Besa lost his company, which was merged with the Nieuport firm, but he set up new factories in Sèvres and Cognac to produce the Breguet, Sopwith and Caudron planes ordered by the French military. Those factories employed over two thousand people by 1918. Though we have no further details of his career, José Luis Sánchez-Besa was still living in Paris when he died in 1955.

CHINA

Date: September 21, 1909
Location: Oakland, California
Plane: Feng, pusher biplane
Length of flight: ½ mile (800 m.)

Feng Yu (1883–1912)

Around the beginning of the century's second decade, aviation took a sudden leap from the western lands of its development to what might justifiably be called its true home in the Far East. In the second millennium B.C., the Chinese had originated the art of flying with the invention of the kite. Kite-flying didn't reach Europe until a century before the Renaissance, some 2,400 years later. Though there's no concrete evidence for the assertion, some have suggested, based on the sophisticated designs of modern Chinese kites, that manned flight was a lost art in China. By a hundred years ago, however, China's days as a progressive intellectual, artistic and technological center had long passed. The Ch'ing Dynasty of the Manchus, conservative since its birth in 1644, had stagnated and was under attack from the inside by progressive forces, from the outside by trade-hungry Europeans and land-hungry Japanese. By 1911, when a man named Feng Yu traveled to his homeland to demonstrate aviation for the leaders of a successful uprising, China had been in decline and turmoil for 70 years. At a time when many European countries still had not flown, and years before aviation would spread to most of Asia, a revolution brought the airplane to China.

Feng Yu first flew in Oakland, California, close by San Francisco, where he had lived since his family immigrated to North America some time around 1895. We don't know why the Fengs left China, nor how they made a living in California, nor how Feng Yu spent his youth. It seems safe to assume that one of the Fengs had a successful business or some other form of income, for Feng Yu reportedly began in 1907 building himself an airplane, not a cheap prospect then or now. However, Feng later had wealthy Cantonese sponsors in California, and it may be that their money also covered his early work. About two years later, September 21, 1909, Feng flew his machine, which by now resembled a Curtiss *June Bug*, over the city of Oakland. The San Francisco papers make no mention of this flight, but it is possible that a member of the Chinese community could have experimented without too much attention from the mainstream press. A German sportsman's index which lists early fliers confirms a 1909 flight of a half-mile by a Chinese national called Fung Quay in San Francisco. This is almost certainly Feng, who was called Fung Guey and Fung Joe Guey in the United States. On Feb. 21, 1911, the *New York Times* noted his departure for China and referred to him as Fung Guey. These various accounts, though naming him differently,

agreed in date and detail, and it's probably safe to conclude that there was only one Chinese national in northern California who had already flown his own plane by 1911 and was embarking for China to demonstrate his machine for the officials of the Guangdong Republic.

The future Chinese resistance leader, Sun Yat-Sen, was not in China during the successful Guangdong uprising in early 1911. Although he had been involved in ten similar actions, he was traveling in the United States when the rebels finally succeeded. Sun had been exposed to aviation during his time in the West, and he promptly called on his countrymen around the world to bring planes and piloting experience to China.[24]

Besides Sun's appeal to expatriate aviators, the revolutionaries had also ordered several airplanes from Austria in 1910. By the time either the planes or Feng Yu had arrived, however, the new Guangdong Republic had been set up in the south of China (the last Manchu emperor, Pu-yi, waited until 1912 to abdicate). When Feng arrived in China, he was immediately appointed the head of the republic's Air Force. The records break there, though Feng would presumably have had his plane uncrated for scheduled demonstration flights in Hong Kong and Canton, stops he had announced before leaving the United States with his sponsors. He seems to have stayed in China, for the next August we find him giving another demonstration, again in his own plane, at an unnamed military base. In front of a large gathering of Chinese troops he had just lectured on aviation, Feng tried twice to get his plane off the parade ground and over a high wall of vegetation. On the third attempt, he pulled up too sharply and stalled, dropping the plane and himself into a stand of deadly sharp bamboo. Feng died later in the hospital.

Even post-revolution, Feng is still honored by the Chinese, as is Sun Yat-Sen. The monument to Feng in Huanghuagang Martyr's Graveyard reads, "China's Great Pioneer in Aviation."

COLOMBIA

Date: April 4, 1922
Plane: *Caudron G-3*, monoplane

Colonel José Ignacio Forero F.
(1903–?)

If it seems those pilots who christened their national aviation after the First World War had things any easier than those who started twenty years earlier, harken to this testimony from our first Colombian pilot:

> As I passed over Lloro I was in total control of the instruments, and I began to fly over the Isthmus of Choco. All of a sudden my front engine quit, and then seconds later the engine in the rear quit. I was in quite a predicament, concerned about certain death since the impact would also cause the conflagration of the 400 gallons of gasoline I was carrying. Fortunately, I was able to land in the trees. But a few minutes later the plane fell from the trees slowly, and I was gravely injured. Luckily none of my passengers were hurt … I must say that people don't appreciate the ability to land in trees and the cool-headedness and skill required for such a maneuver.[25]

José Forero had the benefit of 30 years of aviation development when this incident happened, and he was lucky to be piloting a relatively modern Junkers W-34 flying boat. Although by the 1930s aero-engines had become somewhat reliable, Forero survived numerous breakdowns like this during his 35 years in aviation. What he gained in modern wings and engines was offset by the brutal terrain and the isolation of the country in which he did most of his piloting. Forero spent a good portion of his flying time over high peaks, flooded valleys and desolate rain forest. After 12 years as a pilot, he had become expert at a sort of emergency maneuver never anticipated by his European and American predecessors—the treetop landing.

Colombia got a slow start in aviation. The country's first pilots immigrated from Europe after the war. They set up commercial enterprises carrying mail, cargo or passengers, and for a while they didn't hire native pilots. "They tried to convince us that only Europeans had an aptitude for flying in Colombia," Forero wrote in his 1964 account of Colombian aviation, "that the country was inferior, intellectually and physically, for flying." The country's military seemed to buy into this argument for a number of years. It wasn't until early 1922 that an aviation school began operating tentatively in Flandes. The military had hired German flight instructors, but it never paid them, so Forero received his training from a colonel who had no more flying experience than he. He studied with a number of cadets, and it has become impossible for us to determine who among them made the first qualifying solo flight in the school's Caudron G-3 biplanes, an early war-era two-seater. However, on April 4, 1922, Forero was chosen by his colonel to make Colombia's first official military flight in front of the Minister of War and numerous other dignitaries.

The graduation ceremony went off without a hitch. For their ingenuity and tenacity in flying completely without qualified instruction, Forero and his fellow cadets expected to be rewarded with high-level promotions and rich overseas commissions. But the new air force was not popular in elite military circles. It had been whispered that the Military Air Branch was plotting against the government. The school's director had hoped that seeing Colombian cadets take to the air would fire the Minister's imagination and erase the months of intrigue and doubt, but the cadets did not get commissions. Three weeks later, the military shut down its first flying school and dispersed the students. Forero was assigned the sad task of warehousing the school's materials at a base in the town of Madrid.

At the end of 1922, Forero was a marginally trained military pilot without an air force or planes on which to practice his skills. He was offered a spot in the army's official military school and promised a commission at the end of six months. Still smarting from the closing of the Flandes school, Forero had decided to visit the United States for further training as a civilian pilot, but about the time he was preparing to leave, a friend arranged an interview with a German businessman just starting a commercial enterprise in Barranquilla. The company's president spoke Spanish well, which impressed Forero, and he offered Forero a position in the engine repair shop of Sociedad Colombo-Alemana de Transportes Aeros, or SCADTA. Forero accepted the position and moved to Barranquilla in early 1923 to work in one of the company's two small wooden hangars with a crew of mostly German mechanics and engineers.

The company's director of pilots gave Forero his big break one day when he walked into the shop and invited the Colombian out for some co-pilot practice. The SCADTA routes followed Columbia's two most important rivers, the Cauca and the Magdalena, which still link a majority of the country's population centers. Accordingly, the company had outfitted itself with hydroplanes so its pilots would have an emergency runway at almost any point in their flights. On this particular day, the director of pilots took Forero up in a Junkers F-13 and promptly landed the plane in the middle of the Magdalena River. It was Forero's job to climb onto a wing, let himself down 6 feet to a pylon, crawl out to the propeller and give it a spin while the plane bobbed in the current. Then, avoiding the howling prop, he had to scramble back into the cockpit for take-off. On the third yank the engine engaged, and Forero climbed back to his seat. Thus he had passed his co-pilot's examination. The next day he co-piloted his first SCADTA flight from Barranquilla to Girardot, 800 kilometers up the Magdalena River.

So that mail and supplies could be delivered directly to cities that weren't located right on a river, the company acquired its first wheeled planes early in 1924. This gave Forero a new job locating emergency landing strips along the rivers and establishing runways at delivery points. Forero experienced his first tree landing in late December of that year on the first non-hydroplane flight to Medellín. After repairs had been made, he and pilot Ferruccio Guicciardi, one of the first foreign fliers to work in Colombia,

headed toward the company's new Medellín landing strip, nothing more than a clearing on the farm of Jesús Sierra. It would appear the company had not yet examined the strip, for when the pilots arrived in the Fokker F.II, already with four holes from their tree landing, they found a stand of willows and a stone wall in the way of a safe landing. Despite Forero's protests, Guicciardi insisted they had enough room and proceeded to put the plane down a mere 40 meters from the wall. "After we recovered," Forero wrote later, "we worked out an agreement with Jesus Sierra to rent us another clearing so we could lengthen the landing strip and not hit our noses on the damned stone wall."

SCADTA completed its new route on the Cauca River in 1925 with flights to Cali and Manizales. Forero and Guicciardi seem to have been stationed in Cali, making mail flights up and down the river. Guicciardi had another interesting landing on a passenger flight from Zarzal to Cartago, where a group of railroad officials were headed for the opening of a new line between those cities. Forero had gone ahead to Cartago to locate a landing spot, but his partner didn't arrive on schedule that afternoon, nor even by the next morning. It turned out that Guicciardi had encountered turbulence so violent outside Zarzal that a fuselage screw had broken. Forgetting it was the wet season and that the muddy river had overflowed its banks, Guicciardi tried to put the Fokker down on what looked like a particularly smooth, light brown piece of farmland. The water stopped the plane by its landing gear and flipped it tail-over-nose. The four passengers found themselves hanging upside down from their seatbelts, heads immersed in the water. When Forero got word of the accident, he backtracked to Zarzal, where he found Guicciardi in the lobby of the Hotel Pacífico with his passengers in rags and "scared spitless." The two pilots spent four days standing in water up to their waists dismantling the Fokker and sending its parts by canoe to an airport at San Fernando.

That year the Colombian military began instructing pilots again at a new flight school in Madrid. Commercial aviation slowed over the next couple of years, and in 1926 Forero traveled to the United States for further flight instruction. Studying at the Curtiss school in New York, he earned U.S. pilot's license number 6594 on the famous Curtiss JN-4 "Jennie," a trainer dating to World War I. He then took a course in hydroplanes at Rogers Air Lines in Miami and went to work in the experimental department of the Sikorsky company in New York.

Forero remained in the U.S. for several years and continued to study flying at the Curtiss school, specifically on the Curtiss Sea Gull. The glut of pilots that had hit the market after the war, along with the liabilities inherent in flying passengers and the technological advances in machines, had changed the nature of commercial flight instruction. Rather than simply earning a license to fly, pilots were now beginning to specialize in flying certain machines. In 1930 Forero got a call from his old boss, the president of SCADTA, who wanted him to take on a fixed route between Girardot and Ibagué, with occasional flights to Bogotá. Forero flew this short but mountainous mail route in a variety of de Havilland moth-type planes for two years until war intervened. He was just preparing to ship for Germany to train on multi-engine Junkers planes when he woke one morning to sirens all over the city of Barranquilla. At six in the morning, the president of the company called to tell him that Peru had occupied the southern corner of Colombia and that the military had requested three of SCADTA's pilots. Nearly ten years after he had given up on the Colombian military, Forero finally got his officer's commission in the national air force. He became Lieutenant José Forero on September 3, 1932.

The Colombian air force consisted of eight planes, several of which, according to Forero, were down for repairs at all times. Forero flew daily mail and supply flights from what was now the Madrid Air Force Base, up the Magdalena River and over the mountains into the jungles of the Amazon River Basin, a route that approached 1500 kilometers. Forero refers to the planes they flew only as "Wilds," about which we have

no details. These machines must have been remarkably reliable, considering the frequency and length of this supply route. As the Colombian troops made progress southward, Forero would fly Junkers hydroplanes that could use the Putumayo River as a landing strip. The hazardous jungle flying claimed several of Forero's fellow pilots and friends. The war officially ended on June 23, 1933, but Forero stayed on with the air force to keep the southern portion of the country well supplied.

Three years later, Forero was appointed the head of the air force's Technical Department, which consisted of nine employees—two assistants, two engineers, two doctors, a secretary, a mechanic and a topographer. Forero held this post for six years. In 1946, he became Colombia's Director of Civil Aeronautics, with jurisdiction over 18 airlines now operating in the country. Under his watch, the civil aeronautics department standardized radio communications and instituted a central system for controlling commercial flight nationwide.

José Ignacio Forero F. retired a full colonel in 1962.

COSTA RICA

Tobias Bolaños

Tobias Bolaños may have flown as early as 1914, or he may not have made a successful flight until the 1920s. Just after World War I, in which he claimed to have flown as a pilot for France, Bolaños began working to get both military and commercial aviation started in Costa Rica.

Bolaños had very little success with his promotions work until 1929, when he managed to interest a San José newspaper in his cause. La Tribuna organized a conference on national aviation, on September 22, 1929, in the capital city. The country's leadership had just changed, authorities were more open to the idea of aviation, and the conference led to the establishment of a national aviation committee chartered to raise funds for the new Escuela de Aviación Militar. In addition,

President Cleto Gonzales Viquez made Bolaños a major in full command of the new
school.[26]

Not long after, a two-seat biplane
promised the year before by the Mexican
government arrived in Costa Rica. It was an
Avro 504, a famous British trainer from
World War I. On December 19, 1929, Bolaños
took his country's only plane for its maiden
flight. The propeller, perhaps damaged during its shipping from England, shattered and
landed Bolaños in a tree.[27] The plane was reportedly fixed and in 1930 served as the
school's training machine for its two new
cadets.

Press reports from this period refer to
Bolaños as the only licensed aviator in Costa
Rica, but the origin of his license is unclear.
Perhaps, as he claimed, he served with the
French air service in World War I, in which
case he would have held a French military
brevet. However, this cannot be substanti-
ated. News reports also say he received a
French pension after the war, which, if true,
would certainly lend credence to his claim
for earlier flight.

CROATIA
(AUSTRIA-HUNGARY)

Date: November 13, 1911
Location: Zagreb
Plane: Rusjan monoplane

Mihajlo Merčep (1864–?)

Mihajlo Merčep was born a Serb in
Dubrovnik, a port city on the southern Dal-
matian coast, then a part of the Habsburg
Dual Monarchy. We have no details of his
early life, but he shows up in the flight literature in 1910, running a machine shop in the
capital city of Zagreb. Here, Merčep worked
with Slovene pioneers Edvard and Josip Rusjan to build their second flying machine, a
Blériot-type monoplane.[28]

Edvard Rusjan died piloting that plane
early in 1911 when he collided with a bridge
abutment over the Save River in Belgrade.
According to Serb historians, Merčep restored the Rusjan plane and flew it himself.
He also began producing monoplanes in
partnership with a man named Dragutin
Novak. Whether it was the Rusjan plane or
one of his own that Merčep flew on November 13, 1911, we don't know, but this is the
earliest concrete date we have for a first
flight. He may have flown much earlier.

Merčep constructed his first monoplane
that same year, and apparently produced several designs after that, though we know very
little about these planes. His last was completed in 1914, after which we know nothing
of his life.

CUBA

Date: August 1, 1911
Location: Troy, New York, USA
Plane: Moisant monoplane

Ferdinand E. de Murias

Ferdinand de Murias earned his United
States pilot's license, number 38, on the first
of August, 1911, at the Moisant flying school
in Troy, New York.[29] This is all we know of de
Murias. We don't even know his birth date.
He may never have flown in Cuba, and he is
definitely not known by his countrymen as
the first Cuban to fly. In fact, flight historians have been unable to determine whether
he ever returned to Cuba after earning his
license.

The man recognized by Cubans as their
first aviator is Captain Augustin Parla. Parla
studied flying at the Curtiss school in Hammondsport, New York, in 1911, but he never
earned his pilot's license. There is no evidence he flew until nearly a year after de
Murias. His instructor at the Curtiss school
later said he "did not make much progress"
while there. Nevertheless, Parla returned the
next year to purchase a plane and later made
flights in Miami and Havana. His most notorious exploit was an attempt to complete
the first flight from Key West to Cuba. A
member of the Aerial Experiment Association, John McCurdy, had tried the crossing
in 1911 and been forced by engine mal-

function to ditch a mile off the Cuban coast.[30]

In 1913 Cuba offered a $10,000 prize for the first flight from Key West to Havana, and Parla signed up with a Spaniard named Domingo Rossillo. The aviators had agreed to make it a race, and they arranged to leave at the same time on May 18, 1913. Some kind of confusion occurred that morning, with Parla wanting to postpone the start and Rossillo taking off before the appointed time. By the time Parla found out that Rossillo had already gone, the winds at Key West had picked up and take-off had become dangerous. Parla wouldn't hear of quitting, however, and when his friends tried to restrain him, he put a pistol to his head. They finally let him go. The wind was so nasty that it snapped several support wires in the wings of the Curtiss biplane. Parla made a water landing 15 miles out. The authorities helped him back to shore and promptly arrested him for attempted suicide.

The next day, Parla repaired his plane and set out after Rossillo, who had successfully landed in Havana after more than two hours, then a world record flight over water. Where Rossillo had been able to follow a line of ships all the way to the island, Parla was now on his own. He lost his way and never made it to Havana, but crash landed on the beach at Mariel, Cuba. Later that year, he set a Cuban duration record in Havana, and in 1916 he was sent by the Cuban Army to the Curtiss school in New York for further instruction with an eye to establishing the country's first military flight school. Later in life he served as Cuba's Director General of Airports. Augustin Parla died July 31, 1946.

2nd Lt. Frederick William Stent, August 31, 1915. Royal Air Force Museum, Hendon, London; Royal Aero Club of the United Kingdom certificates, Rac 2748.

CYPRUS

Date: August 31, 1915
Location: Farnborough, England
Plane: Maurice Farman biplane

2nd Lieutenant Frederick William Stent (1890–?)

Like so many British colonials who flew in World War I, the only information we have about Frederick William Stent comes from his pilot's license. Second Lieutenant Stent earned his brevet, number 2748, on the last day of August, 1915. At the military flying school in Farnborough, Stent soloed the famous World War I training plane constructed by Maurice Farman, the "Longhorn." Although we have been unable to place him in one of the Royal Flying Corps squadrons, his name does not appear in the war-end list of casualties, so we can surmise that Stent survived aviation through at least the end of 1918.

CZECH REPUBLIC (AUSTRIA-HUNGARY)

Date: April 12, 1910
Location: Pardubice, Austria-Hungary
Plane: *Blériot XI*

Jan Kašpar (1883–1927)

Jan Kašpar and his cousin Evžen Čihák quit their jobs to build an airplane. In mid–1909, no one had yet flown in the region of Bohemia and Moravia, and the young engineers were unsatisfied with their work at an auto factory in Mladá Boleslav. Both men came from prosperous middle-class backgrounds. Jan Kašpar was born May 20, 1883, to the well-known Pardubice hotel owner Frantisek Kašpar. He had sampled the life of a wealthy sportsman, spending his teens and twenties racing horses, rowing, cycling, ballooning, and racing various newfangled motorized craft. He earned a degree in mechanical engineering from the Czech Higher Technical School in Prague, then went to Germany for further training in auto engineering. Once he received his certification in 1907, Kašpar stayed in Germany to work for the automobile manufacturer Basse & Selve. Here, he met Czech inventor Otto Hieronymous, who was completing his own aero-engine and starting to design a Wright-type airframe. In early 1909 Kašpar returned to Bohemia to work as head factory engineer at the Laurin & Klement autoworks with his cousin, Čihák.

The management position in Mladá Boleslav may have been a let-down after Kašpar's recent motorcycle and auto and boat racing in Germany. Perhaps his contact with Hieronymous had inspired him toward aviation work, or maybe automobiles weren't the cutting-edge pursuit they had been only five years earlier. Whatever their motivations, Kašpar and Čihák left their comfortable positions at Laurin & Klement and began designing a monoplane based on the French Antoinette. A few weeks later (July 25), Frenchman Louis Blériot flew his *Blériot XI* monoplane across the English Channel, an incredible feat of luck and daring. Blériot beat out the Antoinette pilot, Englishman Hubert Latham, who landed two planes in the water on separate attempts. With the benefit of hindsight, we can say the Antoinette was actually the fitter machine. It was more solidly built and had a more powerful engine and a safer control system. It was, simply, much easier to fly. But for extraordinary *bon chance* on the part of Blériot, the Antoinette should have won the Channel contest. However, experimenters in 1909 didn't have the benefit of decades of aerodynamics and design testing to tell them to stay away from the frail, wing-warping Blériot. Like many others, the Czech cousins modified their designs to favor the Blériot.

The first test of the Kašpar-Čihák monoplane wasn't until March of the next year. With their original engine design, the machine didn't have enough power to stay off the ground. A succession of mishaps (and, maybe, the steady progress of Hieronymous on his own machine) convinced Kašpar they should mount a commercial engine on their airframe. He brought back from Paris an Anzani engine and propeller. As Hieronymous was preparing for his first test flights, Kašpar took their monoplane into the air for several short hops. Like many aviation experimenters before him, he was testing his machine while at the same time learning to steer. On one rather successful take-off he ran the machine into a tree on landing. The frame was severely damaged. Hieronymous had the same sort of luck. On April 4, 1910, he wrecked his promising new machine in a test flight, destroying the airframe altogether. Fed up with the laborious process of developing his own design, Kašpar

Jan Kašpar standing at the front of his Blériot monoplane, c. 1910. National Technical Museum of the Czech Republic, Prague.

decided to import a factory-built Blériot to Bohemia. His father, worried about his son's life and the family reputation, had offered to bankroll Jan's purchase of a proven flying machine. Čihák, who wanted a successful design of his own, split with his cousin at this point.

Blériot monoplanes would dominate

the international aviation scene that year. The larger Wright, Farman and Voisin biplanes would continue to do well, but ever since the Channel flight, the Blériot monoplane had become one of the most desirable machines in Europe. And despite the difficulty of flying the Blériot, it did have two advantages over most of its competitors. It had much less wing surface than the predominant biplanes, and it was also lighter than the other large-engine planes available. In particular, it was much lighter than the Antoinette, which had a wooden fuselage. At the time, the safety of the monoplane was still being debated (after many wrecks, there had been a call in some quarters for banning them), but the *Blériot XI* would dominate speed, altitude and distance competitions for two years.

Kašpar's practice in his own plane seems to have helped him when it came time to pilot his new *Blériot XI*. In a matter of a few weeks he progressed from taxiing it around the airfield, to taking off and landing, to making airborne turns. According to Czech sources, his first really successful flight was April 12, 1910. Although we have no details of that flight, it seems a reasonable claim, since only four days later he made a two-kilometer flight in Pardubice. Kašpar kept up his practice and began making demonstration flights that summer. His first, in Pardubice on June 19, drew 20,000 spectators. In August he flew in Prague, attracting another 30,000 people. That summer, Hieronymous also ordered a Blériot and began flying using the aero-engine he had built while working at Basse & Selve.

In between exhibition flights, Kašpar began to design another plane, this time with a friend named Frantisek Novotny. It was essentially a larger Blériot that could carry a passenger and more fuel. When they unveiled the new machine the next spring, Kašpar dubbed it a "Kašpar JK-System Blériot." He flew that plane on April 22, 1911. On May 13, he made the first cross-country flight in the Czech region, flying 90 kilometers (56 mi.) from Pardubice to Prague. This flight is now heralded as the first great accomplishment of Czech aviation.

During this time Kašpar started the region's first aviation school and at some point even taught his cousin Čihák to fly. He made the first Czech passenger flight, carrying a journalist from Mělnick to Prague. Kašpar seems to have done well through 1912, but a string of bad luck, including a fire that destroyed two planes and much of his raw material, put him out of the aviation business in 1913. When his father died that spring, Kašpar took on the management of his family's property full-time. Evžen Čihák and his brother, Hugo, would go on to manufacture a successful monoplane, the *Rapid*, which featured a rotary engine of their own design. Kašpar's other partner, Novotny, went on to work for Avia Works and in the 1930s would serve as their chief aircraft designer.

When World War I began, Kašpar signed up with the Austro-Hungarian railroad corps. When the new country of Czechoslovakia was formed after the war, Kašpar worked briefly for the new public works ministry. He went into the lumber business for a short time, then took over his father's hotel in Pardubice. Details are scarce, but somehow Kašpar's business dealings took a bad turn in the mid–1920s. Facing financial ruin, Jan Kašpar committed suicide on March 2, 1927. His funeral four days later was attended by all the leading figures of Czech aviation, and during the ceremony the planes of the Prague First Air Regiment circled the city overhead.

DENMARK

Date: January 14, 1908
Location: Tivoli Gardens, Denmark
Plane: *Ellehammer IV*, tractor biplane
Length of flight: 170 meters (558 ft.)

Jacob Christian Hansen Ellehammer (1871–1946)

On September 12, 1906, working with no detailed knowledge of experiments in the United States and France, Jacob Christian Ellehammer got his *Ellehammer II* biplane 18 inches off the ground for 42 meters (138 ft.). That was the day before Paris resident Alberto Santos-Dumont made his first hop in the plane that would captivate Europe two months later.[31] Although Ellehammer's machine was tethered to a pole at the center of a circular track, his mostly Danish adherents still say he made the first flight in Europe. At the time, Ellehammer was working away from the press and the public on a private island belonging to Count Knuth. The island of Lindholm was too small for a straight runway, and Ellehammer's planes were tethered so that he could test his craft without risking repeated baths in the Baltic Sea.

Having harnessed enough engine power to overcome gravity, Ellehammer clearly considered the September 12 flight his solution to the problem. As he wrote in his memoirs 25 years later, "Flying was no longer a preposterous and fantastic idea, it was a reality. Proof had been given ... and purely technical improvements were all that remained to bring about improved performances."[32] However, the inventor had neglected to count the added acceleration he got by tying his apparatus to a center post. *Ellehammer II* had wings with no camber, and it had no effective flight controls, making it essentially a man-carrying kite. Ellehammer would make numerous short hops in the next year and a half, but he wouldn't achieve true flight until 1908.

Born in Bakkebølle, south of Copenhagen, Jacob Christian Ellehammer grew up one of nine children on the island of Falster in southeast Denmark. His father worked as a ship's carpenter and a contractor. One of young Ellehammer's first inventions was a wind-powered coffee grinder, with which he hoped to get out of grinding the beans by hand every morning, but which instead littered the kitchen with coffee and grinder parts on its second trial.[33] The Ellehammer children together built four-season sailing sleds on which they could exchange the runners for wheels in the summer. They were

Jacob Christian Ellehammer, c. 1906. Nordisk Pressefoto/ Archive Photos.

fascinated with flight, or just height, long before Jacob began his aviation work, for, like Alexander Graham Bell and Samuel F. Cody, the Ellehammers built kites large enough to lift themselves into the air using cast-off arms from their father's windmill.[34]

When he was 14 years old, Ellehammer apprenticed as a watchmaker, then became interested in the science of Benjamin Franklin and Thomas Edison, eventually pulling his service in the Dutch Navy as an electrician. Pictures show Ellehammer with a thick goatee, widely protruding moustaches and a stout build. He was a good-humored man, and later photos of him with a short white beard look like prototypes for Old Saint Nick. In 1896, he opened his own shop, from which he sold a number of coin-operated machines, including an x-ray machine, an early jukebox, moving-picture screens and, oddly enough, an electroshock device that tested the customer's tolerance for jolts of increasing intensity. As a present to his fiancée, he built a steam engine the size of a thimble, which was operated by holding underneath it a lit match. It was in this shop that Ellehammer began the project that would lead him back into the air, a one-cylinder engine for his *Elleham* motorcycle. After several successful years in the motorcycle business, during which he set up a school to teach his customers to ride the machines, Ellehammer realized that he could finally produce an engine light and powerful enough that it might get a machine into the air.

So he added two cylinders to his motorcycle engine in a radial pattern to give it nine horsepower. The engine was air cooled, making it extraordinarily light. Once Ellehammer had begun testing his first flying machine, he realized he would need more power and enlarged his engine to give 18 horsepower at only 45 kilograms (99 pounds), more horsepower than the original Wright engine, at one-half the weight of the Wright motor. Beginning in 1905, Ellehammer worked on Lindholm with his brother Vilhelm and cousin Lars, who built a hangar and a workshop. Their first test was a success—an unmanned monoplane with a pendulum mechanism to keep the craft balanced. According to Lars, his cousin Jacob went through 14 designs in the summer of 1906 before the biplane configuration emerged that would get a pilot off the ground, albeit tethered. Once he had what he considered a success, Ellehammer left the island and began untethered trials at Tivoli Gardens in Copenhagen.

It must have been a frustrating period for Ellehammer. He had left the ground already, he had what was possibly the world's lightest airplane engine, and yet he could not keep his biplane in the air for more than a few meters. The tether on Lindholm had allowed him to use a machine with no wing camber. This required a very high wing angle (angle of attack) and resulted in a large amount of drag, which would slow his machine drastically as soon as it angled up and left the ground. A properly cambered airfoil can operate at much shallower angles to the wind than a kite. A modern plane's wings are designed to meet the oncoming air at approximately 5 degrees from horizontal. Not only is this a much shallower angle than Ellehammer's 12-degree wing, but a cambered airfoil has even less drag than a flat wing. Ellehammer's wings suffered from at least six times as much drag as a similar cambered wing would have. A flat wing surface is also susceptible to irregular air flows that give uneven lift and make controlled flight difficult. Ellehammer's true innovation, and the device that had allowed him to launch the Lindholm biplane, was that air-cooled radial engine. The first version of that engine, produced in 1903, had an astounding power-weight ratio of 2.5 kilograms per horsepower, better than anything else available, including the much praised Antoinette engine (3 kg./hp.). Ellehammer had upgraded the original radial in 1905 to provide double the power and shave another kilogram off the power-weight ratio.

No amount of engine power, however, would carry flat wings into sustainable flight. Ellehammer produced another biplane, *Ellehammer III*, with the same problem, then tried turning that machine into a triplane. Throughout 1907 he made short, uncontrollable hops. It was on *Ellehammer IV*, another biplane, that he finally added camber to the lower wing. In Tivoli Gardens on January 14, 1908, the inventor made a flight of 170 meters (558 ft.) at 2–3 meters altitude, his first real flight. Even that machine had no form of lateral control. Ellehammer was still trying for automatic stability by hanging the engine and pilot on a pendulum below the wings, an effective device for balancing the pilot, but not for controlling the wings in a turn or a crosswind. This is why one historian grudgingly calls the 1908 successes "hop-flights."[35] Indeed, the longest flight in the *Ellehammer IV* was only a few hundred meters despite the extremely light, five-cylinder, 35-horsepower engine Ellehammer was now using. Nevertheless, the inventor took his machine to the north–German port

Ellehammer 1907 triplane. National Air and Space Museum, Smithsonian Institution (SI Neg. No. 78-15846).

city of Kiel that summer and became the first man to fly in Germany on June 28, 1908, earning 5,000 German mark ($22,500 today). This flight, the longest made by the 1908 biplane, lasted only 11 seconds but attracted an estimated 30,000 spectators.

Within a month of the Wright brothers' first public demonstrations in August, European designers were adding either wing-warping (after the Wright device) or ailerons (after the Farman) for lateral control. In 1910 Ellehammer produced his most successful plane, the Ellehammer *Standard*, a wing-warping monoplane with a new six-cylinder, 40-horsepower engine, a more efficient propeller and the cruciform tail rudder and elevator that were then becoming widespread. The *Standard* was such a reliable machine that in the early 1950s the Danish Air Circus flew an exact replica at airshows.

The *Standard* was Ellehammer's last plane. The inventor had trouble finding capital to keep up with the pace of aeronautical development, but he stayed in the aero-engine business for a while. He invented the modern carburetor and went on to manufacture automobiles, also. In the 1920s and 30s, Ellehammer returned to some of his early helicopter experiments and produced models of helicopters and convertiplanes, a hybrid design with a rotor operating inside a top-mounted wing. During his busy 75 years, Ellehammer also produced numerous machines for firefighting, including water pumps and foam fire extinguishers. He built racing boats and quiet lake boats for Tivoli Gardens that ran on compressed air. On the lighter side, he made a cigarette roller and an "egg-opener" that could take the top of an eggshell off without disturbing the membrane. The Danish inventor amassed 400 patents, earning him comparisons with Edison.[36] In 1926, 20 years after his first tethered flight, he was made a Knight of Dannebrog. Both the Danish Aero Club and the Association of Danish Aviators awarded him honorary lifetime memberships. Jacob Christian Ellehammer is remembered in Denmark not only for his many engineering exploits, but also for the opening lines of his memoir, published in 1931: "Life is worthless in itself; it is what you make of it. The more you make, the more it is worth living."[37]

Dominican Republic

Date: 1930
Location: Campo Columbia, Cuba

Captain Aníbal Vallejo Sosa

In 1930 the Dominican Republic sent a group of soldiers, including Captain Aníbal Vallejo Sosa, to flight school in Cuba. The Cuerpo de Aviación Ejército at Campo Columbia served as a training ground for cadets from all over the Caribbean. Not unlike its neighbors, the Dominican Republic had never had a national aviation program. There had been, in fact, not a single Dominican-owned plane operated in the country from 1913 until 1928, perhaps not ever. Vallejo graduated from the Cuban school in 1930 and was placed in command of the country's new air force, El Arma de Aviación, Ejército Nacional. The air service purchased two Bellanca *Pacemakers*, one hydroplane and one with wheeled landing gear.

Vallejo worked closely with representatives from the United States Marine Corps, who had given the captain much of his early military training, and who now flew his planes and helped train his new cadets. Of course, Vallejo had not made the original decision to involve U.S. soldiers in the Dominican military. That had been going on since shortly after World War I, but Vallejo would suffer for his association with them. In the early 1930s, the country's new dictator began working to remove foreign influence from his armed forces. He sent several American pilots home, and in 1934 he replaced Vallejo with one of his fellows from the

Cuban flying school. These are the last details we have of Captain Vallejo.

Ecuador

Date: August 24, 1912
Location: Turin, Italy
Plane: Chiribiri monoplane

Lt. Colonel Cosimo Rennella
(1890–1937)

As might be guessed from his name, the man Ecuador recognizes as its first flier was actually of Italian descent. And not only of Italian parentage, but born near Naples as well. Rennella's parents moved him to Ecuador when Cosimo, known thereafter as Cosme, was two years old. He grew up in the port city of Guayaquil, Ecuador's largest city, among the nation's wealthiest and most prominent families. Although it's entirely possible that Rennella naturalized, we have no evidence that he did. His ties with Italy remained strong throughout his youth. When the Guayaquil Shooting and Flying Club voted to send him to Europe for pilot training, Rennella attended the Chiribiri school in Turin. Most non–European aviators traveled to Paris or Buc or Pau for their training, since France had the most varied manufacturers, the most numerous schools, and bestowed the most respected brevets. When he happened to be in Italy in 1915, Rennella joined the Italian air service for the duration of World War I. Despite his birth and long connection with Italy, however, Rennella spent the majority of his life in and around Ecuador, and he served in the Ecuadorian military over a period of 28 years. Because he is universally recognized as the first aviator of Ecuador and because no citizen of Ecuador makes a competing claim, we've chosen Rennella as the first.

In 1912 the Club Guayas de Tiro y Aviación shipped Rennella to Italy and paid for his pilot training. A sporting group of men from Ecuador's political and economic elite, the club was interested in training young men for a new air wing of the army.

Rennella received his civil license on August 24. What Rennella did during the next year varies according to different accounts, but he seems to have sailed back to Panama with a pair of Nieuport planes. Whether those machines had been purchased by someone in Panama, whether they were for the government, whether Rennella flew them in Central America when they had been reassembled, we can't tell from the record. But shortly after he arrived home, the club sent Rennella back to Italy to pick up a Chiribiri monoplane that had been purchased for Ecuador's first flying school. Before shipping out, Rennella met with Ecuador's president and vice-president, who pledged to provide financial support for the new national aviation school, Cuerpo de Aviación Ecuador. Once in Italy, Rennella was to oversee the production and testing of the plane, but he also found time to study for his Italian military license, a much more difficult certification than a civil license. He earned the higher brevet, Italian license number 212, in late July, 1913.

Rennella arrived in Ecuador with the new plane on September 29, 1913. On October 8, the school's first flying machine was named *Patria I* after a 1909 battalion raised at Rennella's school for a brief conflict with Peru. Rennella took the plane up for close to an hour, flying over a distinguished crowd of spectators and crossing the Guaya River to the small town of Duran, where he landed without incident. After clearing a runway and refilling his tank with petrol brought over by motorboat, Rennella flew back to Guayaquil, suffering on his return a cattywhompus landing that put the plane out of commission for a short time. Another demonstration on the 19th didn't go so well, however. Rennella wrecked the plane and completely destroyed it.

The club apparently began collecting funds for another plane, while Rennella visited Peru, Chile and Mexico. During this time, he may have flown reconnaissance or supply missions during Ecuador's Esmeraldas War with Colombia, though it's unclear what plane he would have used. In 1915 we find Rennella back in Italy on another purchasing mission for the club. This chore,

however, he would never complete. When Italy entered World War I, Rennella begged the Italian War Ministry for special consideration and was allowed into the air service. He entered flying school in September of 1915 training on a Farman biplane. After stints at three different schools on a variety of planes, he joined the 31st Squadron on April 14, 1916, and flew his first sortie the next day. By the end of August, he had been transferred three times and promoted to sergeant in the 45th Squadron. The next summer Rennella passed the physical exam for fighter training and in late August had joined his final squadron, the 78th. He flew a Nieuport *Ni17*, a small French biplane with the gun mounted atop the upper wing, and later the smaller and faster Hanriot *HD-1*. In the last year of the war, flying from bases in the Italian Alps at Aviano and in the far south at San Luca, Rennella would become Italy's seventh ace and garner more confirmed kills (seven confirmed for 17 claims) than any other pilot in his squadron. He was decommissioned as a sergeant major in early 1919, having earned War Merit Crosses from Italy, France and Belgium.[38]

In 1920, the war hero returned to Latin America to fly exhibitions in Venezuela. He started a military pilot school at Maracay, Venezuela, and served with the Mexican army. He finally went home to Ecuador in 1924, where he resumed his military service as a captain. Rennella's official rank, however, didn't make Ecuador's air force official. The country wouldn't organize a true military air service for another 11 years, so Rennella seems to have freelanced government and commercial flights. He worked at a flight school and made commercial trips for a company called Travel Air.

In 1926 Rennella flew Ecuador's first airmail, and he pioneered the mountainous route from Guayaquil to Quito for Travel Air in 1929. Because of the expense of maintaining the equipment, flying time was sparse even as a commercial pilot. In 1932 one of Travel Air's pilots wrecked its last plane, presumably ending the company's operations. Fortunately for Rennella, the Minister of War ordered two new Curtiss *Ospreys*

2nd Lt. Ernest Ayscoghe Floyer, Jr., Royal Flying Corps (Captain, Indian Army Reserve) June 2, 1916. Royal Air Force Museum, Hendon, London; Royal Aero Club of the United Kingdom certificates, Rac 3038.

instructors. For a short period, Rennella served as director of the school's curriculum.

Rennella was promoted to major in 1937 and in the same year attended a Dayton, Ohio, convention for World War I aces. He was struck down at the age of 47, not on a mission, but by pneumonia. He died in a Quito hospital on May 3, 1937. After his death, the military gave Rennella, already the holder of the Abdòn Calderòn Medal, Second Class, the honorary rank of Lieutenant Colonel. An aerobatics flight school in Salinas has been named after him (Escuela Superior Militar de Aviación "Cosme Rennella"), and one wing of an Austrian plane he shot down in the Italian Alps in 1917 has been preserved at the Museo de la Fuerza Aeria Ecuatoriana.

EGYPT

Date: June 2, 1916
Location: England

Captain Ernest Ayscoghe Floyer, Jr. (1888–1967)

The name Floyer comes from the Saxon word "flo" for arrow. Hence, an arrowmaker, in Saxon, was a "floyer," perhaps a fitting name for one who pilots war planes. Unfortunately, our Floyer was to spend most of his military service as a prisoner of war in Turkey. He was shot down behind enemy lines a little more than a year after joining the Royal Flying Corps, only nine months after getting his pilot's certification. He wouldn't be released until near the end of the war, and he never flew again.

Ernest Floyer, Jr., was born in Cairo, the son of two Lincolnshire natives, on the last day of June, 1888. His father, Egypt's Director-General of Telegraphs, served the Egypt-

a couple of months later. At least there was still government flying to do. As far as can be ascertained, the only military flying logged by Rennella during his years in Ecuador consisted of dropping leaflets over Quito during a brief troop rebellion. In 1934, the flight school was shut down because of difficulties training on the *Osprey*, but this turned out to be a temporary setback. The next year, Ecuador's new president reorganized the entire military. President José Maria Velasco Ibarra personally selected the staff for a military flying school in Guayaquil. He purchased planes and hired experienced flight ian khedive, the ruler of Egypt who at that time had been set up and was protected by the British. Sometime around 1910, his son moved to the Moran Tea Estate in Assam, India, and attached himself to a colonial cavalry unit called the Assam Light Horse. In 1911 the younger Floyer went with this detachment on a Himalayan expedition that seems to have been a natural history excursion to collect plants and insects from the area. By the beginning of World War I, Ernest Floyer, Jr., had reached the rank of captain in the Indian Army, where he served with the 7th Cavalry. In August of 1915, he entered the Indian Army Reserve. Not long after, probably at his own request, Floyer was seconded to the Royal Flying Corps. He remained a captain in the British Indian Army, but he would serve the rest of the war as a second lieutenant in the air wing. During his pilot's training in England that spring, Floyer married Lena Cecile Vost, another offspring of colonial British parents, born in Kanpur, India. The pair were married in Surrey on April 8, 1916.

Floyer completed his British military brevet, number 3038, on June 2. When he began his military flying in the Middle East two months later, 14 Squadron had just been outfitted with older Airco and Martinsyde scouts, perhaps transferred from the European front where they had become obsolete. The air work on the Ottoman front consisted mostly of reconnaissance, and Floyer apparently spent much of his time scouting around Palestine from various bases in Egypt. The Allied forces were attempting to work their way around the southeast corner of the Mediterranean into Palestine. The 14 Squadron bombed Ottoman supply lines and gave the engineers cover who were constructing a water pipeline into the desert to support the advancing troops. Floyer might have been flying a variety of planes, from older biplanes with no mounted guns or guns mounted on the upper wing to fire over the propeller, to more up-to-date two-seaters with bomb racks on either side of the fuselage. He apparently told his daughter in later years about carrying a small bomb in the cockpit for dropping by hand on a

convenient target. This would place him in a small scout for at least part of his flying service. Floyer was made a full lieutenant in October, 1916.

In March of 1917, Floyer was shot down in enemy territory and held as a prisoner at Kedos, Turkey, until the end of the war. He was awarded the Military Cross in absentia in August of that year, but he wouldn't return to England until late in 1918.

The next year Ernest and Lena Cecile had their first child, a girl. Ernest left the service in the autumn of 1919, and the family moved to British Columbia. Two more children, a boy and a girl, were born on the Floyer's Nine Mile Ranch in Canada. Their last child, however, came in England as the couple's marriage was disintegrating. They were divorced in 1925, and Ernest Floyer married Dorothy Castle, who had worked at the ranch in Canada. Floyer took his new bride to Kenya, where he managed the Kerichio Tea Plantation for the African Highlands Produce Company. During the Second World War, Floyer served as the officer in charge of Nyanza Province for the King's African Rifles.

According to his family, Floyer retired in 1953, and he and Dorothy moved to his mother's house in Surrey. Having spent most of his life much nearer the equator, Floyer couldn't tolerate the cold and damp in his ancestral country. He eventually went back to Kenya with his wife and purchased a small coffee plantation. Here he stayed until his death from appendicitis in 1967.

EL SALVADOR

Date: 1914
Location: San Francisco, USA

Julio Yudice

In the summer of 1914, a Salvadoran flier appears in the brief notes of the Chilean Aero Club. The club's bulletin mentions "a beautiful biplane," capable of carrying a pilot and two passengers, designed and constructed by a man named Julio Yudice. The

Henry Farman, January 13, 1908, completing Europe's first kilometer circuit to win the Grand Prix d'Aviation, Issy-Les-Moulineaux, France. National Air and Space Museum, Smithsonian Institution (SI Neg. No. 89-19606).

only additional information concerning Yudice is that he earned his *brevet* at a flight school in San Francisco, but there is no American license in his name before World War I.

ENGLAND
(GREAT BRITAIN)

Date: October 15, 1907
Location: Issy-les-Moulineaux
Length: 285 meters (926 ft.)
Flyer: *Voisin-Farman I,* pusher biplane

Harry "Henry" Edgar Mumford Farman (1874–1958)

When the Royal Aero Club of the United Kingdom met in 1928 to determine who had been the first Englishman to fly, it didn't even consider the man we've cho-sen. In fact, Henry Farman wouldn't have claimed that distinction for himself. Farman, who preferred to be called after the French, Henri, was born in Paris and lived there most of his life. He called himself French, and flew rarely on British soil. He spoke only halting English. The Royal Aero Club wouldn't have taken his name in 1928, for he hadn't lived or flown on English soil in the early days. Farman's father, the wealthy Thomas Farman, served as Paris correspondent for the London *Evening Standard* for 30 years. Thomas Farman and his wife were decidedly British, and they registered their son with the British consulate at birth. However, the deciding detail is this: When the French government wished to recognize Henry Farman's contributions to flight with an appointment to the Légion d'Honneur in 1909, Farman had to apply to the British Crown for permission to accept such an honor from a foreign government.[39]

Henry Farman (holding anemometer) and Louis Blériot (with binoculars). National Air and Space Museum, Smithsonian Institution (SI Neg. No. A-31990-L).

Henry Farman took up aviation in 1906, the year after a wreck that soured him on automobile racing. He had already been a cycling champion in 1892 and an auto racer for eight years. From 1901 through 1905 he competed with the best drivers in the world, including our first Belgian flier, Baron Pierre de Caters. Claiming the dangers of racing upset his family, Farman walked away from cars. In the fall of 1906 the highly publicized success of Alberto Santos-Dumont inspired Farman, and he decided to take up the nascent sport of aviation.[40] His family seems to have agreed that the air was safer than the automobile, since his wife and brothers eventually joined him in the aviation business. Farman purchased his first glider that fall. When he felt sufficiently practiced, he bought a powered airplane from the Voisin brothers, who ran the only commercial airplane factory in the world.

Farman's experience piloting rickety cars on bad roads evidently stood him well when he turned to aircraft. On his very first attempt in September of 1907, Farman managed to get his new *Voisin-Farman I* into the air for 30 meters. His first sustained flight was only his second try at piloting a powered craft. This was a flight of 285 meters (926 ft.) on October 15, 1907. By the end of October, he had set a new European distance record of 723 meters (2,350 ft.), and in November he tried for the 100,000-franc Grand Prix d'Aviation for the first closed circuit, one-kilometer flight.

To fully appreciate the difficulty of this flight, keep in mind that European planes at this time had no ailerons or other means of controlling side-to-side balance. The wings were build with a slight upward angle from the fuselage (dihedral) to help keep the machine right-side up, but they still had to be

Henry Farman in a vintage biplane for a 1942 French movie. A stuffed bear is lashed to the pole behind him in the same way as "Madame X" 33 years earlier. Technical Reports & Standards Unit, Library of Congress, L'Aérophile Collection.

flown in zero wind. When one of the Parisian experimenters wanted to make a test flight in 1907, he would visit the military parade ground at Issy-les-Moulineaux very early in the morning, say, five or six o'clock. This suburb was surrounded by the smokestacks of Paris industry, and only if the smoke from those factories rose vertically into the air without the slightest disturbance would a pilot consider rolling his machine out of the hangar. By mid-morning, it would probably be too breezy to fly. Not only was a wind

Opposite: Henry Farman in an August 13, 1909, exhibition flight with "Madame X," who rode standing up behind the pilot. The stuntress is probably Farman's wife. Technical Reports & Standards Unit, Library of Congress, L'Aérophile Collection.

dangerous because it might tip a plane side-ways, but turns were dangerous because the plane could not be intentionally tipped side-ways. Like a bird, an airplane leans into a turn so that the lift of its wings can help make the corner. When Farman tried for the Grand Prix that fall, he flew several times the required distance because it was so delicate a maneuver to turn the machine with only a rudder like that on a boat. His tail slipped and slid to the side as he gave it as much rud-der as he could without letting his machine get out of control.

Farman did not win the Grand Prix that month. The judges ruled that his wheels had touched the ground during the loop and that he had not quite closed the circle. That prize he won two months later, on January 13, 1908. Farman's aerial steed saw numerous modifications that year, even becoming a tri-plane at various short intervals. Henry Far-man made the first passenger flights in Eu-rope on May 29 and 30. He set several distance and altitude records and made the world's first cross-country flight, or *raid*, as the French called it, from Buoy to Reims northeast of Paris on October 2. This 40-kilometer (25 mi.) flight lasted 44½ min-utes and was the first time an aviator had ventured away from his airfield to fly over the open countryside. After seeing Wilbur Wright demonstrate the advanced controls of the *Flyer* at Auvours that fall, Farman added the world's first effective ailerons to his plane.

Not long after, Farman commissioned the Voisin brothers to build a new plane to his own specifications. When he was ready to pick up the new machine, however, he found that the Voisins, in need of ready cash, had already sold his design to another English-man, J.T.C. Moore-Brabazon. Incensed, Far-man struck out on his own in February of 1909, establishing a factory and school near where he had started his historic cross-coun-try flight the previous fall. This location on the vast Plain of Châlons, thereafter known as Camp-de-Châlons, soon became a popu-lar spot for new manufacturers. Fittingly, Farman's firm would be the Voisins' great-est competitor. The first Farman plane, the

Henry Farman III, was so stable and easy to fly that it became, with its descendants, the world's most popular design in the years leading up to World War I.[41]

The year 1909 ushered aviation onto the world stage, and Henry Farman occupied the spotlight with three other great pioneers. The Wright brothers were still the toast of Europe when they headed back to the United States in May. Louis Blériot stole the head-lines in July when he beat Englishman Hu-bert Latham in the race to cross the English channel. And Henry Farman won the Cham-pagne Grand Prix with a flight of 180 kilo-meters (112 mi.) in a little over three hours at the world's first international air meet that August. The Reims flying week, August 22–29, hosted some 30 flying machines, 18 of which actually flew. An estimated half a mil-lion people came to see the spectacle of ma-chines racing each other through the air. For his distance win and his placings in other contests, Farman took home 63,000 francs ($227,000 today).

In all, Henry Farman set more records for altitude, endurance and distance than any other single flier in the years 1907–1910, 13 total, including a four-hour flight to win the Michelin Prize in November of 1909.

The next year, he would set an en-durance record of more than eight hours and make the first night flights, using Chinese lanterns hung from the tips of his wings.[42] His wife may have been the world's first stunt passenger. Mrs. Farman, posing as the mysterious "Madame X," made exhibition flights standing upright behind her hus-band, lashed by the waist to a vertical pole. Henry's brother, Maurice, began to be suc-cessful in marketing his own designs, and a third brother, Dick, helped his siblings keep the books at their jointly held factory. Henry and Maurice sold their machines indepen-dently of one another until they merged their companies at the beginning of World War I. During the war, the Farmans finally spent some time in England and even flew on English soil.

Perhaps because of his instinct for sta-ble planes (and his famous preference for low altitudes), Henry Farman avoided the fates of so many pilots in the second decade of the century. Though many of his fellows— including Charles Rolls (of Rolls-Royce), Samuel F. Cody and Captain Ferdinand Ferber—died piloting, Farman continued to fly until his retirement. In 1926 the French government memorialized his kilometer circuit flight with a monument at Camp-de-Châlons. There are also monuments on the parade grounds at Issy-les-Moulineaux, where Farman made his first flights, and at the spot where he touched down in Reims after the world's first cross-country flight. Although the first Englishman with wings, Farman died a much-decorated Frenchman at the age of 84 in Paris, having finally gained his French citizenship in 1937.[43]

But who did the Royal Aero Club, when it convened in 1928, decide was the first Englishman to fly? Surprisingly, the committee had only a short stack of names to sort through. This is notable when one considers that England had been the rightful birthplace of heavier-than-air flight and the center of aviation work for the whole of the 19th century. One hundred years before the Wrights, Sir George Cayley had begun designing models that would set the basic criteria for modern airplanes: not flapping wings, but fixed planes ("aeroplanes") with a separate engine to provide thrust. Cayley published his extensive findings in 1809 and spent another 45 years testing successful models and man-carrying gliders. Englishmen like John Stringfellow, Francis Wenham and Horatio Phillips elaborated on aspects of Cayley's work throughout the rest of the 19th century. But by the advent of the motorcar in the 1890s, the British elite had become ensconced in imperial comfort. The automobile so scared English society that for a while every car on city streets had to be preceded by a man walking with a bell and a red flag. Likewise, aviation experimenters who lacked large, unforested estates on which to test their contraptions were considered a public safety hazard. As a consequence, Alliot Verdon Roe, one of the more serious candidates for first English aviator, lived with his airplane under bridges and in makeshift hangars during the years when pioneers in the rest of Europe were experimenting in public parks or on land provided by sponsoring aero clubs and government agencies.

Others with formal claims to the first English flight were American expatriate Hiram Maxim, who launched a 4-ton, steam-driven craft in 1894, and Horatio Phillips, whose venetian-blind–like multiplane made what was eventually judged to be an uncontrolled hop in 1907.[44] Samuel F. Cody, another American expatriate and purveyor of a Wild West show, who became an English citizen only years after he first flew, did as much as anyone to develop aviation in England. And then there was the aristocrat and long-time officer in the Royal Air Force, J.T.C. Moore-Brabazon, who undisputedly flew in the spring of 1909 on the plane that Henry Farman had designed.

The committee ruled that Hiram Maxim and Samuel Cody, not British citizens when they flew, couldn't be considered. A lack of evidence prompted the committee to dismiss the claims of both Horatio Phillips and A.V. Roe. On the overwhelming evidence that he had flown at the Aero Club's field at Shellbeach on the weekend of April 30–May 2, 1909, Lt. Colonel Moore-Brabazon was named the first English aviator. A distinguished flyer and the leading light in British aviation for half a century, Moore-Brabazon served in various ministry posts and in Parliament and was the Chairman of the Royal Aeronautical Society for many years in the 1930s. He was made a peer and titled Lord Brabazon of Tara in 1942.

ESTONIA

Date: June 30, 1910
Location: Riga, Latvia
Plane: Grade monoplane

Theodor Wilhelm Franz Meybaum (1864–?)

Theodor Meybaum is one of those transient personalities who show up occasionally in early aviation, floating from place to

Mishka Babitcheff, September 1, 1930. Royal Air Force Museum, Hendon, London; Royal Aero Club of the United Kingdom certificates, Rac 14497.

take off, land and keep a plane in the air for that long.

Meybaum was born in the port city of Pärnu on the Gulf of Riga on October 5, 1864. He did most of his recorded flying in Latvia and Germany, making him an obscure figure in Estonian aviation history. After his test flights in Leutner's machine, Meybaum gave a public demonstration on July 19, 1910. He began another exhibition flight on the 20th, but a nasty wind pushed him toward the spectators and he ditched the plane into an embankment, giving himself a concussion, a broken thumb and several wire-cuts on his face.

The Estonian shows up in Prussia next, where he earned German pilot's license number 74 on February 17, 1911. He was 46 at the time and the oldest person to earn a German license before 1913. He then went to work for the Albatros company teaching students at their flying school, mostly German officers. Many of the earliest German military pilots received their training from Meybaum.

When the Prussian army invaded Latvia in 1915, Meybaum went to Russia, returning to Riga after the war when Latvia became independent. We have no details of his life during the brief period of free governance in the Baltic republics. In 1939 the Soviet Union signed a non-aggression pact with Nazi Germany, effectively dividing Eastern Europe between the two great powers. Meybaum's experience with the Bolsheviks in 1917 had been so bad that when the Soviets occupied Latvia he fled in the opposite direction, choosing Nazi Germany over the Soviet Union. This is all we know of Meybaum.

place flying exhibitions, often in rich men's planes, and giving lessons to support themselves. The first record of a flight by Meybaum is from the Latvian newspaper *Rigaer Tageblatt* in mid–1910. It seems Meybaum was hired by a Riga bicycle manufacturer named Leutner to test his newly purchased Grade monoplane.[45] According to the newspaper account, Meybaum flew the little 25-horsepower machine for 4–5 minutes on June 30 at the Solitude hippodrome just outside Riga. The Estonian pilot had obviously flown before that day if he could successfully

ETHIOPIA

Date: September 1, 1930
Location: Jijiga, Ethiopia

Mishka Babitcheff (1908–?)

Ethiopia has been fortunate to escape all but a very short brush with European colonization, and this may help explain why Ethiopia has one of the few first pilots of at least partial African descent. Mishka Babitcheff was born in the capital city of Addis-Ababa on October 14, 1908, as Wilbur Wright was demonstrating his *Flyer* to enthusiastic crowds in France. Babitcheff's father was Russian, his mother, Ethiopian.

According to an Ethiopian Airlines publication, Babitcheff trained as a commercial pilot in 1930. He completed his training in September and made demonstration flights in Addis-Ababa on the 15th of October. Babitcheff apparently stayed with the company and was made Chief Pilot in late 1935. He traveled to England to get his international pilot's license, number 14,497, which he earned at the Brooklands Flying Club in a de Havilland *DH-60 Gipsy Moth* on October 11, 1936.

Nothing else is known of Babitcheff's life except that at some point he served as the Ethiopian Chargé d'Affaires in Moscow.

2nd Lt. Henry Vernon Worrall, September 30, 1915. Royal Air Force Museum, Hendon, London; Royal Aero Club of the United Kingdom certificates, Rac 1878.

FIJI (GREAT BRITAIN)

Date: September 30, 1915
Location: Eastbourne, England
Plane: Grahame-White Type XV

Captain Henry Vernon Worrall (1888–?)

Captain Henry Worrall may be our only first flier to work from an early "aircraft carrier," more specifically a seaplane carrier, during World War I. Worrall was stationed on the ship *Ben-my-Chree* in 1916 and flew raids on the Ottoman front around Palestine. In the second decade of flight, planes were still severely limited in range. Only one World War I machine could stay in the air for more than four hours, and its maximum speed was 112 kilometers per hour (70 m.p.h.), giving it an effective range of little more than 500 kilometers (315 mi.). Only this one plane, the Vickers FB5 fighter, could hope to attack a target or check enemy troop movements 250 kilometers (156 mi.) from base and have enough fuel to return safely. So British merchant ships were enlisted to carry seaplanes to within striking distance of a conflict or a reconnaissance target. These earliest carriers had no flight deck, at least nothing more than a space to tie down the aircraft when they weren't in use. When it was time to fly a mission, a crane lowered the aircraft into the water one by one. On their return, the pilots landed in the sea and waited their turn to be taken aboard. A handy setup in the relatively calm Mediterranean, perhaps, but hardly useful in the North Atlantic.

Worrall was born in Levuka, the old capital city of Fiji, on June 2, 1888. At the age of 27, he earned his military pilot's brevet, number 1878, at the Eastbourne flight school in the Royal Naval Air Service, September 30, 1915. Like his fellow trainees, Worrall began his flying as a second lieutenant. Until his move to the Mediterranean in June of 1916, he patrolled the English Channel for the R.N.A.S., probably on the same Grahame-White Type 15 biplanes on which he had trained at Eastbourne. From *Ben-my-Chree* in the Mideast, he flew bombing raids and served as a scout in late 1917 during the Gaza Battle, the turning point for the Allies on the Ottoman front. His World War I service earned him the Distinguished Service Cross. After the war, Worrall taught cadets to pilot flying boats at Felixstowe until 1922, when he entered the reserves as a captain. In 1926 he began working for the Blackburn Aeroplane Company demonstrating machines in Brazil.

As far as we've been able to discover, Worrall's last aerial adventure may have been a six-month survey of the African coast with Sir Alan Cobham. The expedition left Kent on the 17th of November, 1927, in a Short Brothers S5 flying boat named *Singapore I*. They pioneered an air route up the Nile River from Cairo to Khartoum to Kampala, over Lake Victoria to Nairobi, then clockwise around the African coast, through Cape Town, Luanda, Accra, Dakar, the Canary Islands, and Casablanca. Worrall served as Cobham's co-pilot and second in charge and often stayed with the plane when Sir and Lady Cobham went off to collect parts for the engine or to attend diplomatic soirées. Cobham and his crew returned to England on May 5, 1928, having traveled 32,000 kilometers (20,000 mi.).

FINLAND

Date: April 20, 1911
Location: Pyhäjärvi Lake
Plane: *Demoiselle*-type monoplane

Karl Adolf Aarno

The only information we have about Finland's first successful flights comes from the history of a Finnish airline. According to the *Finnair* publication, a Tampere sculptor named Karl Adolf Aarno flew a *Demoiselle*-type monoplane on "ice-covered Pyhäjärvi" on April 20, 1911. Tampere and Pyhäjärvi Lake are located north of Helsinki in the southern central portion of the country.

FRANCE

Date: March 30, 1907
Location: Bagatelle Park, Paris
Length: 80 meters (262 ft.)
Flyer: *Voisin-Delagrange I*, pusher biplane

Gabriel & Charles Voisin
(1880–1973, 1882–1910)

When the Aéro-Club de France announced in 1910 the names of 16 international pilots who would receive the club's first licenses, only three of the men were working or had worked outside Paris. At the turn of the century, Western industry and culture revolved around the French capital. For years before the club awarded its first brevets, inventors and sportsmen from around the world had converged on France to watch the experiments at Issy-les-Moulineaux, to buy airplanes, and to consult with leaders in the field. In the spirit of collaborative invention that permeated France during that time, Parisians would dominate the rolls of early inventors and pilots. It should only be surprising, then, that a Frenchman took his turn, not as the first man to fly, but as the fourth.

As it happened, the first French aviator was Charles Voisin, an airplane manufacturer with his brother, Gabriel, and in early 1907, a test pilot. A wealthy Parisian sculptor named Léon Delagrange had agreed to purchase a Voisin Brothers plane if it could be shown to fly. (One built for another customer that year had never left the ground.) On March 30, 1907, Charles Voisin took their newly finished biplane into the air over Bagatelle Park for about 6 seconds, traveling 80 meters (262 ft.) and setting the machine back down to collect payment. Looking back on that cloth-covered contraption, half canard, half boxkite, held together by piano wire, one can hardly fault the cautious Delagrange, whose proof cost him the chance to become his nation's first flier. The Voisin's success paid their overdue bistro tab, but it also marked the birth of a distinctive biplane that would figure prominently in the first decade of powered flight.

Natural pilot though he was (it would take Delagrange more than seven months to get the same machine into the air), Charles Voisin had not been particularly smitten with aviation himself. It was Gabriel who had lured Charles into the aircraft business from his more or less full-time amorous pursuits. Without an aviation success of his own and more than a year before most Europeans were convinced a man could fly, Gabriel had started the continent's first commercial airplane factory in 1905 with fellow Frenchman Louis Blériot. With vastly different approaches to invention and testing, the two men clashed, and when Blériot left, Gabriel convinced his daring and dexterous brother to join the venture, making it the historic Appareils d'Aviation Les Frères Voisin.

The sons of a middle-class business owner who committed suicide when his children were young, the Voisin brothers grew up around their grandfather's gas works on the Saône River in the east of France, near Lyons. They taught themselves joinery and mechanics, and experimented with autos and engines and man-lifting kites. They even converted a sailboat into a sluggish steam launch that provided much amusement for the local populace. In his 1963 book *Men,*

Women and 10,000 Kites (translated from *Les 10,000 Cerfs-Volants*), Gabriel remembered his brother as a charismatic, happy-go-lucky young man with a well-developed sense of humor. Charles could make accurate distance measurements by eye, which made him a remarkably good shot with a homemade bow and arrow in the local park, as well as with a pea shooter in the opera house. He often used the popular "red Indian" lingo of the era, addressing his co-conspirators by the title, "All-powerful chief," while referring to himself as "the Sun."[46] The brothers performed a war dance after the successful trial of any new Voisin device.

Gabriel was inspired to take up aviation during a working visit to the Universal Exposition of 1900 in Paris. He was a student of architecture and had landed a contract to supervise the plumbing going into the Exposition buildings. One of the featured displays was Clement Ader's *Avion III*, the original version of which (*Eole*) had made the world's first manned take-off from level ground in 1890. Awestruck by the complex machine, the elder Voisin climbed inside and peered around its massive steam engine at the spreading wings, imagining the roar of the wind in his ears and the ground fleeing underneath him. Gabriel returned to his studies but kept aviation in the back of his mind, occasionally attending a lecture on the subject, until he had completed his architecture degree in 1904. At a lecture by the French airship pioneer Charles Renard that year, Gabriel approached the lectern and introduced himself. Impressed by his enthusiasm, Renard referred Gabriel to the foremost French experimenter at the time, Ferdinand Ferber, who finally sent Voisin to Ernest Archdeacon. A wealthy Paris attorney and the president of the Aéro-Club de France, Archdeacon was just finishing his first glider design, and he hired Gabriel Voisin to fly it for him.

On Easter Sunday of 1904, on a beach north of Paris, Voisin took the Archdeacon machine into the air for glides of up to 25 seconds.[47] Like the Wright gliders, the Archdeacon had a front elevator and a rudder in the back, but it had no form of lateral con-

trol. Nor did it have other features, like wing dihedral, for example, to help stabilize its flight. Gabriel finished the day battered but enthusiastic.

Archdeacon finished building his second glider in early 1905. The well-connected Archdeacon arranged to test his machine on the military parade ground at Issy-les-Moulineaux, a south–Paris suburb that would become the center of European aviation two years later. Archdeacon would tow the glider aloft with a motor car, and Gabriel wanted to be onboard. Archdeacon, however, insisted on a trial run with sandbags in place of the pilot. When it had risen 10 meters, the glider disintegrated in the air, convincing Archdeacon and Voisin that they should make further tests over water. When the glider had been repaired and strengthened, it was hitched behind a motor boat on the Seine in early June and towed into the air for more than 600 meters (2,000 ft.). Immediately after this success, Voisin began collaborating with one of the greatest names in early aviation, French engineer and successful headlight manufacturer, Louis Blériot. Voisin had a Blériot glider built a month later. Although uncomfortable with his client's design, Voisin tested the glider on the Seine as he had the Archdeacon machine. The Blériot rose from the water for a mere 30 meters before it plunged into the river, fell apart and trapped Voisin underwater in a web of support wires. His boat crew dove into the river and extricated their pilot.

Voisin went into official partnership with Blériot for the next year or so, producing a number of unsuccessful, even bizarre,

Frenchman Clement Ader, inventor of *Eole*, the first machine to make a manned take-off from level ground (1890). National Air and Space Museum, Smithsonian Institution (SI Neg. No. 93-4217).

powered craft designed by Blériot. The two grew apart, and in 1906 Gabriel invited his brother to join him in the business. Their first success was the plane ordered by Brazilian Alberto Santos-Dumont that made the first flights in Europe that fall. Santos-Dumont, an independent and unflappable dandy, attracted a rare bit of ridicule in the press when he tested *14-bis*, first beneath a balloon, then on a guywire with a donkey pulling. Although Gabriel Voisin probably had a strong hand in the design of *14-bis* (at that time Santos had little background in the

Opposite: Clement Ader's steam-powered *Avion III* at the Paris Salon d'Aviation, c. 1909. Technical Reports & Standards Unit, Library of Congress, L'Aérophile Collection.

Charles Voisin (left) and Henry Farman with a Voisin Brothers fuselage, c. 1908, possibly the Farman design that was sold to someone else, causing a split between Farman and the Voisins. Technical Reports & Standards Unit, Library of Congress, L'Aérophile Collection.

A Blériot monoplane, Issy-les-Moulineaux, France, restrained by spectators while the engine warms up. National Air and Space Museum, Smithsonian Institution (SI Neg. No. 80-15345).

Early Henry Farman biplane, the most popular brand sold before World War I. Rotary engines often spewed castor oil everywhere. This one may be burning more than normal. Technical Reports & Standards Unit, Library of Congress, L'Aérophile Collection.

A Henry Farman factory, c. 1910, the world's most popular plane in the foreground. Technical Reports & Standards Unit, Library of Congress, L'Aérophile Collection.

science of heavier-than-air flight), Voisin distanced himself from Santos and his design so effectively that it became impossible to determine which of the plane's features came from which designer.

Unlike most aeronautical experimenters at the turn of the century, the Voisins didn't have the money to build their own machines. They had to wait for a wealthy patron to finance their construction. The next such man to happen along was Henri Kapferer, who ordered what would be the first in a line of standard Voisin biplanes, a large machine with an elevator out front and a boxkite-style tail with rudders inside. Although the Kapferer machine never flew, the next one, *Voisin-Delagrange I*, took Charles up for his first flight at the end of March, 1907. This machine, built for the world's fifth

pilot, was refined further for their next client, Henry Farman, the world's sixth pilot.[48] Farman turned out to be a gold mine. A Paris-raised Englishman who preferred to be called "Henri," after the French, Farman was a gifted aviator and began attracting publicity immediately. Farman also had a knack for plane design, and he worked with the Voisins to alter his machine little by little, improving its performance and keeping himself and the Voisins in the headlines. Farman flew the *Voisin-Farman I* for nearly a year and a half, making the first circle kilometer in Europe, carrying the first passengers in Europe and making the world's first cross-country flight. The Voisins tried a couple of intermediate designs with Farman, a tandem and a monoplane, but neither were finished. In late 1908 Farman commissioned

Gabriel (left) and Charles Voisin. ©Musée de l'Air et de l'Espace / Le Bourget.

a new plane utilizing the modifications he had made to the first.

Meanwhile, Delagrange had wrecked his original Voisin and purchased another. He began traveling France and Italy giving demonstration flights. In the fall of 1908, the Voisins built three triplanes, two in collaboration with Ambroise Goupy and a very similar machine for our first Belgian flier, Baron Pierre de Caters. None of these did particularly well. That winter, when Henry Farman went to the Billancourt factory to pick up his new *Voisin-Farman II*, he found that Gabriel had already sold his design to someone else. Incensed, Farman broke with the Voisins and very shortly set up a factory and flying school at Camp-de-Châlons east of Paris. This falling out did irreparable damage to the Voisins' business. Farman's first plane, *Henry Farman III*, quickly became the most popular plane in Europe. Farman had learned the lesson of lateral control from Wilbur Wright's demonstrations in 1908. Up to that point, European flying machines made flat, rudder-only turns, and they had no provi-

sion to correct a sudden tilt. With wing-warping for lateral control, Wright had been able to fly graceful, bird-like corners and even fly in winds that were considered too dangerous on European machines. Farman added ailerons to his old Voisin, and when it was time to build his own plane, it included ailerons also. *Henry Farman III* was a remarkably easy plane to fly, compared to a Voisin or a Wright or a Blériot, and the Farman biplanes would be the most popular planes before World War I.

The Voisins ignored the Wrights' exhibition flights. They were among the first in the fall of 1908, even as Wilbur continued to fly figure-eights in the French sky, to discount the achievements of the Wright brothers. Later they would trumpet the French claim to first flight (Clement Ader's flying machines of the 1890s). When every designer in Europe added either wing-warping or ailerons for lateral control, the Voisins stuck stubbornly to their "automatically stable" design. Although Gabriel Voisin and Wilbur Wright approached the problem of flight from opposite angles, in some ways they were very much alike. Wright would never have risked his life testing another man's flying machine; Voisin made his living that way. Wright worked empirically, Voisin by intuition. But both worked closely with a sibling and were suspicious of outsiders. Although Wright was frugal and Voisin a spendthrift, both had worked their way to success with few resources. After 1908 each seemed more concerned with defending himself and his system than with developing better aircraft. While the Wrights stuck inexplicably with their derrick-and-rail launching system and their intentionally unstable wings, Voisin continued with vertical panels in his biplane wings ("side curtains") and refused to make provision for lateral control. Other builders struck a balance between these two extremes, getting rid of needless wing panels, adding wheels to Wright-style biplanes, and adding a little dihedral for stability while making provisions for lateral control. Over the next couple of years, the businesses of both men would suffer for their inflexibility.

Before the slump, however, the Voisin factory would turn out planes for many of the world's first and most famous aviators. Voisin planes opened the skies in Sweden, Ukraine, Russia, Poland, Turkey, Egypt, India, Mexico and Argentina. Escapologist Harry Houdini flew a Voisin when he made the first flights in Australia.[49] For his contributions to aviation, Gabriel was awarded a cash prize of a million francs in 1909 and was made the youngest Chevalier of the Légion d'Honneur.

Business began to slow noticeably in 1910, and Charles quit the firm to exhibit and race planes on his own. Gabriel struggled to regain his lost market share and eventually added ailerons to some of his models. He also produced what may have been the world's first aluminum-framed machine in 1911 and a canard-style hydroplane the next year. Tragically, Charles died in an automobile accident in Belleville in 1912. He was 30 years old. Gabriel fought to reestablish his position in the industry but had little success before the First World War. His big break

may have been a couple of bombers he sold to the French military eight months before the conflict. When the war began, the French government endorsed only a few aircraft designs for military use. Voisin won one of the military licenses. Formerly competing factories around the country began producing Gabriel's bombers. By war's end, more than 10,000 had been built.

Despite his own previous talk of the military potential of airplanes, Voisin was shocked by the direction aviation took during the war. The war itself was shocking enough. The tactics and weapons of the Great War heralded the end of any chivalric code in armed conflict. But for the free, soaring airplane to be turned into a flying coffin, it was unthinkable. Voisin began to take the deaths of aviators very personally, and when the war ended, with all his bomber designs belonging to the French government, Gabriel exited the aviation business for good and began to manufacture automobiles.

In *Men, Women and 10,000 Kites*, Gabriel portrays his brother, Charles, the first French aviator, as a man of appetites and impulses with an irrepressible humor. Judging from his writings, Gabriel was less good-humored than he portrays his brother. His memoir is a casebook in chauvinism and bitterness. Gabriel spends most of his energy defending himself, denigrating the Wrights' claim to first flight, and disparaging almost anyone who wasn't a Voisin, even those we might call his friends and associates. Perhaps he was embittered by the losses of his later years. His only son, 22 years old, was killed in World War II. Gabriel had lost his automobile company not long before.

But at the end of his days, Gabriel Voisin had lived a life of remarkable successes. He had built many of the world's first airplanes, machines that dominated early records and competitions. His company, the first in the world to sell airplanes, lasted 14 years and thrived for most of them. And his later venture into automobiles was an incredible success, gaining him worldwide recognition for his visionary designs. In 1909, at the age of 29, he was the youngest Chevalier, and his company was bringing in millions of francs a year. He was known as a kind and conscientious employer, and his writings show a deep humanity regarding the development of wartime aviation and his own place in that destructive trend.

Despite his successes, Gabriel was nearly broke by the 1950s, and only the timely return of an old girlfriend, who gave him a cottage he had bought for her years before, kept him from penury. He died in 1973, maintaining to the last that his planes, indeed, that world aviation, owed nothing to the Wright brothers.

GEORGIA

Date: August 29, 1910
Location: France
Plane: Blériot

Vissarion Kaburov (1877–?)

There is a legend that the father of a very well-known and colorful Georgian pilot was the first person to fly a private airplane in the Russian Empire. Born in Tbilisi, the capital city of Georgia, Alexander Procofiev de Seversky is supposed to have learned to fly his father's French plane in 1908 at the age of 14. We know little about the father, but the younger de Seversky went on to earn his military brevet in the Imperial Russian Army in 1915, to lose his right leg below the knee on his first bombing mission, to fly fighter planes and to earn every possible decoration during his two years of Russian military service. When the October Revolution began, de Seversky had been sent to Washington, D.C., with a military delegation, and he stayed in the United States from then on. The Seversky Aero Company, founded in 1922, produced the first automatic bomb sight. De Seversky served on numerous U.S. advisory panels on aviation, produced famous racing planes and wrote books on the use of air power in war.

Unfortunately, the legend of the first flight in the Russian Empire may be just that: a legend. There do not seem to have been any working airplanes in the Russian Empire in 1908. European planes wouldn't begin to show up in Russia until almost 1910. Nor does the family name appear in lists of Russian airplane owners anytime before 1914. It is possible that de Seversky or his father flew before his lesser known countryman, Vissarion Kaburov, but it's a claim we cannot substantiate.

Vissarion Kaburov is the first Georgian to earn an international pilot's brevet, and the information contained in his license is all we know of Kaburov. He passed his flying test on the 29th of August, 1910, flying a Blériot monoplane, and was awarded brevet number 210 from the Aéro-Club de France. Kaburov was born on September 21, 1877, in the east–Georgian city of Koutaisi.

GERMANY (PRUSSIA)

Date: December 31, 1909

August Euler (1868–?)

August Euler is the holder of German pilot's license No. 1, but he is not recognized by Germans as their first flier. Because of the changes to the world map since 1918, particularly in Eastern Europe, the man widely credited for the first German flight, Hans Grade, has been listed in this book under Poland, for he was born a few miles to the east of what is now the German border. August Euler was the first pilot who had been born within the modern borders of Germany.

Euler was also the first to manufacture airplanes in Germany. An entrepreneur on the cutting edge, Euler had worked in the bicycle industry starting in the early 1890s. One source claims he "introduced the bicycle to Russia." When the Wrights made their first powered flight in 1903, Euler was just setting up what would be a successful auto parts business in Frankfurt. He was an enthusiastic athlete and, like many of our first pilots, raced bicycles and cars for years before aviation grabbed his attention. In late 1908 when it had become apparent to close observers that flying would soon become a practical means of transportation and sport,

Euler began producing airplane parts in his Frankfurt auto factory. Immediately, he applied for the rights to produce the French Voisin planes and arranged through a high-ranking military friend to locate a new factory and a flying school on the military field at Darmstadt.

Euler jumped into the aviation business with both feet, but he took a little more time to actually learn to fly. Had he begun testing a new Voisin as soon as he started selling airplane parts, Euler may well have been the first citizen of Prussia to make a sustained flight. (Hans Grade's first success was February 18, 1909.) Instead, Euler built himself a glider and spent several months mastering that art before he took up powered flight. We don't know exactly when he made his first sustained flight. He seems to have had a Voisin plane in the summer of 1909, but his first recorded hop wasn't until September. He participated in the first German air meet at Frankfurt the next month, but we have no details of his performance. He was reportedly the only German aviator to leave the ground. We do know that Euler fulfilled the requirements for a German pilot's license on December 31, 1909, only hours after the criteria were announced. He had probably flown a couple of months earlier, but this is our first concrete date.

Eventually, Euler began producing Wright planes in Germany. Whether he ever got the rights to sell Voisins, we don't know. Starting in 1910, Euler's flying school would train many of the first German military aviators and even the Kaiser's brother, Prince Heinrich. Beyond this point, however, we know nothing of Euler's career or his life.

GHANA

Date: August 27, 1946
Location: Essex Aero Club, England
Plane: de Havilland *Tiger Moth*

Peter Ayles

Peter Ayles was born in the town of Kumasi, in what was then known as the Gold Coast. We have no birth date, but Ayles earned his pilot's certificate, number 21,686, on August 27, 1946, at the Essex Aero Club in England. He flew a de Havilland *Tiger Moth*.

GREECE

Date: August 9, 1910
Location: France
Plane: Sommer biplane

Michel Paul Molla (1886–1951)

The legend of Icarus is certainly one of the best recognized tales in Greek mythology and has become a universal Western metaphor for artistic creation and the joy and danger of artistic freedom. A brilliant inventor named Daedalus, imprisoned by King Minos on the island of Crete, fashioned wings for himself and his son, Icarus, out of a wooden frame, bird feathers and wax. It must have taken years to collect enough feathers to build two sets of wings, setting each quill individually in the wax and letting it harden again, adding another next to it, until finally the wings were finished. Daedalus, thinking of the wax he worked so many times with his hands, warned his son to stay low, nearer to the cool ocean and away from the radiance of the sun. They flew from the island, but Icarus's heart swelled at the feeling of his new wings and he soared too high for the soft wax. His wings melted. Icarus plunged into the sea. Heartbroken, Daedalus lived out his days in exile in Sicily. Icarus washed ashore and was buried on what is now the Greek island of Ikaria.

A contemporary Greek writer thinks there may be some fact behind the myth. Minos II ruled Crete around 1400 B.C., and the remains of what may have been his labyrinthine palace—the legendary home of his son the Minotaur, half-bull, half-man—were excavated early in the twentieth century at Knossos. The residents of Crete were known to waterproof fabric with wax. Perhaps, says Elias Katralamakis, Daedalus used the wax to windproof a pair of cloth wings in the way that early twentieth-century avi-

Michel Paul Molla. Technical Reports & Standards Unit, Library of Congress, L'Aérophile Collection.

ators used various compounds to coat theirs. Could Icarus's wings, otherwise successful, have lost their lift when the wax melted out of them? "Radiance of the sun" aside, it doesn't seem likely, especially since the air gets colder at higher altitudes, not warmer. Nor is windproof doping necessary to the functioning of cloth wings. It simply improves their efficiency. But maybe Daedalus did manage to build a successful set of wings for gliding. Several aeronautical experimenters from the 1800s are credited with short, uncontrolled glides in tailless craft, even with artificial wings. Could Daedalus have

The Paris-Amiens race board, July 15, 1912: "Molla took off at 4:03:22 in an R.E.P. monoplane. Gastambide, in a Bayard-Clement, left at 4:11:33." Technical Reports & Standards, Library of Congress, L'Aérophile Collection.

managed a successful downward glide from a prison wall, while Icarus pulled up too soon and, having no tail to correct the violent pitch, fell backwards to his death? Presumably having little knowledge of aerodynamics, Daedalus would have blamed his son's fall on his lingering at too high an altitude, or attempting to fly higher, rather than keeping a downward glide.

The first Greek to fly motorized wings was born more than three thousand years after Icarus would have died. Though he did his flying everywhere but in Greece, Michel Paul Molla was born in Athens in 1886. The existing record tells us nothing of his parents or when he left Greece, only that he earned his pilot's brevet alongside his brother, Henri, in 1910 in France. Michel-Paul Molla earned Aéro-Club de France license number 166, Henri, number 172, on August 9 of that year, both in Sommer biplanes. The Mollas had probably done a healthy amount of flying before that day, since they seem to have leapt right into exhibition flying. Thirty days later, Michel Paul garnered attention with a flight around the capital city of Romania in a Henry Farman biplane, while Henri took his machine up at Reims, France, with auto headlamps and flew for an hour in the dark.

Opposite: Michel Paul Molla, center, at the Port Aviation aerodrome in Juvisy, France, after winning the Paris-Amiens race, July 15, 1912. National Air and Space Museum, Smithsonian Institution (SI Neg. No. 2001-6614).

2nd Lt. Edward McTurk, September 9, 1918. Royal Air Force Museum, Hendon, London; Royal Aero Club of the United Kingdom certificates, Rac 7699.

From 1911 through 1912, Michel Paul flew as the head racing pilot for the R.E.P. company, and he probably worked with Algerian racing pilot Eduoard de Nieuport on an early design, though that could have been Henri. Later Nieuport planes became very successful World War I fighters. Michel Paul won the Paris-Amiens race for R.E.P. and took second in a speed competition in Austria. In January of 1912 he set a world record by carrying five passengers aloft for over an hour. His brother Henri shows up for the last time in 1913 in the second annual seaplane race in Monaco. Further details of the brothers are missing. In fact, most Greek

aviation authors don't mention the Mollas, tending like most writers to focus on their countrymen who worked on aviation at home.

Michel Paul's death was recorded in August of 1951 in Peru, though the obituary says nothing of how he came to be in Peru or whether he flew in his later years.

GUYANA
(GREAT BRITAIN)

Date: September 9, 1918
Location: England

2nd Lieutenant Edward McTurk (1899–?)

Edward McTurk earned his pilot's license in the British military two months before the end of World War I. We do not know if he flew any wartime missions, but he seems to have survived whatever type of service he pulled, since his name does not appear in the British casualty lists. Born in Kalacon, British Guyana, on April 10, 1899, he was only 19 years old when he completed his pilot's training on the 9th of September, 1918, and was awarded brevet number 7699. The information on his license is all we know of McTurk.

HAITI

Date: June 10, 1910
Location: Camp-de-Châlons
Plane: Farman biplane

Charles Terres Weymann (1889–?)

"Charley" Weymann was a citizen of the world, to use an expression coined long after

Above: Charles Terres Weymann. National Air and Space Museum, Smithsonian Institution (SI Neg. No. 2001-6618). *Below:* "Charley" Weymann registering for an unknown seaplane race. Technical Reports & Standards Unit, Library of Congress, L'Aérophile Collection.

he started flying. When he was chosen to represent the United States in the third Gordon Bennett race in 1911, there were loud protests regarding his true nationality. Weymann had been born in Port-au-Prince, to American parents, and had grown up in France. He flew French planes with French motors. His win at Eastchurch that year, with an average speed of 113 kilometers per hour (70.5 m.p.h.), was generally considered a win for French aviation rather than the United States.

Weymann always called himself American. He once asked a newspaper that had referred to him as Haitian to "kindly rectify certain erroneous statements ... about my nationality." However, the proper little pilot with the pince nez, always immaculately dressed, had rarely been in the United States, either. Weymann's Haitian birth (August 2, 1889) made him a citizen of that country, even if he was also a citizen of the United States through his parents. Despite his protests, he fits our criteria for the first Haitian pilot, and we can find no good reason not to list him.

Weymann earned his American brevet, number 14, on June 10, 1910, flying a Henry Farman biplane with a Gnome rotary engine. Within three months he was competing with the best aviators in the world, including our first Russian and Peruvian aviators, Mikhail Efimov and Georges Chavez. In fact, Weymann was the only other aviator to make an attempt at the Alps crossing that killed Chavez in late September. Weymann made four attempts to take off from the airstrip in Brig, Switzerland, but an icy carburetor sent him back to the field on each try. Chavez made the crossing but was mortally injured in a crash landing.

Before the Alps race Weymann had already set a record by carrying a passenger 370 kilometers (231 mi.) across France. He flew the Paris-Rome race twice and the Circuit of Britain in 1911. He won a 300-kilometer race late in 1911, won the Saint-Malo race in 1912 and set two more distance records with a 600-kilometer (375 mi.) passenger flight from Amberes, Belgium, to Vernon, France, in September of 1912. He continued to race into 1914, but his interests seem to have shifted gradually toward airplane design. After his 1911 Gordon-Bennett win on a Nieuport monoplane, he had served on the board of directors of the Nieuport firm. He resigned that position in 1913 and began to work with the French government on a tiny fighter plane that could fly at 192 kilometers per hour (120 m.p.h.). We don't know if this plane was ever manufactured.

In December of 1913, Weymann read at the British Royal Aeronautical Society a paper entitled "The Science of Fast Flying." He served on the rules committee for the 1914 Gordon-Bennett race. During World War I, he flew as a test pilot, though we don't know for which firm. Weymann entered the manufacturing side of the business after the war when he started the company Avions Weymann-Lapere with a partner. After a couple of years he started his own company and produced several designs before closing his doors in 1934. He retired to Paris, and we have no details of the rest of his life.

The second Haitian pilot wouldn't take to the air until after Charley Weymann's career had ended. The man usually recognized as the first Haitian pilot, Lt. G. Eduoard Roy, earned his license in the United States in 1937.

Honduras

Date: 1929
Location: Tampa, Florida, USA

Captain José Raphael Aguilar

The Honduran government sent José Aguilar to Tampa in 1929 to study flying at the McMullen School. Captain Aguilar, apparently an insider in elite military circles in Honduras, appears in a telegram that year to the U.S. Secretary of State from the Wright Aeronautical Corporation. Aguilar had shown up at Wright headquarters asking to be sold an airplane. The Wright executives, put off by his supercilious manner, decided to check with the government as to Aguilar's identity.

The captain eventually got the plane for his government, a Wright-Standard *Aristocrat*, for he flew the first Honduran air mail in it on December 19, 1930. In 1931, he made demonstration flights in several locations across Central America. Another government plane, probably a Lincoln *Standard*, was crashed by Aguilar at Siguatepeque, in central Honduras in June of 1931. This is all we know of José Aguilar.

HONG KONG

Date: June 17, 1911
Plane: Avro biplane

Herbert Stanley-Adams (1884–?)

Herbert Stanley-Adams, born January 5, 1884, in Hong Kong, earned his British pilot's license, number 97, on the 17th of June, 1911, flying an early Avro biplane. The information on his pilot's certificate is all we know of him.

HUNGARY
(AUSTRIA-HUNGARY)

Date: November 26, 1909
Location: Hamburg, Germany
Plane: *Voisin-Rougier*, pusher biplane
Length of flight: 1.5 minutes

Ehrich Weiss (Harry Houdini) (1874–1926)

Harry Houdini's short time as a pilot, like his long career as an escape artist, was

Ehrich Weiss, alias Harry Houdini. American Stock/Getty Images.

full of contradictions and mysteries. Houdini flew for roughly seven months beginning in late 1909, in an airplane that may or may not have been flown by the famous French pilot, Henry Rougier. Houdini never stayed in the air more than a few minutes at a time, and he never flew again after May of 1910. The historical record shows him to be the first Hungarian to pilot a heavier-than-air craft, but the record contains a gaping hole and a competing claim that has placed another flier first in the eyes of their fellow Hungarians. To complicate matters, Houdini not only changed his name from the more Germanic Ehrich Weiss, but also claimed years later that he had been born in Appleton, Wisconsin.

Harry Houdini's Voisin biplane, c. 1910. National Air and Space Museum, Smithsonian Institution (SI Neg. No. 90-383.)

In August of 1909, when the first international air meet was held at Reims, France, no one from the Hungarian side of the Dual Monarchy had piloted an aircraft. Five months later, in January of 1910, as many as four Hungarians are reputed to have flown, and one had already died flying. The choice of first aviator is made more difficult by the fact that starting during this autumn of incredible growth in the sport, most pilots weren't mentioned in aviation journals until they had covered several kilometers in the air. The man generally recognized as the earliest Hungarian flier, Dr. Agoston Koutassy, had his first recorded flight on December 2, 1909, in Budapest, a distance of 5 kilometers (3.2 mi.) according to one periodical. Other sources say he had flown in France even earlier but didn't fly in Hungary until late 1910. Only six days before the earliest reported flight by Koutassy, another Hungarian had stayed aloft for a minute and a half in his Voisin biplane in Hamburg, Germany. The lengths of these flights leaves little doubt that both pilots had flown before these dates, but Houdini has the earliest recorded flight by a Hungarian.

Houdini later said he had become interested in aviation when he saw the Prussian, Hans Grade, fly that previous summer. At other times he credited Blériot's channel crossing or the Reims meet as inspirations. In any event, his show was touring Europe in the summer of 1909, and at the Reims meet he seems to have purchased his Voisin biplane and retained the mechanic who later followed him on a stage tour to Australia. Much about the famous showman can only be deduced from his own contradictory statements, as he consciously embellished or obscured the details of his life. During World War I, for example, Houdini claimed to have been born in Appleton, Wisconsin, the town to which his family had emigrated in 1878. He may have chosen this alternative birthplace to help squelch rumors that he was a spy for the Central Powers. In his 1926 obituary, the *New York Times* noted that he was either from Appleton or Budapest, and later biographers have settled on the Hungarian capitol.[50] Young Ehrich Weiss grew up on the streets of Appleton, then Milwaukee and New York City, even at one point living with another family that mistakenly thought he was an orphan. His father was a rabbi and had a hard time finding work that paid. When Houdini wasn't on the street, his days were taken up with athletics. He was a lifeguard, a champion swimmer and a runner.

By the end of December 1909, Houdini had progressed far enough with his piloting that he had an insurance policy, possibly the first in aviation, and was flying passengers in Germany. He used his aerial exploits to help promote his nightly music hall shows. In 1910 the showman had a tour scheduled in Australia, and the Australian Aerial League asked Houdini to bring his plane to the Antipodes for some exhibition flights. This fit in with his already established approach to flying as a sort of advertisement for his shows, and Houdini accepted. Several Australians had worked on designs already, with the incentive of a huge government prize of £5,000 ($450,000 today) for the first Australian citizen to pilot his own plane. A man named Colin Defries had even tried to pilot a Wright *Flyer*, but no one had had any success. At Digger's Rest, a plateau outside Melbourne, the Aerial League set up a showdown between Houdini and local businessman Ralph Banks, an American who had imported another Wright plane. The winner would ostensibly be the first person to fly in Australia.

Despite an unfavorable wind on March 1, Banks became impatient and decided to try for a take-off. Houdini's mechanic had only just begun putting their machine back together from its shipping crate. It would be many days before it could possibly be ready, but Banks couldn't wait. He set off taxiing and made the mistake of turning the wings at a bad angle to the breeze. The wind lifted Banks's *Flyer* off its wheels and slammed its nose into the ground, destroying the plane. Houdini could now relax and await his mechanic's progress. However, the overprotective mechanic (a Frenchman named Antonio Brassac who slept with the machine) kept Houdini grounded for 17 days, a nearly impossible wait for the hyperactive showman. On the 18th, with Brassac's permission, Houdini finally took the Voisin into the air and became, in the eyes of those witnessing,

the first to fly in Australia. As it turned out, however, an English mechanic in Adelaide shortly after made a claim to have flown a Blériot monoplane only the day before.[51]

Instead of inaugurating his public career as an aviator, however, Houdini's flights in Australia, of which he made many more, turned out to be his swan song. Perhaps because his plane was boxed rather severely for the trip home (it was cut in half), perhaps because he didn't have time for regular practice, Houdini never flew again after he left Australia. However, there may be another reason for the end of his flying. Even after seven months of practice, Houdini in his three take-offs on March 18 only managed to stay in the air for a maximum of three and a half minutes. The man who he claimed had sold him the Voisin biplane, Henry Rougier, had flown the same type of machine 90 kilometers and well over an hour at the Reims meet. Houdini may have sensed he wasn't the best pilot, or he may simply not have liked the sensation of flying a wire and wood motorized boxkite. Readers used to modern flight may forget that the airplane during its first decade was still a highly unpredictable machine. There were no stabilizing or safety features like auto-pilot, wing slots and artificial horizons. Reliable engines didn't exist. The Voisin biplane of 1909 had no provision to control the tilt of the machine, meaning that rough-weather flying and smooth turns were impossible. On any but the most perfect day, flight would have been a moment-by-moment test of the pilot's nerves. Another of our first fliers, Baron Pierre de Caters of Belgium, compared piloting his Voisin triplane to riding a bowl of jelly. As a long-time auto and boat racer, de Caters had an edge on someone more used to the speed of horse-and-cart transportation. As the very early insurance policy suggests, Houdini left very little to chance. Every aspect of his stage show was in fact minutely scripted so that, despite the spectacular appearance of, say, a chained underwater escape, he took very few risks. Flying was simply a sidelight for Houdini, and perhaps too dangerous a sidelight.

The escape artist did continue to follow

aviation, attended several competitions and met the Wright brothers and American pioneer Glenn Curtiss. Houdini died of peritonitis on October 31, 1926, having finally sought medical attention many days after his appendix burst. The situation was probably exacerbated by an obnoxious fan who challenged Houdini to a test of abdominal strength and clobbered him before the reclining Houdini had a chance to get off a couch. When doctors finally operated, 12 days after the first sign that he was ill, the infection had spread uncontrollably.

ICELAND

Date: 1931

Sigurd Johsson

The only thing we know about the first Icelandic pilot is from a brief reference in an English periodical concerning the 1931 British Arctic Air Route Expedition. A member of the expedition had gone missing near Greenland, and one of the search pilots was from Iceland. His name was Sigurd Johsson, and he flew a Junkers plane and was accompanied by a "parent ship" in the search.[52]

INDIA

Date: May 1, 1912
Location: San Diego, California, USA
Plane: Curtiss biplane

Man Mohan Singh

The license records for Man Mohan Singh are rather confusing. The same reference book lists an M. M. Singh as the holder of American brevet number 123, earned on May 1, 1912, and British brevet number 123, earned on May 18, 1912. An American newspaper article refers to a Mohan Singh who is supposed to have finished his training at the Curtiss flying school on San Diego Bay on May 19. In fact he seems not to have earned a British license at all, since the Royal Club

of the United Kingdom was, chronologically speaking, well past awarding license number 123 in the spring of 1912.

At any rate, when Singh was done, he bought a Curtiss seaplane and headed back to India. It may only be coincidence, but the name reappears in the flight literature in 1928, when a 22-year-old Man Mohan Singh earned his brevet at the Bristol and Wessex Aero Club in England. Again in 1930, a Man Mohan Singh, this time a 17-year-old, shows up in the British press preparing for a race from London to Karachi. The Aga Khan had offered a £500 prize for the first pilot to connect England and India with a solo flight. This youngest Singh was the first to try, but he was delayed by a forced landing in a bog near Marseilles and exceeded the 30-day time limit on the flight. We have no idea if either of these younger men are related to the first Indian pilot.

INDONESIA

Date: July 29, 1910
Location: Ede, Netherlands
Plane: *Blériot XI*

Jan W. E. L. Hilgers (1886–1945)

In the Netherlands there are monuments to two different pilots who were "the first Dutchman to fly in Holland." In Ede, one monument commemorates the July 29, 1910, flights of colonial-born Jan Hilgers. A hundred kilometers away in Heerenveen, the citizens have erected a monument to Clement van Maasdijk for his flights on July 30, 1910. The disagreement has nothing to do with the fact that Hilgers came from Probolinggo on the island of Java. It has to do with company profits, public relations and civic pride. In the minds of the antagonists, however, it has to do with the definition of the word, "flight."

In the spring of 1910, an Ede engineering firm named Verwey & Lugard hired mechanic Jan Hilgers and sent him to the Blériot school in Pau, France, to learn to fly. Hilgers had experimented with flying a couple

Above: Man Mohan Singh, 1912. National Air and Space Museum, Smithsonian Institution (SI Neg. No. 2001-6617). *Below:* Man Mohan Singh at a Curtiss School in San Diego, California, 1912. National Air and Space Museum, Smithsonian Institution (SI Neg. No. 85-18317).

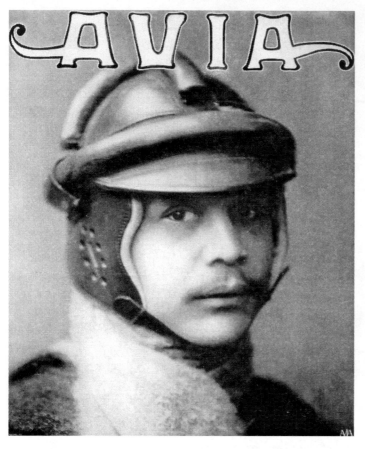

Jan W. E. L. Hilgers, c. 1911. Thijs Postma Collection.

to bring aviation to maturity in Holland, and the company felt it must put the first Dutch pilot in the air. At the country's first airfield, no less. Though he hadn't received his license yet, Hilgers traveled from southwest France back to Holland with a new, still boxed *Blériot XI*. He arrived in late July and began working frantically with the Verwey mechanics to get his plane put together.

The machine was ready on July 29, and Hilgers took to the air in front of a small audience of dignitaries and military officials. He would start the Blériot at one end of the aerodrome, take off, fly straight to the other end, and land. Then he would turn the plane around and repeat the performance in the other direction. His training hadn't progressed to the point of making mid-air turns. These were not the first flights in Holland, but it was the first time a Dutch citizen had flown in his homeland. Hilgers's most dazzling stunt that evening was to swing the plane's propeller himself, duck under the wing as the machine began to move, and leap aboard for take-off. Many of the naive spectators didn't know until much later, after they had seen others fly, that Hilgers's demonstrations were rather primitive. Van Maasdijk had earned his brevet five weeks before, and his exhibitions in Heerenveen included airborne turns and 15-minute flights. Heerenveen boosters, perhaps annoyed by Verwey's sneaky tactics, seized on the fact that Hilgers was unlicensed, and that his display had not included turns, to claim they had actually put the first Dutch pilot in the air. Needless to say, Verwey & Lugard stood by Hilgers's demonstrations in Ede.

Hilgers stayed at the Verwey plant in Ede and kept practicing on the *Blériot XI*. Sometime that year, he built a sesquiplane of his own design. The company held an air meet

of years previous, when he built a glider which he planned to fly from his roof. In preparation for his first test, however, Hilgers had fallen off the house and destroyed his new machine. In 1910 the Verwey & Lugard company was building the country's first aerodromes in the cities of Ede and Soesterberg in the hopes of turning a profit with air meets and exhibitions. The company was clearing and grading runways and parking lots, building hangars and stands for spectators, even putting in restaurants and tram lines to the fields. When finished, they would need capable fliers to attract the crowds, and Hilgers would be their first pilot. That summer, however, when the company's owners learned that the town of Heerenveen had retained a Dutch pilot to make exhibition flights starting in late July, they immediately sent for Hilgers. Verwey & Lugard intended

Jan W. E. L. Hilgers, right, with what is probably a Fokker *Spin III* monoplane, c. 1913. Thijs Postma Collection.

that November to celebrate the opening of its aerodromes and invited three experienced Dutch aviators who had until then spent their flying time abroad. The first Dutchman to fly, Gijs Küller, shared the marquee with Frits Koolhoven and Henri Wijnmalen. The next spring Koolhoven was appointed Verwey & Lugard's chief of operations. Wijnmalen became chief instructor, and Hilgers ran the company's manufacturing in Soesterberg. A series of airshows kicked off the 1911 flying season and attracted famous French and Belgian fliers, along with the various Dutch pilots. Hilgers stayed at Soesterberg that year and finally earned his brevet at the company's school on August 12, 1911.

He taught flying also, but when the demand for pilot training and exhibitions didn't cover the company's vast expenditures on its two new airfields, Hilgers migrated to the Fokker firm in Germany. The aviation branch of Verwey & Lugard declared bankruptcy early in 1912. Hilgers stayed in Germany until offered a position as a Fokker demonstration pilot in Indonesia. In 1913 he shipped for Java with two Fokker monoplanes, one 100-horsepower, one 80-horsepower, and an assortment of propellers. He docked at Surabaya, not far from his hometown of Probolinggo, but this homecoming would prove to be one of the biggest challenges of his flying career.

His first flight in Indonesia, on February 18, ended on top of a house after he had unexpected trouble keeping his machine at altitude. After repeated difficulties getting into the air, he switched to the flying field Küller had used to make demonstrations years earlier, but nothing in the area of Surabaya seemed conducive to flying. Another aviator who was touring the islands at the time, a Ukrainian named Kuzminski, had similar problems. Leaving aside the rotten shape of the fields, both pilots complained that the air was thinner and gave less lift than in Europe. The flying, said Kuzminski, is "like you are floating in a vacuum and cannot maintain any altitude."[53] At an exhibition in Semarang, Hilgers landed himself and a passenger in a swamp, submerging the plane. Despite all his trouble, however, Hilgers had returned to the

place of his birth for good. After the demise of the second Fokker, Hilgers seems to have stopped flying for some time. The Dutch company that organized flying exhibitions in the East Indies folded in 1915. Though we know little of his activities after 1913, Jan Hilgers apparently stayed in Indonesia the rest of his life. He died July 21, 1945, in a Japanese prison camp at Ngawi, about 250 kilometers from his birthplace.

IRAN (PERSIA)

Date: January 6, 1924
Location: Villacoublay, France
Plane: *Breguet 19*

General Ahmad Khan Nakhjavan (?–1944)

Colonel Ahmad Nakhjavan became the head of Persia's fledgling air force before he had even earned his pilot's license, in fact, while he was away at the Breguet flying school in Villacoublay, France. A military air force had been created only the year before, in 1923, but it had no pilots to fly the Junkers F-13 aircraft it had recently purchased from Germany. Probably because of his quick progress in pilot's school, the former Royal Guard infantry officer was chosen to head up the new air branch. Nakhjavan passed his solo flight tests on January 6, 1924, and received one of the most challenging missions a newly breveted pilot has probably ever been assigned.

The Persian government had just purchased another plane, a *Breguet 19* reconnaissance and bombing craft with a 450-horsepower engine. The colonel, with a mere 200 hours in the air, was to fly Persia's new craft from Paris to Tehran. The bomber had the red lion and sun emblem emblazoned on its tail and Persian flags on its wings. Nakhjavan left Paris in late January, 1925, and made stops in Italy, Turkey and Iraq. The only trouble he encountered was a muddy landing in Turkey that damaged his machine. He flew into a makeshift airstrip on private land in Tehran on February 5, 1925, and stepped out of his plane to kneel victorious at the feet of his king.

Lord John Carbery, 10th Baron Carbery, in London, July 1914. Technical Reports & Standards Unit, Library of Congress, L'Aérophile Collection.

Nakhjavan became a brigadier general in 1926. Someone apparently decided the country's first pilot should be out flying rather than working at the War Department, for another officer took over command of the air force until Nakhjavan returned to that position in 1933. He made full general ten years later. Our sources are unclear, but General Nakhjavan appears to have died in 1944. At the time, his air force consisted of 80 pilots and a total of 493 personnel.

of Iraq and says he served the Allied cause on the Ottoman front during World War I. Es Said seems to have flown Handley-Page machines, probably the famous bombers, in the Persian rebellion aided by the British and Colonel T. E. Lawrence. Several years earlier in the same publication a highly decorated military official with a similar name, al Sa'id, is mentioned in connection with a state luncheon at the Savoy in London. We do not know if this is the same gentleman.

IRAQ (GREAT BRITAIN)

Date: World War I
Location: Middle East
Plane: Handley-Page

General Nuri Pasha Es Said

In western flight literature there is one reference to General Nuri Pasha Es Said, who seems to have been an Iraqi diplomat in 1932. An article in the British journal *Flight* refers to the general as the former prime minister

IRISH REPUBLIC (GREAT BRITAIN)

Date: August 14, 1913
Location: France
Plane: Morane-Saulnier monoplane

Baron John Evans Carbery (1892–1970)

Few men, certainly few English lords, could have developed such a reputation as John Carbery and lived to be almost 80, yet have left behind so few personal details. For almost three decades of the twentieth century, Carbery was notorious on three continents. Stories abound of his exploits in Kenya's "Happy Valley" and of his inhuman treatment of wives, associates, children and animals. Yet it is difficult now to determine where he was born and what he did during his life other than torment his fellow beings.

John Evans-Freke became the tenth Baron Carbery in 1898 at the age of six. The ninth Baron, Algernon Carbery, was only 40 years old when he died, a lieutenant in the Northants Regiment and the husband of author Mary Carbery, who wrote the nonfiction books *The Farm by Lough Gur* and *Happy World*. We do not know for certain where the younger baron was born, but the family castle was located in the southwest of County Cork, a stone's throw from the south shore of Ireland. Even if he wasn't born there, John Carbery grew up in Castle Freke, and County Cork is also the seat of the Carbery baronage. Mary Carbery was remarried three years after her husband's death, to a physician named Arthur Sandford.

John Carbery attended school in England and Switzerland and graduated from Trinity College, Cambridge. When he was 21, he earned a French pilot's brevet, number 1437, dated August 14, 1913. He quickly became an accomplished pilot and in 1914 represented the U.K. in the prestigious Schneider Trophy race. He made the first exhibitions in southern Ireland, thrilling the crowds with unexpected dives and aerobatic maneuvers. He was much admired in County Cork during this time. At Castle Freke, he flew the flag of Irish independence, and when the town of Clonakilty organized its own branch of the Irish National Volunteers, it was named the Lord Carbery Branch. During World War I, Carbery served as a pilot and second lieutenant in the Royal Naval Air Service.

The early twentieth century would have been a difficult time for a young Irish lord. The influence of peers in British society was on the wane. Certainly in Ireland, the idea that the titled few should lead the rest, or that a lord deriving his position from the authority of English kings had anything to say worth listening to, would have been openly questioned. From his youth Carbery had taken the side of the Irish republicans, but no matter his sympathies, a young baron would never be one of the common lot of Irishmen. His position on Irish independence only ensured his complete isolation from his fellow noblemen.

We don't know whether Carbery's war experiences were the root of his later troubles, or whether the war encouraged certain aspects of his personality. The signs had certainly been there in his younger days. When told one St. Francis's Day that he should be especially kind to animals, John later reported back to his mother that he had been very kind to the cat: He had fed her the canary. John had once made the gardener stand still while he shot an apple off the man's head with an air gun, and a photograph of John and his brother Ralfe from 1910 shows them wielding "the instruments of animal slaughter."[54] Around the end of World War I, probably in response to the heightening conflict in Ireland, John Carbery became determined to reject everything English. He traveled to the United States, acquired American citizenship and affected an American accent. In 1919, his first wife, the former José Metcalf, was granted a divorce on the grounds that he had cheated on her and beat her with an ox whip. His American citizenship was reportedly revoked after he was caught bootlegging. Carbery sold the family castle and moved to East Africa, in what is now Kenya. He renounced his hereditary title and took the name John Evans Carberry (with an extra "r"). In 1922 he married Maia Anderson of Nairobi, and the legend of Happy Valley began to grow around his homes and those of several other wealthy noblemen in the area. These transplanted lords and ladies, cut loose from the strictures of noble European society, had found a place where their influence was restored and their power unbounded. They became known for their week-long parties and for the quantity of booze, sex and hunting one could expect when visiting. Carberry owned an airstrip and a bar and distilled his own gin and rum.

He had a house in Malindi and another in Nyeri at the historical scene of a bloody tribal battle, a place the Masai called Seremai, meaning "Place of Death." John Carberry was known to his servants as Msharisha, "the long whip."

John's second wife died in a 1928 plane crash that her daughter later suggested was suicide prompted by her father's treatment. (To be fair to her father, though, Juanita Carberry was only three at the time of her mother's death.) Two years later, Carberry married his third and final wife, June Weir Mosley, who won his heart by taking off her seatbelt when he offered to show her some stunts in his open-cockpit plane. June seems to have been better matched to Carberry's temper. She met his infidelity with infidelity. She is said to have lived mostly off brandy and soda. The couple had ferocious rows, but they stayed together until his death. A fuzzy picture from this time period shows a tall, gaunt man with dark brows and a domed forehead sitting on his front steps with a cigarette. He looks 70 years old, though he couldn't have been 50.

According to those who visited his ranch, Carberry would put gramophone needles in his horses' bits and run them until they could barely stand, or tie tin cans to their tails, which would spook them so badly they would run into things. His daughter Juanita lived in a separate "children's wing" that he had built for her alone, and her father made bets on her ability to swim, matching her against older boys and giving her a beating when she lost. Sometime during the 30s he spent 18 months in jail for smuggling currency into the country. He later said it was the happiest time of his life. His hatred of his mother country had developed to such an extent in 1940 that, at a wedding party, he offered a toast to Germany and "to hell with England." He was, of course, reported to the authorities, but his position and reputation apparently convinced the police to overlook his comments. In her biography of aviatrix Beryl Markham, Mary Lovell wrote of Carberry, "During nearly a hundred interviews conducted for this book not one person could find a good word to say for him. He was thoroughly disliked ... and Beryl at eighty-three still hated him."[55] Carberry was a skilled flier, however, and his airfield and stable of planes kept aviation alive for many years in East Africa. He personally flew an early de Havilland *Moth* from Kenya to England 1924, and he met the historic Cobham expedition around Africa in 1928 to shuttle Sir Alan Cobham to a governor's conference in Nairobi. Despite her feelings about him, Beryl Markham used one of Carberry's planes for her 1936 flight across the Atlantic, the first westward crossing by a female pilot.

With the advent of the Second World War, the aging of Happy Valley's noble denizens, and the scandalous 1941 murder in Nairobi of Josslyn Hay, Earl of Erroll, the public began to feel the errant lords and ladies had gone too far. The Happy Valley legend, as well as its reality, was on the wane. We know nothing more of the former Lord Carbery or his wife, except that he lived until 1970, she until 1980.

ISRAEL

Date: 1940
Location: England

Schlomo Shamir (1915–?)

Since every person of Jewish faith, regardless of ancestry, is a potential citizen of Israel, and since Israel did not formally exist until many years after flight had been well established, choosing a "first" pilot for this country presents interesting challenges. Pilot's certificates do not list the religious faith of the holder. Even if they did, we could hardly pick the first Jewish pilot and call that person the first Israeli, since becoming a citizen requires either residence or application. Since Israeli citizenship is not bound by birthplace, the criterion we use in the rest of the book also seems rather meaningless in this case. Instead, we have chosen the earliest pilot we can find with concrete ties to the Israeli state.

Schlomo Shamir was born in Russia in

pilot aboard and landed Calderara in the hospital.

The young lieutenant would build no more gliders, but the next year the navy allowed him personal leave to visit the aviation experiments going on in Paris. Calderara sent regular reports back to Rome, and that fall the navy made his activities official. Mario spent his time at the Voisin Brothers factory, helping to build and test several different machines, including the Goupy triplane design.[58] He saw the flights Wilbur Wright made for the French government near Le Mans in the fall of 1908, and he made astute observations on the practicality of the Wright design versus the French designs, telling his superiors that while the Wrights had a temporary advantage, the stability of the French designs would eventually make their machines much easier to pilot. Mario worked on the Goupy biplane that winter, hoping that what he now knew about stability and lateral control would yield a machine far ahead of its competition. Things may have turned out differently if Calderara had been able to make more test flights on *Goupy II*. Or if he had stayed in France to work with Goupy on the next machine. As it happened, Mario returned to Italy immediately after his only test flight. His partner went on to develop a similar machine with ailerons which flew well but which, despite its cutting-edge design and its far-ranging influence on other inventors, would never be commercially successful.

The Wright brothers, following successful demonstrations in the U.S. and France, had contracted with different governments and franchises to provide planes and pilot training. When he had finished training a group of Frenchmen at an airfield in Pau, at the base of the French Pyrenees, Wilbur Wright traveled to Italy to fulfill his contract with an Italian group that would be selling Wright planes. We don't know what sort of arrangement was made with the Italian navy, but the Real Aero Club of Rome paid Calderara's tuition, and, about the beginning of April, he began training under Wright at Centocelle parade ground.

The Wright *Flyer* apparently made as big a sensation in Rome as it had eight months earlier in Paris. Beginning the day before Wilbur's first flight in Italy, the road to the parade ground swarmed with "automobiles, wheelchairs, bicycles and every means of transport."[59] True to character, Wilbur's preparations went on entirely unaffected by the excited throngs. All day, he walked to and from the hangar where his mysterious plane was billeted, whistling carelessly. The next day was the same, with irregular engine sounds emanating from the hangar and the crowd growing ever more impatient. When finally ready to fly, Wright set up his launching derrick and plane, went through his painstaking examination of the machine, and flew away from the gawking spectators.

The next day, Calderara began flying with Wright for ten minutes at a time, and by the 23rd of April (only three weeks after starting ground school), he had progressed enough to handle the controls with the teacher along as a passenger. Calderara later said he hated having to learn with several thousand spectators watching him every day, but by the time Wilbur Wright left for the United States on the 27th, the young lieutenant had made at least one recorded solo flight. Calderara had learned to fly in less than a month. A week and a half later, flying in a stiff wind for his family and a journalist, Calderara crashed when one wing hit the ground in the middle of a turn. He dislocated one shoulder and suffered head injuries that kept him grounded for more than a month, during which time he was visited in the hospital by King Victor Emmanuel III. Another student, Lieutenant Umberto Savoia of the Italian Military Engineers, had begun training the day before Wilbur left, and he was able to rebuild the plane while Calderara convalesced. Wilbur Wright, who was something of a puritan, received the news of the wreck with little sympathy. "After sailing we learned that Lt. Calderara at Rome had met with an accident but we have no reliable information regarding it as yet," Wilbur wrote to a friend. "I left him with greater misgivings than my other pupils, because he was a cigarette fiend, and was being badly spoiled by the attention and flattery he was receiving."[60] While this could have been a veiled expression of concern, it was true that neither of the Wrights could abide cigarettes.

Once the plane had been repaired, Calderara kept practicing at Centocelle and began giving Savoia lessons. The aero club organized a meet to be held in early September in the north, near Verona. Despite a storm that destroyed their hangar and damaged their plane, Savoia and Calderara managed to rebuild in time for the Air Circuit of Brescia. They worked in an old church in Brescia, where they neglected to measure the front door before starting. When they had finished reconstructing the *Flyer*, the church's entrance had to be knocked out to remove the plane. Calderara competed against five accomplished pilots from the United States, France and Italy. He won five of the eight prizes, including the King's Cup for the longest flight, 60 kilometers (38 mi.).

That fall, Mario met his future wife, Emmy Gamba, who had followed his travails in the newspapers earlier that year. They met at a palace ball, and Emmy fell in love immediately. The next spring, Mario had shaved his mustache, which had been the subject of some dissention with her father. On May 18, 1910, he took Emmy for a flight. Family lore has it that Mario refused to land the plane until Emmy had promised to marry him. They would be engaged later that year and married on August 20, 1912. We cannot determine if Emmy Gamba was the first woman in Italy to take a flight, but she was certainly one of the earliest.

In order to keep his seniority in the navy, Calderara had to make up the officer's exams he had missed while spending time in Paris in 1908. He took the early part of 1910 to study. During this year, his past conflicts with his superiors worsened. Ambroise Goupy released their biplane into Calderara's custody, but it was ruined when someone had it removed from a hangar and stored outside. The officer he had been having problems with ordered Calderara to have the crippled machine removed from the base at his own expense. Also that summer, Savoia traveled to Europe to learn to fly different types of planes. Because Calderara had only been trained on a machine that was now obsolete, he was considered a specialized pilot of little practical use to the military. Savoia returned home and made the first cross-country flight in Italy to great public acclaim. Meanwhile, Calderara was assigned to a Naples firm to flight test an experimental machine that could hardly fly. Having had enough for one year, he requested a leave of absence that September and traveled to France and England, where he would spend the year building a new hydroplane.

If possible, Calderara ended his long leave in Europe on an even worse note than he had started it. In September 1911, he went to Camp-de-Châlons in France to try his hand at piloting different airplane designs. The French press, which knew Calderara from two years before, gave him all sorts of coverage. One of his superiors, who happened to be at Camp-de-Châlons at the time, ordered Calderara, though he was still on leave, not to fly in public again. That was September 25. Several days later, a French newspaper erroneously reported that he had flown on the 27th. Calderara was put under arrest for disobeying a direct order. In the end, a military court of inquiry cleared him, but this was hardly the note on which Mario had hoped to resume his active duty.

Nevertheless, he had finished building his hydroplane by that fall. There was a delay in ordering a proper engine, so that Calderara made his first successful take-off on March 2, 1912. The plane made dozens of flights at La Spezia and Venice that year and saw numerous adjustments and improvements. In April of 1913, Calderara was able to carry four passengers. The navy commission looking into the purchase of airplanes issued a favorable report on Calderara's flights, but at the time it didn't recommend reproducing the design. In fact, by the time the commission had gotten around to viewing the 1911 design, many of its features had been outstripped by foreign machines. The navy bought five French seaplanes. Calderara applied for another leave of absence and in June of 1913 returned to England to try to sell his plane there. This was his last effort as

Lieut. Calderara's Hydroaeroplane on her first flight with passengers 2 Sept. 1912. Pilot: Lieut. Calderara

Calderara hydroplane, first passenger flight, September 2, 1912. National Air and Space Museum, Smithsonian Institution (SI Neg. No. 2001-6006).

a designer. After a few months, Calderara returned to Italy as the technical manager of the Savoia Aeronautical Company.

Calderara's leave was interrupted by the start of World War I, and he returned to service on the ship *R. N. Etna*, which immediately occupied a small island off Albania. In early 1915, his crew returned to Italy, and Mario began organizing the air defense of Venice, a task for which he later received a commendation. That fall he boarded the *Lanciere*, the very same destroyer that had towed his hydroplane glider underwater eight years earlier. The next year, he directed the naval flying school at Sesto Calende for seven months, then served on a torpedo boat in the Adriatic. Finally, he served as director of the seaplane school at Bolsena, training mostly American pilots, a duty perfect for Calderara, who spoke flawless English, as well as French.

Calderara was promoted to Corvette Captain and stayed on at the Bolsena school until it closed in mid–1919. When he was placed on leave, Calderara began his first true business venture, taking out a patent on replaceable filaments for light bulbs and directing a small light bulb factory. He was made a Knight of St. Maurizio and a Knight of St. Lazzaro for his military service. In 1920, he became an Official of the Crown of Italy, and in 1922, he was awarded the silver medal of military valor for his persistent and long-term work in aviation.

The next year, Mario, Emmy and their two children traveled to Washington, D.C., for Mario's new position as Italian Air Attaché to the United States. They lived near the White House and spent two years socializing with presidents and Italian princes. When Calderara returned to Italy in 1925, he immediately began to scout around for a position in the aeronautics industry. He found a spot with the Pioneer Instrument Company and moved his family to Paris, where he would stay until the outbreak of World War II. Calderara seems to have enjoyed Paris, where he knew many names from the early days of aviation and was included in the group of pioneers who greeted Charles Lindbergh on the completion of his transatlantic flight. Calderara's business flourished, even though he personally suffered from the stock market collapse in 1929. During the 30s he was able to move the family into a villa outside Paris.

Things went well until 1940, when Italy became an enemy of France, and Calderara was recalled to Rome. The Paris villa was seized by the French. Calderara served briefly with the Italian navy, but his health was poor from years of heavy smoking. A private firm offered him a position in Bologna, and Mario Calderara stayed there with his family until his death on March 16, 1944. Emmy outlived him by 38 years. She died on her 91st birthday, August 5, 1982, in Bagni di Lucca.

Captain Albert Alexander Kartham, June 9, 1916. Royal Air Force Museum, Hendon, London; Royal Aero Club of the United Kingdom certificates, Rac 3048.

JAMAICA

Date: June 9, 1916

Captain Albert Alexander Kartham (1887–?)

Alexander Kartham already held the rank of captain before he earned his Royal Flying Corps license, number 3048, on the 9th of June, 1916. That means he had probably served in the British military for some time before transferring to the new air wing. Captain Kartham had been born in Kingston, Jamaica, on November 13, 1887. His name does not appear on British casualty lists, so it's presumed he survived his World War I flying career. His pilot's certificate is our only source of information about Kartham.

JAPAN

Date: November 8, 1910
Location: Étampes, France
Plane: Farman

Lt. General Yoshitoshi Tokugawa (1882–1963)

During aviation's pioneer years, few countries followed an aeronautical path as consistently military as Japan. Perhaps because of that society's long samurai heritage, perhaps because of ongoing conflicts with Russia and China, perhaps simply because

Japan was so far physically removed from aviation schools and factories in Europe that only the government could afford to train pilots: Whatever the reason, beginning with the army's Provisional Balloon Unit in 1904, Japan's earliest endeavors in the air were invariably associated with its military.

In 1909, Army First Lieutenant Yoshitoshi Tokugawa became a charter member of the Provisional Military Balloon Research Society, a group of air-minded army and navy officers organized by Japan's War Minister. With its budget of ¥600,000, the society selected two men to attend flying school across the globe. The chosen ones—Tokugawa and his fellow army lieutenant Kumazo Hino—left Japan for France and Germany, respectively, during the spring of 1910 to learn aviation from two of our earlier first fliers. Tokugawa attended a school founded in France by the first English pilot, Henry Farman, while Hino learned from the Prussian pioneer Hans Grade. While in Europe, the officers purchased planes for the empire, one Farman biplane with a 50-h.p. Gnome engine for a price of ¥18,000 ($86,000 today) and one Grade monoplane with a 24-h.p. engine for ¥8,090 ($45,000 today).

Tokugawa earned his Aéro-Club de France license on November 8, 1910, while still in France. Hino never became a licensed pilot in Europe, so the date of his first solo is unknown. The Japanese officers must have shipped out of Europe soon after, for they were back in Tokyo the next month assembling the army's new planes, a difficult task in the case of the Farman. The technicians began uncrating the machines on December 11, with the intention of flying three days later. Beginning on December 14, an estimated 100,000 people a day showed up at the canvas hangars on Yoyogi Parade Ground to see if the planes were ready. Hino apparently had his monoplane out taxiing on the first day and actually left the ground when a wind gust caught the Grade's wings and lifted it into the air. It was Tokugawa, however, who got the honor of giving the first demonstration flight. When his plane had finally been reassembled, on December 19, Tokugawa taxied around the military grounds 27 times,

testing the controls and making sure everything was in place. At 7:55 that morning, with the wet-cell battery strapped to his back, Tokugawa made a short take-off run and flew two circuits around Yoyogi in four minutes, covering 3.3 kilometers, or a little over 2 miles, to the tumultuous applause of the spectators. Later than day, Hino flew his monoplane a kilometer (0.6 mi.). Both had by now become captains in the Japanese army.

The name Tokugawa became synonymous with Japanese aviation. After the new Tokorosawa airfield was christened in Tokyo the next April, he and Hino gave daily flying demonstrations for the masses. The military ordered more planes from Europe—Wrights and Blériots and Nieuports and Maurice Farmans—and sent more cadets for training. On June 9, 1911, Tokugawa made the nation's first cross-country flight from the Tokorosawa airfield northwest to the town of Kawagoe and back, traveling 42 km (26 mi.) on his original Farman plane. That same day, he took a new Blériot monoplane on the same route but crash-landed the notoriously difficult machine. A couple of months later, Tokugawa flew the first successful Japanese-built airplane, a modified Farman-type of his own design dubbed the Kai-1 or "Tokugawa-type." The Japanese word, "kai," means "society," and during the next several years Tokugawa would work on five more designs for the Provisional Military Balloon Research Society. Hino also designed a number of planes, including a float plane, but none were particularly successful. In 1912, Hino was promoted to major and left to take command of a battalion at Fukuoka, on the south Japanese island of Kyushu. Tokugawa ran the army's flying school in Tokyo, turning out his first class of pilot-officers in 1913. As their final exam, the new fliers had to complete a 90 kilometer (56 mi.) round-trip flight between the Tokorosawa airfield and the Tokyo suburb of Ichikawa.

Tokugawa remained active in aviation for decades. During the First World War, Japanese forces bombed German outposts, and Tokugawa with two other pilots made the first crossing of the Hida mountain range, from Tokyo to the west coast of the island of Honshu. The troops under the Provisional Military Balloon Research Society became the Air Battalion in 1915, the Army Air Division in 1919. Tokugawa was made a lieutenant general in 1935 and the First Commander of the Army Air Corps in 1936. During a failed 1937 offensive in China, Tokugawa served as Commander of the Army Air Force.

On May 21, 1960, Tokugawa sat again in the original Farman biplane that had taken him aloft in Japan for the first time. At the conclusion of World War II, United States intelligence officials had taken the remains of the plane, still damaged from a 1913 crash that killed two men, to the Wright Patterson Air Force Base in Dayton, Ohio. Air Museum personnel restored the craft, and it was returned to Japan as a token of good will one hundred years after a U.S.-Japan friendship accord and fifty years after the first powered flight in Japan. On that occasion, General Tokugawa posed in the pilot's seat of the Farman with U.S. Air Force General Benjamin D. Foulois. Tokugawa died three years later, still the avatar of flying in Japan.

JORDAN

Date: July 5, 1950
Location: Hamble, England
Plane: de Havilland DH82 *Tiger Moth*

Issa Nour (1924–?)

In 1950, Issa Nour attended the British Air Service School at Hamble as one of three trainees for his country's new air force. The Royal Jordanian Air Force had been officially established the year before, after the country's loss in the Arab-Israeli War. Ironically, the money for Jordan's air wing came from an annual subsidy of £10,000 from Great Britain, the country that had initiated Jewish settlement in Palestine and long supported the establishment of a formal Israeli state.

Jordan used the yearly grant to purchase its first couple of transport and recon-

naissance planes and to send Hamzeh Ziad Mohammed, Kassim Saad Eddine and Issa Nour to the Royal Air Force flying school. Nour earned his brevet first, number 26,600, on July 5, 1950. The other pilots finished their training later that fall. A native of Amman, Nour had been born the first of November, 1924.

Nour may not actually be the first person from Jordan to fly, but he is the earliest we can verify. In fact, King Ali Husein, the beloved ruler of Jordan from 1952 until his death in 1998, is rumored to have begun flying in the late 1940s when he was still very young. (He was 17 years old when his reign began in 1952.) We cannot, however, find any evidence to support this.

KAZAKHSTAN

Date: November 23, 1911
Location: France
Plane: Blériot

Gorchkov (1881–?)

The first Kazakh flier was born in Ural'sk in the extreme northwest of the country on August 10, 1881. We have only the information from his license, Aéro-Club de France brevet 626, which does not even include his first name. Gorchkov passed the license test on the 23rd of November, 1911, flying a Blériot monoplane.

KENYA

Date: January 13, 1932
Location: London Aeroplane Club
Plane: de Havilland DH60-G *Gipsy Moth*

Patrick Theodore Stuart King (1909–?)

Although several residents of what is now Kenya were flying commercial routes in the early 1920s, it wouldn't be until 1932 that someone born in Kenya earned a pilot's license. Patrick King earned his brevet,

Patrick Theodore Stuart King, 1932. Royal Air Force Museum, Hendon, London; Royal Aero Club of the United Kingdom certificates, Rac 10309.

number 10,309, at the London Aeroplane Club on January 13, 1932. He flew a de Havilland DH60 *Gipsy Moth*, the famous two-seat biplane that served as a military trainer and a touring plane for numerous aero clubs. King was born on the 8th of March, 1909, on a coffee plantation in Kenya.

KOREA
(SOUTH OR NORTH)

Date: 1927
Location: Japan

Keigan Boku

Keigan Boku may have been born in what is now North Korea, or she may have been born in the South. In the early 20th century, there was no division between the two, and we do not know the name of her hometown. She appears in three places in the Western flight literature: once in 1927 in Japan when she had just begun flying, again the next year in a Tokyo air meet, and finally in 1933 on the event of her death. The accounts generally refer to Boku as Korea's only female pilot, so there may have been men flying earlier, but she is the earliest pilot we can find.

The first two articles include snapshots of Boku with her two-seater biplane and, in 1928, with her female mechanic. The pair had flown from Korea to the Yoyogi Airport in Tokyo for a meet, in which Boku participated. Boku was 28 years old when she died in a crash near Kyoto on a cross-country flight, August 7, 1933.

LATVIA

Date: Winter 1910
Location: St. Petersburg, Russia
Plane: Farman

Vladimir Victorovich Slusarenko

A native of Riga, Vladimir Slusarenko reputedly learned to fly a Henry Farman biplane in 1910. That's when Imperial Russia's first aviation school opened at a military airfield in Gatchina outside St. Petersburg. Slusarenko is listed as a member of the St. Petersburg Imperial Russian Aero Club, an official arm of the international licensing agency, the Fédération Aéronautique Internationale, but we have no evidence that he ever earned a brevet himself.

In 1911 Slusarenko took his wife, Lidia Vissarionovna Zvereva, and a couple of other aviators on the road for exhibition flights across Russia. Slusarenko is reportedly the first aviator to fly in Latvia and the other Baltic provinces. He and his wife also took passengers up for pay, but the money must not have been very good. When a storm destroyed their plane before a show in Tiflis (now Tbilisi, the capital city of Georgia), Slusarenko and Zvereva had to give their engine in payment for the race track they had reserved.

In 1913 the couple established an aircraft factory, repair shop and flying school near Riga. The Russian military contracted for two Henry Farman biplanes that fall, and another eight in the spring of 1914. They were able to produce one or two planes each month. At the beginning of World War I, Slusarenko and Zvereva relocated their company to St. Petersburg. The military continued to place orders, and by 1917 the factory employed more than 450 workers. All told, they produced 47 Farmans, more than 53 Morane-Saulniers, a few experimental craft, and 20 Lebeds (a Russian design). The ensuing political and military chaos took its toll on the company's business, and the Slusarenko-Zvereva factory closed in late 1918. We know nothing about the couple after 1918.

LEBANON

Date: 1924
Location: Villacoublay, France

Joseph Akar

In 1926 Joseph Akar was flying exhibitions in Argentina and trying to raise money for a great transatlantic attempt. Akar wanted to fly from Beirut to Buenos Aires. His story appeared in the English journal *Flight* after his return to Paris the next year. If Akar was able to raise enough money for the trip, he doesn't seem to have actually tried it. At any rate, there are no mentions of such a long flight in the late 1920s. In the next decade, several pilots flew from western Europe to Rio de Janeiro and Buenos Aires, but no one completed a flight from the Middle East to Argentina. According to the 1927 article, Joseph Akar had learned to fly three years earlier in Villacoublay, France.[61]

Interestingly, the first Lebanese-born pilot was a man named Shakir Jerwan, who in 1911 flew at the Moisant Company school on Long Island, after becoming a naturalized citizen of the United States. Since he flew as an American, we have not listed him as Lebanon's first, but Jerwan went on to serve as the chief instructor at the Moisant school, both in New York and Augusta, Georgia, and as the Director of Military Aviation for Guatemala during World War I. Perhaps his most famous exploit as an aviator was dropping a letter to President William H. Taft at an Augusta hotel in 1913. He appears to have stopped flying in 1920 to manage a hotel on the Hudson River in New York.

LITHUANIA

Date: June 1916
Location: Odessa, Ukraine

Ensign Ernst Krislanovich Leman (1894–1917)

Twenty-year-old Ernst Leman enlisted in the Russian army shortly after the start of World War I. Though only a private, he somehow managed a transfer to the army's flight school in early 1915. He trained in Odessa for over a year. Leman graduated in June of the next year as a warrant officer and joined the 19th Corps Fighter Detachment, later a component of the 1st Combat Air Group. He flew missions on the Ottoman front in the Caucasus region of southern Russia. Early in 1917, his unit moved to Romania. In the year and a half he flew Nieuport fighter planes for Imperial Russia, Leman made five official kills and earned the Cross of St. George, 4th Class, the Order of St. Anne, 4th Class, and the Order of St. Stanislav, 3rd Class. He was wounded on the 26th of September, 1917, while shooting down his fifth plane. One of his fellows was killed in that engagement, and Leman was awarded the Order of St. George, 4th Class. He was married during his recuperation. Leman returned to the front lines a couple of months later, but upset over the Bolshevik Revolution, he attempted suicide on December 17, 1917. Ernst Leman died a couple of days later.

Luxembourg

Date: March 1, 1910
Location: Wiener-Neustadt, Austria
Plane: Wright *Flyer*, pusher biplane

Vincent Weisenbach (1880–1911)

In its naissance, the realm of aviation was populated by family teams: the Wrights, the Voisins, later, the three Farman brothers.[62] The Gnome rotary engines, as well as Breguet, Morane, Caudron, Short and Nieuport airplanes, were all manufactured by sibling businesses in Europe. One of the United States' earliest female fliers, exhibition pilot Katherine Stinson, brought her sister Marjorie and her brother Eddie into aviation. Even many of the hot-air balloon pioneers from the previous two centuries had been brothers.[63] The first Luxembourg citizen to fly had a brother in aviation and worked with the first and most famous of the brother teams, the Wrights.

Unlike these other family teams, the Weisenbach brothers didn't go into business together. They rarely worked together, but this sibling pair separately became the first two Luxembourg citizens to fly. Born in Diekirch in the 1880s to a father who later started an automobile factory, the brothers worked together in aviation briefly but spent most of their time in different countries. Because he stayed at home in Luxembourg, younger brother Jacques Weisenbach was for more than 80 years credited by his countrymen as their first pilot. Recently it's been discovered by a Luxembourg historian that Vincent Weisenbach, who lived the last five years of his short life in France and Austria, flew first by several months.

Vincent Weisenbach began his aviation work with no less a figure than Wilbur Wright. It's not certain when he left Luxembourg, but sometime before 1908, he was working as an engineer and mechanic for a man named Léon Bollée in Le Mans, France. He also raced cars with the L'Automobile Club de la Sarthe and may have flown lighter-than-air craft with its sister Aéro-Club de la Sarthe. When Wright traveled to France in 1908 to make his first public demonstrations, the flying machine he would use had been sitting for nearly a year in its crate at Le Havre, where it had been left when a previous round of European sales negotiations had collapsed. Wright needed a flying field, but he also needed a workshop in which to rebuild the *Flyer,* for it had been badly damaged in French customs. Contrary to the expectations of the Paris aviation community, the press-shy Wright accepted an offer from Bollée to use his Le Mans auto factory, located a hundred miles from Paris. During the six weeks it took to reconstruct the *Flyer*, and well into the next year, Weisenbach worked as a mechanic for Wright.

When Wright left for Rome to train an Italian military pilot, Vincent Weisenbach worked with the Wright franchise in Paris, a company named *Ariel*, located on the Champs-Elysées. In April of 1909, the company advertised French-built Wright biplanes for sale at 30,000 francs ($108,000 today). Weisenbach left Paris that autumn. He had been hired as the pilot and mechanic of a Wright *Flyer* purchased by wealthy Austrian industrialist Robert von Lieben. If Weisenbach were hired as a pilot, it only seems logical that he had already flown at that point. Some have speculated that he learned from Wright and may have flown as early as 1908, but his first documented flight wasn't until the beginning of March 1910, when he took his employer up for a spin. His first flight in Wiener-Neustadt reportedly took place a couple of months earlier on January 4, but we have no details of the flight and no way to judge that it was a proper flight. It is possible, after all, that he didn't learn to fly until after he had put together von Lieben's plane, following its shipment from Paris the previous fall. In constructing that machine, Weisenbach worked with a Professor Richard Knoller to design a new wheeled landing gear. The Wright brothers had up to this point always flown from a launching derrick, a sort of level catapult that helped them get into the air faster, and until 1910 they fitted all their craft with landing skids rather than wheels. Weisenbach and Knoller built a sprung landing gear for the *Flyer* that would allow the machine to take off without a catapult launch, a very handy addition if a pilot found himself forced to land some distance from his launching derrick.

Weisenbach got his brevet from the Aéro-Club de France on April 10, 1910, and immediately began giving lessons to officers in the Austrian military. He set several Austrian endurance records and was presented to the Emperor François Joseph. That autumn, the Austrian government bought the von Lieben plane, and Weisenbach continued to pilot in a Sommer biplane belonging to another industrialist, Richard Bader. Weisenbach had also been designing his own airplane, one that resembled the Sommer, though no one knows whether he ever started building such a machine.

The first completed Weisenbach airplane, a monoplane, was finished just in time for an air meet in Wiener-Neustadt in mid–June of 1911. According to one source, Weisenbach had not had much time to test his machine before its debut public flight. On the opening day of the Wiener-Neustadt meet, Weisenbach was in the air with his new monoplane for 22 minutes when, crossing a corner of the flying field notorious for its eddies, he stalled the machine in a downdraft and plunged to the ground. The impact was such that his lifeless body was recovered almost 50 feet from the wreckage.

City officials in Wiener-Neustadt later named a street for Vincent Weisenbach. Barely more than 30 years old at the time of his death, Weisenbach had been a pioneer aviator in Luxembourg, France and Austria.

Anthony St. John Lilley, July 28, 1938. Royal Air Force Museum, Hendon, London; Royal Aero Club of the United Kingdom certificates, Rac 16048.

MALAWI (GREAT BRITAIN)

Date: July 28, 1938
Location: Cotswold Aeroclub, England
Plane: de Havilland DH60 *Gipsy Moth*

Anthony St. John Lilley (1921–?)

Anthony Lilley, then 17 years old, flew the popular de Havilland *Gipsy Moth* for his certificate at the Cotswold Aeroclub in the west of England. He was awarded brevet number 16,048 on the 28th of July, 1938. Lilley was a native of Limbe, Nyasaland, in what in now southern Malawi, born February 7, 1921. The information from his license is all we know of Lilley.

Lt. M. W. Noel, February 18, 1913. Royal Air Force Museum, Hendon, London; Royal Aero Club of the United Kingdom certificates, Rac 416.

sumably training for entry into the Royal Flying Corps as a new officer, but we have no positive indication that he served in the British military. If he did serve, he appears to have lived through the conflict, for his name does not appear in the post-war casualty rolls.

MALTA

Date: December 31, 1910
Location: Hendon, England
Plane: Blériot monoplane

Lieutenant George Bayard Hynes (1887–?)

George Hynes was one of the earliest British colonials to earn a pilot's license. In fact, his brevet, earned on the last day of 1910, was only the 40th given out by the Royal Aero Club of the United Kingdom. Hynes passed his test flying a Blériot mono-plane. He had been born in Malta on April 12, 1887, and the details from his brevet are all we know of him.

MAURITIUS

Date: February 18, 1913

Lieutenant M. W. Noel (1888–?)

M. W. Noel, born in Mauritius on the 30th of December, 1888, was awarded British flying license number 416 on February 18, 1913. New army fliers usually began their service at the rank of second lieutenant. So Noel, who starts his flying one rank higher, seems to have already been an officer in the military. Unfortunately, we know nothing of his career as a soldier or an airman, as his license data is all we have.

MALAYSIA

Date: May 5, 1915
Location: Hendon, England
Plane: Beatty-Wright biplane

Yin Khean Leong

One of our few colonial fliers of native descent, Yin Leong was born in Ipoh on the Semenanjung peninsula, not far from Thailand. He earned his pilot's license on the 5th of May, 1915, at the Beatty school in Hendon, flying a Wright-type biplane. He was pre-

MEXICO

Date: January 9, 1910
Location: Plain of Balbuena, Mexico
Plane: Voisin pusher biplane
Length of flight: 500 meters (1,640 ft.)

Alberto Braniff (1888–?)

A sportsman of independent means, Alberto Braniff began his career in aeronautics with lighter-than-air flights. He spent some time in France working with a balloon manufacturer on different designs, then moved into heavier-than-air flying sometime in 1909. Braniff purchased a Voisin biplane in that year and took lessons while still in France, but he did not get a license while there. On January 10, 1910, he flew his new Voisin a half kilometer (1,640 ft.) on the Plain of Balbuena, near Mexico City, becoming the first Mexican citizen to fly.

Once aviation had become a practical pursuit, Europe had only five years before the First World War changed flying forever, from the sport of aerial matadors to a tool of war. In Mexico the interim between discovery and war was even shorter. In 1906, the turbulent country had enjoyed 30 years of relative peace under President Porfirio Diaz when a depression called public attention to the overwhelming foreign exploitation of the country's resources and resulted in popular pressure for land reform. Just as Alberto Braniff was boxing up his Voisin biplane in late 1909 to ship home from France, the revolution began to foment that would keep Mexico in a state of war for more than 30 years.

Eventually, even the greatest fruits of human invention devolve into tools of war. Einstein's theories, modern chemistry, genetic engineering, electronic communications: All have been enlisted in armed conflict. The airplane, of course, was no exception and provides a ready proof that the human capacity for destruction is fully matched by our ignorance and denial of that same capacity. Many of aviation's pioneers were staunch critics of war and, at the same time that the art of H. G. Wells and others began to predict the massive aerial destruction of the coming World Wars, the first decade of aviation inspired countless forecasts of the end of all violent conflict. Forgetting the eternal question of the balance of power, writers asked how any nation would dare invade another when its own boundaries, its armies, its very capital, were susceptible without notice to attack by air. A similar theory has enforced the nuclear "peace" of the last half-century.

There is some question whether Mexico or Italy earns the distinction of being the first country to use airplanes in armed conflict. In 1911 both countries used planes for wartime reconnaissance, even some ineffective hand-bombing—Italy in a North African conflict at Tripoli, Mexico against its own rebels. Fighting had begun in Mexico the year before when a coup ousted President Diaz. The new military government hired the first Native American pilot, a mercenary named Hector Worden, to do surveillance and bomb raids on guerrilla fighters to the north and Zapatistas in the south. The rugged terrain had made actions against the dissidents very difficult, but Worden's Moisant monoplane overflew the mountains and so impressed the authorities that in 1912 they sent cadets to the Moisant flying school in New York. On the same plain where Braniff had flown, the government also founded in that year a national airplane factory which would eventually produce Blériot and Morane-Saulnier monoplanes for the Mexican Aviation Corps.

We have been able to learn little more about Alberto Braniff except that he was born December 8, 1888, to a wealthy family of old Irish descent. (Braniff Airways was started in the United States by his distant cousin, Thomas E. Braniff, whose family had emigrated from Ireland to the United States.) Alberto raced automobiles and spent a portion of his youth as a bullfighter. Apparently brave but not terribly skilled, he was injured in the ring several times. We do not know the date of Braniff's death, but he was still alive in 1960 for the official 50th anniversary celebrations of his first Mexican flight. Eight years later, the Mexican government dedicated a bust of Braniff at the Mexico City International Airport.

Schwade biplane, c. 1909. National Air and Space Museum, Smithsonian Institution (SI Neg. No. 2001-6610).

MOROCCO (FRANCE)

Date: March 1, 1918
Location: Ellington Field, Texas, U.S.A.
Plane: Curtiss

Robert B. Sewell (1896–?)

Robert B. Sewell was born the 22nd of April, 1896, in Tanger. He first soloed an airplane in the United States, at Ellington Field in Texas, on March 1, 1918, and he was awarded his brevet shortly before his 22nd birthday, on April 10. He apparently flew a Curtiss plane. Though the records don't say which machine, it would most likely have been the famous Curtiss trainer, the JN-4, or "Jennie." The record also lists his nationality as American, though it's unclear whether he was the son of American citizens, whether he had recently naturalized or whether he might have had dual citizenship.

MYANMAR
(GREAT BRITAIN)

Date: June 21, 1910
Location: Camp-de-Châlons, France
Plane: Farman, pusher biplane

James Schwade (1884–?)

James Schwade was born in Rangoon, on the delta of the Irriwaddy River in 1884, just two years before the British Empire annexed what would be called Burma, and later, Myanmar, from the countries of India and Siam. But more accurately, we might say James Schwade was born into aeronautics. Early aviation grew from the ever-varied compost of human ambition. Some pioneers were driven to leave a mark on history, others to make their fortune, many more by a sense of life-or-death adventure. In contrast, James Schwade seems simply to have inherited the flying gene. Some time in the mid–1800s, a German farmer named Oskar Schwade wrote a letter to his son on the aeronautical potential of gyroscopics: "Notice that by giving his hollow felt hat a spinning motion the circus clown can throw it 40 meters with hardly more effort than it takes to throw it ten…," Oskar wrote. "The planets and all other heavenly bodies have a circling movement which prevents collision with other bodies. … A similar trick would probably make a ball or disk overcome gravity and go its way through higher regions."[64] The recipient of the letter, Otto Schwade, lived in Siam at the time. In 1879, this second generation of aeronautical Schwades began studying bird flight and built a model glider. And 20 years later, Otto and his son, James, built a wind tunnel, complete with a steam injector, to test air pressure and its effect on aeronautical designs. Though not in a position himself to experiment with flight, Oskar Schwade's interest persisted through three generations, to his grandson, who would become the first Burmese citizen to fly, and to his great grandson, who would carry on the family tradition.

At some point Otto and James Schwade returned to their German homeland. After the turn of the century, the father ran an automobile factory, Otto Schwade & Co., in Erfurt. When it was time for him to learn to fly, James took his leave from the business to attend Henry Farman's flying school at Camp-de-Châlons, France. He received his Aéro-Club de France license, number 115, on June 21, 1910. Because this brevet was earned under the requirements of the international licensing body, the Fédération Aéronautique Internationale, the German licensing authority also issued him a certificate, number 9a. There were four early German brevets given with the "a" suffix, presumably because the Deutschen Luftfahrers Verbandes wanted to recognize these early German fliers who had earned their certificates abroad. Thus, Schwade ended up with two certificates for essentially one license earned. The German club later dropped these duplicate, "a" license numbers from their rolls, so Schwade no longer appears in the list of early German licenses. After earning his brevet in France,

Schwade returned to Erfurt to manufacture Farman-type biplanes in his father's factory. Though his airframes were similar to the Farman or the Sánchez-Besa, Schwade installed a 7-cylinder aero engine of his own design, called the *Stahlherz*.[65]

James may have been the first person to hunt from a plane, something he did not long after he gained his wings in 1910. He also participated in the Berlin air meet that fall in one of his own machines and sponsored a pair of German racers in other meets. His designs seem to have done well in Germany before World War I. One of his pilots even stayed aloft for eight hours in 1913, an unusual accomplishment for an engine in those days. Although he was a successful pilot and industrialist we know nothing about James Schwade after 1913. We do know, however, that his son also became a pilot and carried on the legacy.

NEPAL

Date: March 2, 1931
Location: Delhi, India

Rana K. S. Jung Bahadur

Prince K. S. Jung Bahadur is one of a very few members of a royal family to lead his country into the air. The son of the Nepalese commander in chief, Jung Bahadur earned his license, No. 164, at the Delhi Flying Club on March 2, 1931. A press report from the time says the prince was the first Nepalese to earn a brevet, but we have little more information about the prince than that contained in his license.

NETHERLANDS

Date: November 1909
Location: Mourmelon, France
Plane: Antoinette monoplane

Gijs P. Küller (1881–?)

The Dutch aristocrat Gijs Küller began flying in 1909 when aviation hit the marquee

in Europe. A Frenchman had just crossed the English Channel; the world's first international air meet had met with spectacular success; the exploits of aviators filled the headlines and loosed champagne corks around the world. A little more than two years later, when the charm was wearing off, Küller quit flying, telling the press, "There is no future in the flying sport, and moreover it is dangerous." This seems a bit disingenuous coming from a man who was notorious for taking off when the wind kept everyone else in their hangars. Küller may have been more honest when he said of his retirement, "If every farmer can do it, what use has it for me?"

Küller was born in Loenen on June 28, 1881. We know nothing of his family or his youth, but we do know he earned an engineering degree, a very popular degree at that time, from the Technische Hogeschool in Delft. Some years later, when he was 27, Küller began experimenting with gliders and seems to have caught the flying bug. In the summer of 1909, he traveled to Camp-de-Châlons in France, the place northeast of Paris where several designers had set up factories and flying schools. He chose what was probably the best looking and the sturdiest of the planes available, the Antoinette monoplane. This needle of a plane with a canoe-shaped fuselage was powered by a 50-horsepower, 8-cylinder engine, one of the first V-8s and one of the most powerful aero motors available. Its fuselage was made of wood, which made it heavier than anything else on the market (590 kg., or 1,300 lbs. loaded). It had a distinctive cruciform tail, 50 square meters of wing surface and could fly 70 kilometers per hour (43.5 mph).

By early October the German aviation press reported that Küller had flown a kilometer in a straight line. A month later, he was able to stay in the air for 15 minutes, indicating that he had probably mastered the airborne turn by then. Nevertheless, Küller wouldn't take his license test until the next spring (French brevet no. 46, April 5, 1910), making him the second Dutchman to be licensed behind Freddy Van Riemsdijk.

He stayed in the town of Mourmelon, near Camp-de-Châlons, and sometime in 1910 began teaching for Antoinette, a job he kept for five months. Küller did some racing and exhibition flights, but the teaching limited his travel time, and his engine apparently limited his success. When he stopped teaching to compete and fly air shows, Küller replaced the Antoinette engine with another V-8, the French 60-horsepower E.N.V. His troubles didn't stop, however, and Küller's only good showing was at the Scottish air meet in Lanark, where his bad-weather flying became legendary. On October 30, 1910, Küller returned to the Netherlands to fly for the official opening of the country's first airfields. He flew at Molenheide for a week, then helped to christen the airfield at Ede, then spent another couple of weeks in Soesterberg, where he got his engine running properly and took several prizes during the closing days of the country's first air meet.

The next spring Küller headed for the Dutch colony of Indonesia with funding from a group of Indonesian businessmen. He spent several months making exhibition flights on the island of Java, the first flights in that country. He traveled from Surabaya to Semarang to Bandung and Jakarta. The Sultan of Java presented Küller with a ceremonial golden kris, a wavy-edged knife favored by the Indonesian military. Küller also gave demonstrations in Kuala Lumpur, where the organizer refused to pay him because he had not flown like a bird, with flapping wings. After more flights in Java, Küller headed home to Holland and announced his retirement from flying. When the war broke out and the Dutch government in Indonesia was looking for airplanes, it surfaced that a man had an old boxed monoplane in Surabaya. The government wanted desperately to buy it, but its owner asked an exorbitant sum for the old machine, knowing that it was one of Küller's Antoinettes and one of the first planes to mount the Indonesian skies. The historical machine remained safely in storage.

Opposite: Gijs Küller. Thijs Postma Collection.

Gijs Küller in his Antoinette monoplane, c. 1909. Thijs Postma Collection.

Küller came out of retirement briefly in 1915 to prove to an American plane manufacturer that a machine could be flown in any kind of weather. He won his bet and never flew again. Obviously, Küller could appreciate that aviation had a future, even if he didn't like the looks of his own future in aviation. We have no details of Küller's life beyond 1915.

New Zealand

Date: October 4, 1910
Location: France
Plane: Sánchez-Besa biplane

Captain Joseph Joel Hammond
(1886–1918)

When aviation had been in the global spotlight for less than a year, British colonial J. J. Hammond packed up his chaps and 10-gallon hat and left Cody, Wyoming, for England. Less than two years out of New Zealand's Victoria College, the native of

Feilding had already spent a summer trapping and prospecting in Alaska, a winter on an Arizona ranch and a season with Buffalo Bill Cody's Wild West Show. The details of his visit to England are scarce, but perhaps he met another American showman, Samuel F. Cody, a recently naturalized Britisher and the former purveyor of his own Wild West Show, who had turned plane designer and pilot. There is no evidence that Hammond worked with Cody the aviator, but whatever he did in England in the summer of 1910, by the time he reached Paris that fall it took him only ten days to procure his Aéro-Club de France license, No. 258, on a Sánchez-Besa biplane. Later that day, October 4, he reportedly flew 40 kilometers (25 mi.). After a brief sojourn in France, Hammond shipped back across the Channel and earned his Royal Aero Club license, No. 32, on November 22.

Although he couldn't have started flying until only a few months earlier, Hammond had apparently become an accomplished pilot already, for he began teaching at the flight school in Eastbourne and developed a reputation as a skilled, fearless and happy-go-lucky flier. He was next hired by the British and Colonial Aeroplane Company (the "Bristol" company) to fly exhibitions in Australia. So with two Bristol *Boxkites*, he and a man named L. F. MacDonald sailed for the other side of the world at the end of 1910. They made an immediate sensation in Perth, for though there had been flights in Sydney and Melbourne earlier that year, no one had yet flown on the southwestern edge of the continent. In between exhibitions, Hammond made some distance attempts, including a 56-kilometer (35 mi.) trip in January 1911, before moving the show east to Melbourne. Hammond made a 72-kilometer (45 mi.) cross-country flight two days in a row and set a continental altitude record in Melbourne, at 7,000 feet. His wife became Australia's first aeropassenger in Hammond's biplane. He and MacDonald continued to Sydney that spring. Hammond and his wife returned to New Zealand later that year, and after a protracted illness, he took up again with Bristol as a flight instructor in Wellington, the dominion's capital.

Joseph Joel Hammond, October 4, 1910. Royal Air Force Museum, Hendon, London; Royal Aero Club of the United Kingdom certificates, Rac 32.

There is an anecdote about Joe Hammond and a couple of showmen who appeared in Wellington's harbor one day in 1912. Two hucksters had acquired a Blériot monoplane for cheap in the United States after it had been totaled in a crash. Upon their arrival in New Zealand, they sold shares in their traveling air show. But before any flights could be made, the man who was supposed to fly the machine quit the partnership and quickly shipped out of the country. The shareholders needed a pilot if they were to see a return on their investment, and Hammond offered to fly the machine for a mere £250 a week, the equivalent of more than $22,000 today. Hammond was a broad, muscular man. Later in the year he would attempt to help a young New Zealander get his biplane out of a wet landing field and fail because his own weight was too much for the machine. Hammond was presumably not told about the Blériot's previous smash-up. At any rate, when it came time to fly, Hammond approached the Blériot like a trusted stallion and put his hands on the fuselage to leap into the cockpit. When he tried to swing his weight onto the frame, the plane broke in

Joseph Joel Hammond on a Curtiss biplane, July 1911. Courtesy of the Library of Congress.

half. Legend has it that the remaining owner wired it back together and toured the countryside charging admission to see his flying machine in a tent.

Near the end of 1913, Britain's Imperial Air Fleet Committee dispatched a *Blériot XI-2* to the New Zealand government. Hammond was hired to pilot the monoplane, which was regarded by officials as the seed of a future New Zealand air corps. In early 1914 Hammond had the Blériot together and began practice flights in it. It was a sound machine, having been the former airplane of Gustav Hamel on his cross–Channel flight from Dover to Cologne. For his new position as government pilot, Hammond received a commission as a second lieutenant in the Royal Flying Corps. Alas, his tenure as New Zealand's only pilot would be very brief. Once he was comfortable with the new plane and word spread that he was soaring over Auckland and the ships moored in the har-

bor, Hammond scheduled a day to take a group of government officials aloft. He had been slated to fly with a journalist the week before. During the take-off run with his passenger aboard, Hammond had learned that the rudder wasn't working. Like most planes at that time, the Blériot had no brakes. Hammond had leapt out of the plane and dragged it to a halt before it hit the fence at the end of the airfield. Once the controls had been repaired, it was the politicians' turn, but the official group was disappointed to learn when they arrived at the field that Hammond had entertained an actress with a flight that very morning. The actress received more publicity than the officials, and Hammond was fired. The disgruntled politicians put the dominion's only plane in storage and later shipped it back to England, ostensibly to aid in the war effort.

A few months later, Hammond shipped to England to teach for the Eastbourne Aviation Company. When the war started, he flew reconnaissance for the British forces at the battles of Mons and Yser. He had risen to the rank of captain by June of 1916 and became an instructor in England again. Hammond must have been at least a part-time test pilot during this period, also. One day that autumn he was piloting an experimental fighter design when his controls failed. Unable to turn the plane, he tried to glide to an open field but found he couldn't make it. Hammond put his machine down on the roof of an asylum. Perhaps damaged during the landing, the plane burst into flame. Hammond walked to the other end of the building and sat down to have a smoke. After watching the frantic rescue effort for some time, he finally got up from his cigarette break and walked back down the roof to inform the fire crew and the spectators that he had escaped the blaze.

In early 1917 Hammond began testing new fighter designs for the Bristol Company, and when the United States entered the conflict, Bristol sent him to its facility in Indianapolis, Indiana, as a test pilot, instructor and exhibition flyer. The war had almost ended when Hammond was killed landing a Bristol fighter on September 22, 1918. Thousands attended his funeral, and his coffin was draped with the flags of both the United States and Great Britain.

NICARAGUA

Date: March 19, 1924
Location: Bresford, California, USA
Plane: Curtiss *JN-4*

Humberto Pasos Díaz (1890–?)

Humberto Díaz earned his United States pilot's certificate, No. 6080, flying the famous Curtiss trainer, the *JN-4* "Jennie," at Varney Field in California on March 19, 1924. His license also gives his birth date, August 4, 1890, but the only thing we know about Díaz beyond his license data is that the Nicaraguan government seized his personal plane, a Swallow, in 1926.

NORTH KOREA *see* KOREA

NORTHERN IRELAND (GREAT BRITAIN)

Date: Spring 1910
Location: Magilligan Strand
Plane: Ferguson monoplane

Harry George Ferguson (1884–1960)

An Ulsterman named Harry Ferguson set himself a nearly unmeetable goal in the fall of 1909. The young engine mechanic and motorcycle racer let it be known around Belfast that he would fly an airplane of his own making by the end of the year. A farmer's son, Ferguson had early on considered emigrating to Canada to escape his hereditary duties on the family farm. Instead, he took a job offer in his brother's garage in Belfast, J. B. Ferguson, Ltd., and studied engineering at Belfast Technical College. With John Lloyd Williams, an English friend from school, Ferguson had begun work on a flying machine in the summer of 1909. The ambitious students based their initial design on motor-journal pictures of the *Blériot XI* monoplane, which had crossed the English Channel that July. They actually finished enough of the airframe to perform some tests that summer, tests that convinced them they needed to know more about plane design. They traveled to France in mid–August for the Reims aviation week and the Paris Salon, hoping to get a closer look at successful flying machines. Ferguson also wrote to the new English journal *Flight* for more details on the Blériot.

Back in Ireland after attending an October meet in Blackpool, England, Ferguson and Williams began overhauling their design, lengthening the wings and modifying the controls and undercarriage. They had gotten permission from Lord Downshire to use his Old Park estate in Hillsborough for flight trials, and by December the rebuilt machine was ready to face the pock-ridden

Harry George Ferguson, 1948, with a model of his original Blériot-type monoplane. AP/Wide World Photos.

moors once again. The weather, however, raged against them. Ferguson ground-tested the machine, making small modifications and waiting for the weather to clear. He fidgeted with the controls and replaced the propeller, but while they sat on their hands, another Irish experimenter was gaining on them. The competition was not an engineer, not a student even, and had no training in mechanics. Worst of all, the other would-be aviator was a woman, the independent-minded Lillian Bland, a sports reporter and photographer who rode straight-saddle, smoked, drank, gambled and hunted, and with whom Ferguson shared a mutual dislike. This unladylike specimen could hardly be allowed to beat two respectable young Irishmen into the air.

On New Year's Eve, 1909, Ferguson and Williams had still not gotten their machine off the ground. Despite the same cold wind that had dogged them all month, Ferguson decided to give it a go. Pushing as fast as possible across the rocky fields of Old Park, Ferguson could barely get the machine into the air in the 25-mph gusts. Finally, he had the plane towed up a hill so he could get more take-off speed. On his first downhill run, Ferguson got the wheels off the ground and flew just over the divots and molehills for 150 feet. One more try got him into the air, this time at an altitude of 15 feet and for nearly 400 feet (122 m.). At last, Ferguson was satisfied that he had flown his machine, during 1909, and that he could control it in the air.

A downhill run, however, falls into the category of assisted take-off, so for our purposes, Ferguson's first true flight wouldn't take place until later that spring in a new venue. Having battled with the moonscape terrain of Old Park, Ferguson realized he would need a smoother airstrip if he were ever going to get enough speed to take off from a level surface and land without destroying his undercarriage. He and Williams accordingly moved their operations to Magilligan Strand, a 6-mile section of hardpack beach on the northern tip of the isle in the sheltering inlet of Lough Foyle. Ferguson had reportedly flown at least a mile by June, when one of his practice sessions nearly landed him in the salty water and thereby made headlines in *Flight*. He journeyed to Newcastle in July for some exhibition flights and returned to Magilligan to continue practicing. When he was comfortable with his abilities, Ferguson took Miss Rita Marr of Liverpool for the first passenger flight in Ireland. This was the peak of his work in aviation.

In 1913, Ferguson was married and returned to his engine work. Williams continued to pilot and to develop their plane, while J. B. Ferguson Ltd. was again associated with

automobiles more than aviation. During the First World War, the company worked in flight once again, producing aero-engines for the British government. While working this government contract, the firm produced an assembly-line machine that boosted its crankcase production from four a week to 28. The government immediately bought a large batch of these machines for its other engine works. The firm next did piecework, manufacturing wings for the military. During this very successful work for the government (the company received a commendation on the quality of its engines), Harry Ferguson concentrated on what would eventually make his name world famous: farm implements. He began by selling tractors to farmers whose horses had gone for war duty. Eventually, he also invented a plough that could be used behind a Ford tractor, beginning the line of farm equipment that lives on today under the name of Massey-Ferguson.

J. B. Ferguson Ltd. was bought out in 1920, but its successful inventor continued to work with the firm. Harry Ferguson lived comfortably in Ireland until 1960, when he died at the age of 76. Lillian Bland, who got her plane into the air a few months after Ferguson, eventually married a cousin and lived first in Vancouver, then in England until her death at the ripe age of 93.

NORWAY

Date: June 1, 1912
Location: Horten, Norway
Plane: Rumpler *Taube*

Commander Hans Fleischer Dons (1882–?)

We do not know when Hans Dons learned to fly or when he made his first solo, but he probably took lessons in Germany. Born in Ekker, Norway, on the 13th of June, 1882, Dons trained on a German Rumpler *Taube* and later purchased an identical machine to take back to Norway. Then a lieutenant in the Norwegian navy, he first appears in the flight literature with four other submarine officers, raising money by public subscription to pay for the new plane. On the first of June, 1912, he flew that Rumpler, christened *Start*, from the naval base at Horten to Frederikstad, 60 kilometers (38 mi.) across the Oslo Fjord. The flight took 35 minutes and was referred to in the press as the first flight in Norway by a Norwegian subject. The Norwegian government had sent two army cadets to flying school outside Paris in 1910, but neither earned a brevet until the fall of 1912. It is, of course, possible that they flew long before Dons and only took their license tests later, but we have no evidence of that. Dons never earned a brevet.

The cross-country flight by Hans Dons apparently convinced the Norwegian legislature that it should resume its plans for an air corps. Shortly afterward, it voted money to send four officers to flying school in France. Dons later flew a seaplane and made it to the rank of Commander in the Royal Norwegian Navy. In the 1920s, he served as a naval attaché to Britain, but that is all we know of his life.

PAKISTAN (INDIA)

Date: 1930
Plane: de Havilland DH-60 *Gipsy Moth*

Aspy Merwan Engineer (1913–?)

When Aspy Engineer was only 17 years old, his father purchased for him and a friend, Ram Nath Chawla, a de Havilland *Gipsy Moth*. The Aga Khan, the leader of an Indian Muslim sect, had offered a prize of £500 to the first person of Indian nationality to connect England and India by air. Engineer and Chawla wanted to try for the prize. The rules of the contest stipulated a solo flight that had to be completed in less than a month. The pair flew from Karachi, then part of India, to England in 17 days during March of 1930. Chawla acted as chief pilot, and though it wasn't a solo flight, the Indian government awarded him a consolation prize (£560, roughly $24,000 today) that was larger than the Aga Khan's original offering. Engineer then prepared to make the return flight by himself to meet the Aga Khan's requirements.

In the early twentieth century, men of Parsi descent sometimes changed their names to a word matching their vocation, even an English word. Engineer's father was a very wealthy merchant named K. H. Irani. In school as a child, Aspy earned the nickname "Engineer" for his fascination with machines, and he decided to change his name permanently. We do not know exactly when Engineer began to fly, though he couldn't have been too much younger than 17 when he did. He had presumably done a bit of piloting before his first intercontinental flight, especially considering the ease with which he and Chawla executed that flight.

Engineer left Croydon for his return trip on April 25, 1930. Another contestant had left the same airfield earlier in the month but had been forced to make an emergency landing near Marseilles, France. Man Mohan Singh, who may or may not have been related to our first Indian flier, apparently had a series of starts and mishaps that would have been comic had he not been such a young and inexperienced pilot. Engineer made the trip in 16 days, landing in Karachi on May 11. Singh had arrived the day before, but had taken 32 days, putting him over the time limit. The third contestant made the fastest flight, taking only nine days, but didn't leave England until May 8. A grateful Engineer took the Aga Khan Prize and sent a cable to the de Havilland company in England congratulating them on "the splendid behavior" of their airplane.

Despite his promising start, we've been unable to find further information about Engineer's career in the air.

PANAMA

Date: World War I
Location: England

Guillermo (William) Lambert (1894–?)

The name of our first Panamanian flier comes to us from historian Germinal Sarasqueta of Panama City. We do not know when he first flew, or even whether he went by a Spanish or English first name for most of his life. Guillermo Lambert was born on the island of Taboga in 1894, the son of an English tugboat engineer and a Panamanian mother. Around the turn of the century, Lambert and his family moved to England, where he would later serve in the Royal Flying Corps during World War I. He apparently wrote to his relatives in Panama during the war, informing them of his promotions and medals, but we have no details. Nor do we know if he survived the war.

PARAGUAY

Date: January 17, 1913
Location: Reims, France
Plane: Deperdussin monoplane

Silvio Pettirossi (1887–1916)

Silvio Pettirossi didn't get his pilot's license until he was 25, but he lived every day of the next four years like a teenager with a new hot rod. Pettirossi was initiated into the aerial community by none other than our first Argentine flier, Jorge Newbery, who predicted Pettirossi would be a great pilot after taking him up in Buenos Aires. As soon as he could get to Europe, Pettirossi enrolled in flying school, and within the year he was challenging the records set by the world's greatest aerobatic pilots. Some have said that until a student is behind the controls it's impossible to say how well he'll fly, but Newbery glimpsed something in his young friend's personality that we can only guess at. His prediction was unerring.

Silvio Pettirossi was born June 16, 1887, in Asunción to a Paraguayan mother and Italian father. Antimo Pettirossi wanted his son to have a quality Catholic education and sent him to school at Viterbo and Spoleto in Italy. Silvio's schooling ended when revolution broke out in Paraguay in 1904. Over his father's objections, Pettirossi returned to his birthplace to serve with the revolutionary

forces. He made his reputation during a particularly nasty battle. When his commanding officer was killed, Pettirossi donned his leader's uniform and led the troops himself, rather than have his fellows lose heart. In the young revolutionary forces, his actions were seen as outstanding initiative rather than impersonating an officer, and this episode earned Pettirossi a full commission. Despite his performance in battle, however, Pettirossi was disgusted by war, and when the revolution was over, he moved to Buenos Aires, then the cosmopolitan center of South America.

Silvio became involved in Argentine politics and mingled with the South American elite. It was in these circles that he met Newbery, but these two didn't become friends until probably 1910. We have no idea what Pettirossi did in the intervening years, though one biography mentions his "ample financial opportunities," suggesting that perhaps he had a sizable inheritance to invest.[66] As soon as he'd been up in an airplane, however, Silvio returned to Paraguay to raise money for a trip to Europe and flying school. His former superiors from the revolution, who were now running the country, eventually found government funds to send him to Reims, France, with the understanding that he would return and open the country's first military school of aviation. He shipped from Buenos Aires on October 4, 1912.

At the aerodrome in Reims, Pettirossi met the world's premier fliers and watched them testing new planes and doing new stunts. He enrolled in the Deperdussin school and learned quickly. In mid–January 1913, after 17 lessons, Pettirossi made his first solo flight, after which he described the feeling thus: "I have felt that I am the sole owner of space, after God."[67] Silvio earned both his French brevet, no. 1128, and a renewed commission in the Paraguayan military, on the 11th of February, 1913. As an official envoy of his country's government, Lieutenant Pettirossi began to tour Europe, where there was little knowledge of his country. He visited an exposition in Turin and flew at the continent's main aerodromes for six months before returning to the Reims area. In October he made a spectacular cross-country flight from Mourmelon to Paris and back, a non-stop trip of 450 kilometers (281 mi.). Not long after, he notified the French flying authorities that he would try for a record in looping.

The first-ever flying loop had been performed by Russian Pyotr Nesterov in Kiev on August 27, 1913. His officers in the Imperial Russian Air Service were so shocked by the maneuver that they threw Nesterov in the clink for endangering government property (the plane). Not quite a month later, Frenchman Adolphe Pégoud showed that a pilot could fly upside down on purpose. At the Brooklands airfield in England on September 21, Pégoud demonstrated several aerobatic moves, including a tail-slide, an inverted loop (starting from upside down), and a flying-S (a downward loop followed by a half-loop). Pettirossi wasn't far behind. His record attempt in October recorded 30 loops in one flight. This was apparently more than anyone had done under official observation, but it's unknown whether such a category of stunting was officially entered in the record books.

Pettirossi remained in Europe until the next summer, flying at aerodromes around Paris and making multi-leg cross-country trips of up to 1,500 kilometers. Supposedly, he would flip upside down whenever he passed over a city along the way, or he would do loops over the entire town. With his Deperdussin monoplane, Silvio returned to Buenos Aires in April of 1914 and embarked on an exhibition tour of South America. He made aerobatic demonstrations in Buenos Aires and Rio de Janeiro, Montevideo and Santiago de Chile. His trademark stunts were a full-speed dive into the aerodrome and a spinning fall from 500 meters that left the crowds gasping. He finally got to perform in his hometown that December. The government created the National School of Aviation upon his return, though it's unclear how involved he was in the running of the school. He was married that December to a woman he had met in Montevideo.

In 1915 he was abroad again, this time at an International Exposition in California to celebrate the opening of the Panama Canal. Unlike many of his compatriots, Pettirossi chose not to join the escadrilles in France. Many pilots without direct connections to the war nevertheless enlisted in the French or British forces, but perhaps Pettirossi had had enough of war. His aerobatic predecessor, Pégoud, was killed over the western front on August 31, 1915. With his new wife, Pettirossi toured the United States for much of that year and did not return to Paraguay until the middle of 1916. He had one mishap of note while flying in the U.S. On his second night in San Francisco, a control cable broke during an exhibition and landed Silvio in the Pacific Ocean. The pilot was unhurt, and his plane was salvaged, but salt damage was suspected in the crash that eventually killed him.

Near Buenos Aires on October 17, 1916, in front of an invited group of officials and prominent families, for the inaugural celebration of President Hipolito Irogoyen, Pettirossi performed his last show. Silvio had been having intermittent problems with the Deperdussin for some time, and he had installed two new wings only five days before. An inquest determined the crash was the cause of failed tension wires to the wings. Years later someone determined that Pettirossi had reused the original wing wires, the same ones that had taken a bath in the Pacific, when he installed his new wings. There is conjecture that one of these broke under the strain of his aerobatics. Silvio apparently dove straight into the ground from 1,400 meters.

Pettirossi received a memorial service in Argentina before his remains were shipped to Asunción for burial. The Argentine government erected a monument on the Arsenal del Rio de la Plata in Punta Lara where the brave Paraguayan fell.

PERU

Date: February 10, 1910
Location: Camp-de-Châlons, France
Plane: Farman biplane

Jorge Chavez Dartnell (Georges Chavez) (1887–1910)

Georges Chavez over the beach in his Henry Farman biplane at the Nice air meet, April 16, 1910. Technical Reports & Standards Unit, Library of Congress, L'Aérophile Collection.

Peru seems a remote origin for a man who would become one of the greatest aviation heroes of the twentieth century, just as seven months seems an unlikely span for a career so celebrated. In the year 1910 Georges Chavez earned his pilot's license and died flying, but his legend lives on in the famous motto of the Peruvian Air Force, "Higher, ever higher."

Like many of our early fliers, Chavez never had to emigrate to pursue flying in the aviation capital of the world. In fact, he never even saw Peru during his short lifetime. Like Englishman Henry Farman, Chavez was born in Paris, but unlike Farman he always claimed the land of his ancestors, not his place of birth, as his home. "Yo soy Peruano," he told people who asked his nationality, "I am Peruvian."[68] Chavez had been a soccer player and was already well known when he took up flying in December of 1909. He qualified for his Aéro-Club de France brevet, No. 32, five days after his first solo flight on

the 10th of February. On the last day of that month, he took his new Farman biplane aloft for nearly two hours, flying until he finally ran out of fuel. By early April, Chavez had won his first prizes flying at an aviation meet in Nice.

After that, the winnings came fast. In his Farman, Chavez took distance prizes at the end of April and in early May. He bought a new *Blériot XI*, a monoplane, and began flying higher, setting a world altitude record of 2,587 meters (8,484 ft.) in early September at Issy-les-Moulineaux. Only a year before, at the first Reims air meet, the altitude competition had been won by the daring Hubert Latham with a height of 508 feet. In the summer of 1910, new marks were set every month by Latham, by Americans Walter Brookins and J. Armstrong Drexel, and by Frenchman Leon Morane. Chavez joined a select group of pilots who jockeyed for every prize and whose names crowded the French newspapers and the Paris social

Georges Chavez (Jorge Chavez Dartnell) aboard his Henry Farman biplane, 1910. National Air and Space Museum, Smithsonian Institution (SI Neg. No. 78-15841).

Georges Chavez in his Blériot at Brig, Switzerland, September 1910. National Air and Space Museum, Smithsonian Institution (SI Neg. No. A-4006).

scene, but the cross–Alps flight that would cement his fame would also be his last.

Italian promoters had envisioned the flight over Simplon Pass—from Brig, Switzerland, to Domodossola, Italy, and on to Milan—as a sensational opener for the inaugural Milan air meet. The meet would feature 100,000 lire ($360,000 today) in prizes, more than two-thirds of which was reserved for the winner of the alpine race. The Società Italiana di Aviazione Milanese called its brainchild "audacious and patriotic" and hoped it would bring Italian aviation onto center stage.[69] "Audacious" was certainly the word for it: Starting on the miniature Brig airfield in near-freezing temperatures, the fliers would take off at a thin 2,953 feet, gain nearly 4,000 feet to cross the pass, outmaneuver the notorious air currents flowing off the sides of the Fletschorn (13,127 ft.) on one side and Monte Leone (11,684 ft.) on the other, and then descend another sinuous, blustery canyon to the safety of the Bognanco Valley leading to Milan.[70]

All this would have to be accomplished in a frail, open-cockpit machine weighing less than a modern automobile. In 1959 on the 50th anniversary of Louis Blériot's crossing of the English Channel, a replica of the *Blériot XI* made the Channel flight again. A commercial airline pilot, examining the plane after its landing in England, is said to have commented, "I wouldn't take that thing up for a solid gold clock."[71] The sheer daring of the alpine flight attracted exactly the publicity for which the committee had hoped. During the three weeks leading up to the event, the tiny telegraph office in Brig sent out half a million words in press dispatches.[72]

The race committee received 13 entries but, perhaps because of high-profile criticism over the dangers of the course, limited the competitors to experienced entrants of their own choosing. Five of the 13 aviators were approved, but three of those dropped out as the race approached, leaving only Chavez and Charles Weymann.[73] The first four days of the competition saw the aviators try time and again to climb the damp, windy canyon. Weymann gave up after an iced carburetor forced his machine back to Brig

three times. The weather only got worse, and Chavez returned often to his telescope to examine the pass. A group of his friends tended a huge bonfire in the mountainous gap. Through his glass, Chavez checked their smoke signal several times a day. On the afternoon of the 23rd, the smoke finally rose straight upward, and Chavez climbed once again into his four layers of wind- and waterproofed clothing. On the day before the race was to close, the Peruvian took off at 1:29 p.m. His crew watched him wind up the forested slopes toward the clouds.

Spectators at Domodossola, where Chavez was scheduled to refuel, scanned the mountain ramparts for a machine that would have been like a distant mosquito against the pines. At a few minutes after 2 o'clock, Chavez's plane would have become visible over the Bognanco, sending up a cheer among the crowd. They watched as Chavez approached, having already completed the dangerous alpine crossing, everything seemingly fine. But just when the onlookers must have let out their breath in collective relief, the plane dove into the Domodossola airfield from only 30 feet. One spectator said he saw a wing fold suddenly, but the rest were convinced that the plane had just turned nose-down and fallen from the sky. Experts would later surmise that his hands had become too numb to work the controls for the landing. From the description of the fall, however, it sounds as if Chavez cut all his speed while he was still too high and stalled the plane—as if he had misjudged the approach of the ground. An experienced pilot could be expected not to make such a mistake, but that same pilot, numbed and disoriented by hypothermia, might easily pull up early and find himself with too little speed to stay aloft. After all, his four layers of clothing consisted of only windproof underwear, waterproof cotton coveralls, a sweater and a leather jacket. His leather helmet and boots would have done little to keep him warm in the freezing mist that had clogged Weymann's carburetor so many times.

His machine destroyed, Chavez was taken to the Domodossola hospital with two broken legs. Perhaps it was unidentified internal injuries, or hypothermia, or a combination of factors to which he succumbed four days later, still semi-conscious and murmuring the words, "Arriba. Mas arriba," the phrase that would later become the motto of the Peruvian Air Force. While still alive, he was awarded a consolation prize of 10,000 lire. He had crossed the Alps in 42 minutes, a trip that had taken Napoleon a day and a half over the lower pass of Great St. Bernard.

The Blériot was restored and is still on exhibit at the Peruvian Military Historical Museum. A monument stands in Lima where Chavez's remains were moved in 1957, and monuments have been dedicated to him at either end of his historic flight. The Simplon Pass would not be dared again for more than two years. Jean Bielovucic avenged his countryman's name on January 25, 1913, when he flew the course in 26 minutes during the least blustery month of the year and in a machine with a protected cockpit.

PHILIPPINES

Date: October 15, 1916
Location: Redwood City, California, USA
Plane: Curtiss biplane

Luis Quimson (1893–?)

If it hadn't been for World War I, Luis Quimson would be much better known in his homeland. A later aviator named Alfredo Carmelo is generally recognized as the first Philippine aviator. However, Quimson earned his pilot's brevet four years earlier than Carmelo, on October 15, 1916, at a Curtiss flying school in Redwood City, California. Quimson flew demonstrations on the West Coast and was called "utterly fearless" by the San Diego press. A native of Manila and the nephew of one of that city's architects, he began making plans to take his aerobatics to the Philippines. Before he could leave, the United States entered the war, and Quimson's departure was held over for two years.

His competition, Carmelo, was in a similar situation in Europe, where he had enrolled in a German flying school in the summer of 1914. Shortly after taking his first passenger flight, however, World War I began and Carmelo had to give up his lessons. Quimson arrived home in the Philippines first, and he contacted a newspaper, the Philippine Free Press, about financing his first exhibitions. The paper seemed interested in the plan, but it was unable to come up with a Curtiss plane. Instead of showing off his talents, Quimson took a job as assistant instructor in the country's National Guard aviation corps. The full instructors in this body would presumably have been Americans, and it's a mystery why Quimson didn't spend the next two years flying machines at the school in Corregidor. Perhaps he did and that fact has since been forgotten. It's possible he may have helped train the man who would later become publicly recognized as the Philippine's first flyer. It's also possible he was given the relatively menial task of ground-training, or that the job with the aviation corps somehow didn't pan out.

At any rate, Carmelo enrolled in 1919 in a new Curtiss flying school at Paranaque and made his first solo flight on January 10, 1920, over the capital city and Manila Bay. Carmelo continued to fly in the Philippines and abroad for more than 30 years. He was still performing aerobatics in 1956. Luis Quimson fades out of the flight literature after 1920, when he's mentioned in a Philippine article as one of several "future Filipino aviators," despite having qualified for his brevet four years previous.

POLAND (PRUSSIA)

Date: February 18, 1909
Location: Magdeburg, Germany
Plane: Grade triplane
Length of flight: 400 meters (1,312 ft.)

Hans Grade (1879–1946)

When Hans Grade began the task of building Prussia's first plane in 1907, he never confronted the personal bugbear of so

Hans Grade, center. Technical Reports & Standards Unit, Library of Congress, L'Aérophile Collection.

Grade 1909 monoplane. Courtesy of the Library of Congress.

many pioneer designers. Grade had followed the work of Otto Lilienthal and Jacob Ellehammer; he had read of the Wrights and the Voisins and Santos-Dumont.[74] Grade had been preparing for this for more than a decade. He knew manned flight was possible. As a fan of Lilienthal's, Grade had constructed his first aircraft in the mid–1890s. At the time, Lilienthal was the world's most accomplished flier. He had spent decades studying the flight of birds, had published an important early paper on his findings, and by 1895 was making glides in excess of a thousand feet on small wood-and-cloth machines that he controlled simply by shifting his weight. During this time, Grade built a glider himself and would practice by jumping off the roof of his parents' house in Koslin, on at least one occasion crashing into the side of the house when he lost his balance. Lilienthal suffered a fatal fall in 1896 when one of his gliders stalled, but his seven years of public work would leave an indelible mark on the science of flight.

Not long after Grade graduated from Charlottenburg's technical university, he established his own motor works, the Grade-Motor-Werke, in the town of Magdeburg in what is now Germany. (Since he did most of his engineering and most of his actual flying not far from Berlin, and since he was born in Pommerania, Grade is widely considered the first German flier. The town in which in he was born, however, has been a part of Poland since World War II.) In Magdeburg, Hans built and raced motorcycles, explaining that motorcycling, "with its lasting dangers, is the best preparation for the flying sports."[75] He volunteered for a year's service with the Magdeburg garrison in 1907 and spent his free time constructing a bamboo and canvas triplane that resembled an early Ellehammer machine. He received financial help from a fund set up by a Mannheim merchant to promote German aviation. The merchant, Dr. Karl Lanz, had also established the Lanz-Preis der Luefte, a 40,000 mark ($180,000 today) reward for the first German citizen to fly a German-built plane at least 2.5 kilometers. In his shop, Grade machined a four-cylinder, 36-horsepower engine for his triplane and on his discharge from the service was ready to flight-test his new machine.

He used the garrison's parade grounds

throughout the fall of 1908, making flights up to 60 or more meters. At first Grade would start his take-off from one side of a large depression in the field and, rather than pulling up on his elevator, would just let the ground fall away from his speeding machine. Once, the captain of the garrison parked his bicycle and his sheathed sword, stuck upright in the ground, just over the curve of the hill. As Grade skimmed over the lip of the depression, his propeller smashed the bicycle and unsheathed the sword, sending both flying up in front of the plane. These hops over a low spot in the field are generally not counted as true flight, since they weren't lift-offs from level ground, and it would be the next year before Grade could fly the triplane a respectable distance. On February 18, 1909, his first machine stayed in the air for more than a quarter mile.

This most successful flight was also the triplane's swan song, as Grade shortly began building the monoplane that would make him famous and bring student-pilots to Germany from all over the world. Grade would follow the lead of two other first fliers in designing small aircraft intended mainly for use by the general public. Unfortunately, because of the necessary costs of building a gasoline engine in those days, economical airframes couldn't bring the cost of the flying machine within reach of the masses. This focus on small, affordable aircraft would eventually relegate Grade, with Alberto Santos-Dumont and Alfred de Pischof, to a back seat in the airplane's development.[76] Only those who could afford the technology would have much effect on its development, and airplane design in its first several decades moved steadily to accommodate military and commercial interests with greater size, range, and carrying capacity. Small machines for personal use wouldn't see a renaissance until much later in the century with the advent of ultralights.

Even in 1909, before airmail and commercial flights and large military air wings, the Grade monoplane was small compared to its contemporaries. Grade seems to have stayed with his roots in Lilienthal, paring his unwieldy triplane down to a monoplane, keeping the weight low and striving for the most stable configuration with the center of gravity below the wings. He took his immediate example from the latest Santos-Dumont plane, the *Demoiselle*, and his inspiration from the *Lanz-Preis der Luefte*.

Already the preeminent flier in Prussia, Grade won the Lanz prize on his second try on October 30, 1909. (His propeller had fractured on the first try a month earlier, bending his crankshaft, stalling his engine and landing Grade in the top of a pine grove.) By this time, Grade had moved his operations a few miles east from Magdeburg to Bork, and he used the Lanz prize money and his subsequent income from air shows and competitions to establish a factory and Prussia's first flying school that winter. In early 1910, he was awarded German pilot's license No. 2, after our first German flier, August Euler.

Grade eventually ran schools in Gelsenkirchen, Johannisthal, Leipzig, Kassel, Magdeburg, Mainz and Munich, and personally taught a total of 350 students. In concert with one of his former students, he organized Prussia's first unofficial airmail, from Bork to Breuck. For a short time, Grade contrived to sell his own private post stamps and place them next to the official stamps of the Prussian postal service.

Grade's career as a builder would span the next nine years and yield numerous plane types. He built small racing planes, two-seaters and a machine (named the Blue Mouse) especially for nose dives and aerobatics. All of his designs aimed for lightness, speed and efficiency. After taking part in military maneuvers in the fall of 1912, Grade wrote: "... it is absolutely necessary to build

Opposite: Hans Grade in his 1911 monoplane at the 25th anniversary celebration of aviation in Germany, September 25, 1934. On the ground are a Junkers G-38 and a Junkers G-38c, the "von Hindenburg." Though born in what is now Poland, Grade is widely considered the first German to fly. Corbis Images.

light and fast machines that can make a short take off and safe landings, instead of heavy juggernauts with wide wingspans and un-economically powerful engines. I proved that one can fly as fast and safely with 30 horse-power as one can do with 100 hp, that one can load a passenger and fuel for four hours and still develop speeds of about 100 kilo-meters per hour and safely land on any terrain…. Perhaps meanwhile the decisive authorities will realize that the machine with impressive dimensions is not the only option…."[77]

After the First World War, Grade stopped producing planes and began manufacturing cars, an enterprise that went well for him until the worldwide depression of the thir-ties. He retired from business in 1932. Two years later, the German government cele-brated the 25th anniversary of Grade's first flights. The inventor flew one of his grease-stained early monoplanes, which he had dubbed Ölsardine, "Sardine in Oil," for a crowd at Johannisthal field in Berlin. This machine had by that time spent seven thou-sand hours in the air. When he finished demonstrating that day, Grade parked the Sardine under one wing of the then-gigan-tic Junkers airliner Hindenburg, to illustrate the size difference in machines built only a quarter-century apart. For the German au-thorities, this was intended to show off na-tional initiative and the country's latest tech-nology, but Grade may have felt he was proving yet again a point that nobody else was hearing.

Many years after Grade had quit build-ing and teaching, a portrait of the aviators' guardian angel continued to hang above the door of a pub in Bork. The following verse accompanied the picture: "This is the holy Sengel, the angel who protects pilots. Soothe him with a little kerosene or seven spark plugs, and he will prevent all pain, kindling, foul weather and emergencies. Keep this in mind, young pilot!"[78] "Kindling" was slang for a wrecked plane, and one of Grade's few boasts was that no one was ever killed in one of his schools.

Hans Grade died in Berlin on Octo-ber 22, 1946.

PORTUGAL

Date: Autumn 1909
Location: Issy-les-Moulineaux
Plane: R.E.P. monoplane

Óscar Blanck (1878–1944)

Óscar Blanck, like many of our pre–1910 fliers, spent much of his life in Paris. At the age of 31, he was a successful antiques collec-tor and insurance agent. He visited an aero-drome near Paris sometime in 1909 and was intrigued by the sight of two men propelling their wood and cloth machines through the air. Although the accounts are unclear, this was probably Port-Aviation, the world's first constructed aerodrome, a dozen miles south of Paris at Juvisy. Blanck was reportedly in-spired by two unnamed aviators, and in sep-arate accounts he is said to have attended an air meet at Port-Aviation in early July. Al-though there was no Juvisy meet at that time, Port-Aviation had opened with a small avia-tion meet a month and a half previous. On that day only two aviators—Frenchmen Léon Delagrange and Henry Rougier—were able to leave the ground in the stormy spring weather. Perhaps these were the men who in-spired the Portuguese businessman to pur-chase an R.E.P. monoplane that summer.

Some have said that aviation was more of a democratic sport in the pioneer days than in later years with the establishment of government regulations and the evolution of more complex, and expensive, technologies. This may have been true for some, for cer-tainly there were those pilots who started their careers working on a ground crew and eventually learned to fly. And some ambi-tious middle class men got themselves hired as test pilots or with good connections and persistence started successful factories. But even at aviation's coming out party in the fall of 1909, it remained for the most part the province of the well-to-do. Most of those who packed the grandstands in Reims that August, at the first international aviation meet, were members of the nobility, wealthy sportsmen, or successful businessmen like Óscar Blanck.

Those who declaim the democratic nature of early aviation are probably speaking in relative terms. It would be nearly impossible at the beginning of the 21st century to start building modern planes with a capital investment of $6.5 million, as American Glenn Curtiss did with an equivalent amount, $360,000, in 1909.[79] But it took Curtiss years of successful work in engines and motorcycles before he had the capital to start building planes. Nor is $6.5 million an amount the average citizen could raise easily in 2003. Even the Wrights, whose work was a model of thriftiness, had a steady income from their bicycle factory and shop, one that allowed them to be away for long periods of time and to spend $1,000 ($18,000 today) of their own cash developing their first powered airplane. The Wright expenditure pales, of course, next to the $73,000 in public money spent by Smithsonian Institution Secretary Samuel Pierpont Langley on his *Aerodrome*, or the $200,000 of his own money spent by American arms manufacturer, Hiram Maxim, on his 4-ton steam-powered machine. Even the Wrights' total, however, was more than the $600 average U.S. income in 1905.

We don't know how much Blanck's R.E.P. cost him, but a Wright *Model A* produced by the licensed Short Brothers firm in England cost £1,000 ($90,000 today) that summer. This money paid for a wooden machine held together by wire cables, with the engine sitting next to the pilot on the lower wing: no protected cockpit, no flight instruments, no wheels, not even a launching derrick like the one the Wrights used. A Blériot monoplane, more like the R.E.P. but with a smaller engine, went for about half the price of the Wright (£480). Nor did these costs include lessons. Two years later, the A.V. Roe company in Weybridge, England, would teach a new pilot to fly for £50 ($4,400 today).

There is some question over when and how far Óscar Blanck flew his expensive contraption. The R.E.P. was only a marginally successful machine, anyway, and the Paris news accounts of Blanck's flying mention only crashes. One Portuguese historian claims Blanck received international pilot's license no. 8 on July 9, 1909. However, we know Blanck does not hold brevet no. 8, and his name is nowhere to be found in the pre-war license records. He reportedly flew his monoplane at the popular flying field in Issy-les-Moulineaux in August. The newspaper *Le Temps* reported a wreck on October 9 that destroyed his propeller and the front of his machine. And at another air meet in Juvisy on October 18, Blanck had a spectacular wreck when his engine failed during take-off and landed him in the middle of a crowded grandstand. His plane, perhaps a new one, since it had only been nine days since his last catastrophe, was destroyed, and five people were injured, two seriously. Though it's rarely noted in the histories, this mishap made Blanck the first aviator ever sued for damages from a crash. The most seriously injured, a woman named Mme. Férand, sued Blanck not for the cut that opened her calf and thigh to the bone, but for the damage to her dress. She lost the suit, and there is no record of Óscar Blanck flying again.

Normally, we wouldn't credit a pilot for achieving flight when all we can find are accounts of his smash-ups. In our working definition, flight only qualifies when it includes a successful landing. However, *Le Temps* mentions in passing that Blanck had been flying his monoplane before the accident, and Portuguese flight historians feel strongly that Blanck did fly successfully. The next successful Portuguese aviator, and the first to get his international brevet, would be Luis de Noronha, who began flying under the tutelage of world-famous air racer André Beaumont in early 1912.

ROMANIA

Date: January 10, 1910
Location: France
Plane: *Blériot XI* monoplane

Prince Georges Valentin Bibesco (1880–1941)

Of all the wealthy gentlemen, and even noblemen, who took up aviation in its early years, our Romanian flier was one of only a couple true members of the European royalty to pilot an airplane before World War I. King Alphonso XIII of Spain had sat in the *Flyer* with Wilbur Wright in 1908, wanting desperately to take a ride but restrained by a promise to his mother. Prince Heinrich of Prussia, brother to the Kaiser, learned to fly in 1910. But Georges Valentin Bibesco, Prince of Romania, began learning to fly at the same time that many of Europe's pioneers were just getting started. He was immediately at home in the new flying machines, and for more than 30 years Bibesco would live quietly at the very center of international aviation.

The 3rd Prince Bibesco was born in 1880, the grandson of the Russian prince who had granted Romania its charter in 1848. His mother descended from Napoleon Bonaparte. Prince Bibesco married at the age of 22, perhaps too young for a rich sportsman with petrol in his veins. His wife, Marthe Lahovary, was only 16. The unwanted female child of the very wealthy Romanian Foreign Minister, she was married off for political gain. The newlyweds did not hit it off. Within a few years they lived, and loved, separately.

In 1902, Prince Bibesco founded Romania's first auto club, and he would still be racing cars seven years later when he founded the country's first aero club and left for France to get his pilot's license. He was a noted hunter, and he practiced that most noble of sports (because so expensive), ballooning. Sometime around 1905, King Carol I sent the prince and princess on a diplomatic mission through southern Russia into Persia to tour and map the area and to sow the seeds of international auto travel. The trip was also an attempt to repair the couple's marriage. It did not. When the tour was over, Princess Bibesco retired to her various estates to write a book about the trip, while the prince left for Paris to see for himself if men were really flying machines of their own building. Bibesco ordered a glider from the Voisin factory in France and began to practice his aerial skills. He witnessed Frenchman Louis Blériot's first monoplane trials at

Issy-les-Moulineaux in 1907, and he returned to France for Wilbur Wright's Auvours demonstration flights in 1908. That year, he purchased an early Voisin biplane, though he seems never to have flown that particular machine. At the prince's invitation, by then world-famous Louis Blériot made exhibition flights in Bucharest the next fall, a few months after his first-ever crossing of the English Channel. Prince Bibesco saw Blériot fly in Bucharest on October 30, 1909, and decided he must enroll in the Blériot flight school immediately. The prince went to the Pau school, in the southwest of France, and earned his license, French brevet no. 20, on January 10, 1910. In later years, Bibesco, descended from Russian royalty and the great French emperor, said of Blériot, the French bourgeois businessman, "I was his pupil, and he was my master and my friend."

As soon as he had his license and a *Blériot XI* of his own, Bibesco began scouting air routes from airfield to airfield, still a very risky endeavor with the inconsistent engines of the era. Engine failure often landed fliers in rutted fields and treetops. Blériot's 1909 demonstrations in Constantinople had ended with a landing on a hotel roof. As he had so many times already, Blériot came out of this life-threatening accident alive. Bibesco seems to have had the luck of Blériot but without all the mishaps. He returned to Romania to establish the country's first aerodrome at Cotroceni and to pioneer several air routes from Bucharest to the country's interior. In Cotroceni he founded Romania's second flying school and managed to license a dozen army officers that year. The country's first air meet was organized in August of 1910 and featured, among others, Bibesco, our first Greek flier, Michel Paul Molla, and Aurel Vlaicu, the first successful Romanian plane builder.

Probably because of his role in training all the army officers who were now Romania's aviation corps, the prince received his army commission as a captain in 1911 when his flying school became the country's first school of military aviation. As commanding officer of the new school, Bibesco received from King Carol that year the Order of Military Merit and the Star of Romania with Swords. In 1912 Bibesco established the Liga Nationala Aeriana to raise money for air corps planes. The Balkan War of 1913, known as the Second Balkan War, sucked Romania into a Europe-wide conflict over the disintegration of the Ottoman Empire and the distribution of political power in the Balkans. Bibesco took command of the three Romanian air squadrons he had by now trained, flying reconnaissance and communications missions in the push for Bulgarian territory. When continued Balkan conflict plunged the world's powers into war again a year later, Bibesco continued to command the Romanian air forces. The prince and his men flew missions against Ottoman oil fields with Britain's Royal Flying Corps, and Bibesco earned the Distinguished Service Order for his service with the British forces.

After the war, Prince Bibesco took several years off sporting to help with the work of reconstruction in Romania. In 1923 he was chosen vice-president of the country's Royal Aero Club (King Carol was president) and acted as delegate to the meetings of the Fédération Aéronautique Internationale (F.A.I.), the worldwide licensing body and flying society. In the 1920s Bibesco founded at least three cross-country air races for military aviators: an English-Romanian London-Bucharest Cup, the French-Romanian Coupe Paris-Bucharest, and the Circuit de la Petit Entente, for the air corps flyers of eastern Europe. At some point he became the president of Romania's aero club, with the king serving as "President-in-Chief." In 1927 Bibesco became the vice president of the F.A.I. and was awarded the position of Commander in the French Légion d'Honneur.

Prince Georges Valentin Bibesco. Technical Reports & Standards Unit, Library of Congress, L'Aérophile Collection.

When King Carol established the new Ordre pour le Mérite Aéronautique in 1930, the prince became the first member. And that year, Bibesco was unanimously elected president of the F.A.I. As the world's premier civil aviator, his message was clear: The air should remain open to civilian flying, airspace should not be restricted. He made extensive air tours spreading this message, including a 1931 journey from Paris to Saigon, a 1934 loop around the Mediterranean Sea, a scouting trip from France to its colony of Madagascar via the Nile River in 1935, and another tour through Algeria and Chad in

1939. The prince was either an extraordinarily careful pilot or an exceptionally lucky one, probably both. After all those years of flying rickety, unreliable airplanes, even in World War I combat, it was a modern airliner that caused the only serious flying injury of his career. On the 1931 Paris-Saigon tour, Bibesco's 16-seat Fokker collided with a vulture over northeast India. The bird hit one of the propellers. The crew descended immediately and checked the engine and prop while the machine was being refueled. Everything seemed fine, so they continued toward Rangoon. Not long after take-off, however, something went drastically wrong with the effected engine, and they were forced to land immediately. The plane hit a ditch and burst into flames. One of the four crew members was killed in the fire, the prince and two others were badly burned. They eventually recovered, but Bibesco's health was never the same.

By now Princess Marthe Bibesco was famous for her literary ability, but also for her many relationships with the powerful men of Europe, including the Crown Prince Wilhelm, the same Alphonso XIII of Spain who had sat with Wilbur Wright in the *Flyer*, even Benito Mussolini. She had gained literary notoriety in 1908 with her first book, *Les Huits Paradis*, the story of the Russian-Ottoman automobile trip with her estranged husband. Since then, she had published a book about Romanian folk life, *Isvor, le pays des saules*, numerous novels including *The Green Parrot* (1924) and *Catherine Paris* (1928), and regular nonfiction pieces in the *Saturday Evening Post*, the *North American Review* and *Vogue*. She had been a close friend of Marcel Proust and had won the Prix de l'Académie Française in 1928. During his last years, the prince and princess at last became friends, and she accompanied him on several of his aerial journeys.

Prince Georges Valentin Bibesco, a senator in the Romanian Parliament, three times a Parliamentary deputy, the president of the F.A.I. and civil aviation's most prominent voice, a constant in the realm of flying for a span of 34 years, died of cancer in Paris in 1941 a few days after the start of World War II.

Marthe Bibesco seems to have become even more active in European circles of power. She had relationships with Ramsey MacDonald, Lord Thomson of Cardington and, last and most prominently, Charles De Gaulle. Her family lost all its property after World War II, and the princess fell to writing popular romances under the name of Lucile Ducaux to support herself. She also managed to publish biographies of Proust and Winston Churchill, another of her friends, and to write screenplays for Robert Bresson. She died in 1975 at the age of 89.

There are many possible candidates for first Romanian flier, and Prince Bibesco started his career several years later than a man who is credited in Romania with actually inventing flight. Depending on your viewpoint, Trajan Vuia was either a visionary designer whose very early monoplane nevertheless didn't amount to much, or he is the first man ever to fly a real airplane. In 1906 Vuia built the first powered monoplane, a design that anticipated the appearance of modern airplanes, as well as the ultralight configurations of Santos-Dumont, Grade and de Pischof.[80] It had four wheels with pneumatic tires and a tail with elevator and inboard rudder. Vuia tested it at Issy-les-Moulineaux near Paris, where the Voisin brothers and Louis Blériot were also working. The *Vuia I* influenced Blériot to move away from the Wright-style biplane and start building monoplanes. Although a forward-looking design, Vuia's craft had two major defects: Its carbonic acid engine was not powerful enough, and it had no form of lateral control. The best Vuia was able to do in nearly a year of testing was a hop of 24 meters (78 ft.). However, Romania recognizes Vuia as the originator of powered flight because he had a short hop (6 m.) before Ellehammer and Santos-Dumont's first hops in the fall of 1906, and because he carried his landing gear with him, which in this argument invalidates the early Wright flights, made either from a rail or with the help of a launching derrick. If these standards were applied universally, however, there were several contenders who got their wheels off the ground before Vuia, most especially that

Aurel Vlaicu's *Vlaicu II*, 1912. National Air and Space Museum, Smithsonian Institution (SI Neg. No. 2001-6625).

perennially ignored Frenchmen, Clement Ader, whose steam-powered machine made a successful take-off in 1890 (and prefigured Vuia's monoplane design, without the tail). It is also hard to argue that someone making a 20-foot hop in 1906 has primacy over the Wrights, who had flown nearly 25 miles the year before.

The other serious contender for first Romanian pilot, at least in early aviation lore, is Henri Coanda. Coanda was a talented but difficult young designer who began work on a helicopter as early as 1906. He designed the world's first sesquiplane and the world's first ducted fan engine (a precursor to the jet), and he went on to a successful career with the Bristol company during World War I. Legends arose many years later that Coanda had flown his helicopter in 1907 and his "jet sesquiplane" in 1910. In fact, no pictures, drawings or other details remain of the helicopter, only a French news article from a year after its supposed testing. The helicopter may even have been a model, but it almost certainly was not successfully piloted by Coanda or anyone else. Helicopters capable of sustained flight didn't exist until the 1920s. Coanda's sesquiplane is supposed to have made a short flight before crashing and

burning up, but there is no contemporary account of the plane being seen in public except on an exhibition stand at the 1910 Paris Salon. And years later, an English historian viewed the sesquiplane, intact and unburned, in a collector's warehouse. Though Coanda may have designed many successful planes, he seems never to have piloted any of them.

The first successful plane built and flown by a Romanian designer was the monoplane of Aurel Vlaicu, pictured on this page. Vlaicu flew this very plane in the first Romanian air meet of 1910 that was attended by Prince Bibesco.

RUSSIAN FEDERATION

Date: January 31, 1910
Location: Camp-de-Châlons, France
Plane: Farman biplane
Length of flight: 33 kilometers (21 mi.)[81]

Mikhail Nikiforovich Efimov (1881–1917)

Mikhail Efimov's star rose with that of his well known Peruvian counterpart,

Mikhail Efimov over the waves in his Henry Farman biplane at an air meet in Nice, April 20, 1910. Technical Reports & Standards Unit, Library of Congress, L'Aérophile Collection.

Georges Chavez. The two men began lessons in the same month at the Farman flying school on Henry Farman biplanes.[82] They made their first solo flights four to eight weeks later and received their Aéro-Club de France licenses on the same day, February 15, 1910. Holding Aéro-Club brevets numbers 31 and 32 respectively, Efimov and Chavez took their first competition prizes at the Nice flying week in early April.

Efimov's career outlasted that of the famous Chavez, but there was an earlier difference between the two men and one that makes the Russian of still rarer material than most of his contemporaries. While Chavez and the rest of the aviation field were almost exclusively men with the extensive financial means required to pursue the latest in technology and fashion, Mikhail Efimov came from the Russian lower class. A syndicate of Odessa businessmen had hired Efimov, the son of a Smolensk laborer, as a sort of turn-of-the-century stock car driver. That arrangement made Efimov one of the few members of his social class who ever stepped foot in an early airplane, much less piloted one. Efimov had already distinguished himself by graduating from a trade school and getting a job with the railroads as an electrical engineer. He had done well enough in this career that he was able to take part in the recreations of the middle class. Before he became one of the world's first hired racing pilots, Efimov had spent his spare time cycling, motorcycling and even flying gliders with our first Ukrainian pilot, Sergei Utochkin.

While his arrangement with the aviation syndicate put him in the seat of an airplane, like other forms of sponsorship it had its drawbacks. Since Efimov's relationship to the syndicate was essentially that of a business investment, he kept only one-tenth of his contest winnings. The syndicate took out an insurance policy on their pilot for £4,000,

Mikhail Efimov aboard his Farman biplane, c. 1910. Courtesy of the Library of Congress.

the equivalent of $360,000 today, so as to re-coup their investment in the case of his death. As it turned out they didn't need the insurance policy, and Efimov won enough in his very first competition (£3,000) to cover all of his costs, including that of an additional plane.

At the Farman school in France, Efimov made a name for himself quickly. By the time the Russian had been in flight school for a month, Farman himself said he'd never seen such a fast learner. Efimov started lessons in December of 1909 and by the end of January had taken his biplane up for a 33-kilometer jaunt around the Plain of Châlons. A crash a few days later apparently left him unfazed, for by mid–February he had passengers in the air for more than an hour at a time. Judging from his progress and that of Chavez, a British periodical speculated in early March that it was the Henry Farman biplane that was the cause of all the incredible piloting at Châlons: "It is astonishing how easily some

of the purchasers of Farman machines seem to learn the art of flying."[83]

Language would have posed an additional barrier for Efimov at the flying school, for he had grown up speaking only Russian. Farman spoke French and some English, but it's highly unlikely he or his instructors knew anything of the Cyrillic dialects. An Englishman who wrote later of his experiences at one of the French schools, however, expressed the opinion that a common language wasn't all that important to flight instruction. Although the Englishman was glad he could speak French, that sentiment was mainly for the rainy days spent around the stove at the school, laughing and joking with the shockingly ribald French students.[84] In the air, he said, the student couldn't have heard a word of instruction even if the teacher had shouted in his ear. He simply put his hands and feet on the controls and observed the instructor's movements. On the ground afterward, a student sometimes got pointers, but those could be understood as much by the instructor's gestures as from his words.

At Nice in April of 1910, while Chavez took the single-flight distance prize, Efimov set records for fastest take-offs with and without passengers and logged the greatest distance flying for the whole meet: 960 kilometers (597 mi.). He won much more than any other pilot, and though he was fined 100 francs for a close fly-over that landed another aviator in the sea, even the 10-percent share (£300) of his total winnings must have seemed a handsome take. His prize money would have been worth about $27,000 today. At the flying week in Rouen, Efimov won the prix de passagères for his 112-mile (70 km.) flight with a passenger. At some time that spring he saved his own life with a maneuver that renowned Frenchman Louis Blériot had executed a couple of years earlier. Cutting his engine for a gliding descent, or *vol plané*, Efimov failed to keep enough speed on his approach to the field and went into a stall at 150 feet. In order to right his diving machine and get himself out of the way of the ground, he clawed his way up the rear fuselage. The weight shift brought the nose up enough to avert total catastrophe, but while Efimov walked away from the crash, the plane was demolished. Perhaps that's why he was flying a Sommer biplane, rather than his old Farman, when he competed at the Reims meet later that summer. To cap his first year in aviation, he returned to his homeland to make the first exhibition flights in the Russian Empire.

Efimov set numerous records during his time in competition. He also pioneered the *vol plané*, a maneuver that later became a requirement for most advanced and military pilot's licenses. He worked as a test pilot and was later appointed instructor at the Russian flying school in Sevastopol. Here, he invented a starter that would get a plane's engine turning without someone having to swing the propeller. Efimov flew for the Russian Em-

2nd Lt. John Munro Rankin, August 26, 1918. Royal Air Force Museum, Hendon, London; Royal Aero Club of the United Kingdom certificates, Rac 6724.

pire during World War I, and he may have served earlier for Bulgaria in the Balkan Wars.

Perhaps in deference to his humble beginnings, Mikhail Efimov sided with the Bolsheviks during the October Revolution and the ensuing civil war. We do not know the circumstances surrounding his death, but we know he was executed by White Guards in 1919.

St. Christopher & Nevis

Date: August 26, 1918
Location: England

John Munro Rankin (1892–?)

John Munro Rankin came to flying late in World War I, receiving his Royal Flying

Corps brevet on August 26, 1918, less than three months before the Armistice. He was not quite 26 years old at the time, and the record does not mention his rank. This makes it impossible to tell whether he had already served in another branch of the military or had just begun his service. His license data is all we know of Rankin, except that he does not appear in the casualty rolls of the Royal Flying Corps.

SAUDI ARABIA

Date: December 28, 1949
Location: England
Plane: de Havilland DH-82A

Said Hashem Hashem
(1931–?)

The earliest mention of a Saudi pilot occurs in the British license records of the 1940s. Said Hashem earned English brevet number 26,290 on December 28, 1949. He was apparently a visiting student and took his lessons at Air Service Training, Ltd. Hashem flew a de Havilland DH-82A during his license test. His certificate data is all we know of Hashem.

SCOTLAND
(GREAT BRITAIN)

Date: April 19, 1910
Location: France
Plane: Farman biplane

Captain Bertram Dickson
(1873–1913)

Our first Scots flier had just come into his own as a competitor when he was involved in one of the most unfortunate incidents in pre–World War I aviation. On

Said Hashem Hashem, December 28, 1949. Royal Air Force Museum, Hendon, London; Royal Aero Club of the United Kingdom certificates, Rac 26290.

October 2, 1910, Captain Bertram Dickson and Frenchman René Thomas had the first recorded mid-air collision during an air meet in Milan. The injuries he received would plague Dickson until the end of his life.

Bertram Dickson was born in Edinburgh on the 21st of December, 1873. We know nothing about his early life, his education or his professional training. He must have served in the British military, but we do not know if he was on active service during his time as an aviator. Dickson earned his pilot's brevet, number 71, on April 19, 1910, at a Henry Farman school in France. He set a record for time aloft with a passenger, two hours, on June 6, 1910. Not long after, he was one of three competitors in the world's first cross-country race with a simultaneous start,

Captain Bertram Dickson, left, and an unidentified man. Royal Air Force Museum, Hendon, London. Ref No. PC 73/61.

the Angers-Saumur race over the Loire River. Dickson finished some time after the first- and second-place fliers, but he provided the comic relief for the day when he landed in a flooded portion of the airfield and had to be "rescued" from the wing of his biplane by a member of the French Horse Guards. Dickson did well at a meet in Rouen that summer, winning several prizes, then flew without particular distinction in a Scottish meet at Lanark, near Glasgow, that August. His luck had a brief but splendid recovery at a meet in Tours, France, where he won all the prizes.

This is where Dickson's life becomes entwined with a persistent piece of superstition. Late that summer, he and his sister had supposedly viewed the remains of the Egyptian priestess Amen Ra, the infamously cursed mummy that went down with the Titanic some years later. At the time, the mummy belonged to a London collector. At the Milan meet on October 2, 1910, Dickson

was making a routine exhibition flight inside the aerodrome when René Thomas, who was competing in a race, came into the aerodrome over Dickson. Neither aviator saw the other. As he descended toward the field, Thomas's *Antoinette* monoplane, one of the heaviest planes available at the time, collided with Dickson's open-cockpit Farman biplane. Locked together in mid-air, the two machines crashed to the ground from 120 feet. Thomas was not seriously injured, but Dickson spent months in the hospital. While recovering, the Scotsman learned his bank had gone under and that he was penniless. To add insult to injury, the Milan committee found Dickson responsible for the accident, since Thomas had been competing in an official event, while Dickson was only demonstrating. The committee fined Dickson £600 ($54,000 today). Also during that time, his sister was shipwrecked in Albania.

Captain Dickson eventually regained his

Barnwell canard-style biplane, c. 1909. National Air and Space Museum, Smithsonian Institution (SI Neg. No. 2001-6612).

feet, but, probably due to his financial troubles, he couldn't fly again until he got a position with the Bristol company in March of 1912. Bertram Dickson died a year and a half later, at the age of 40. Though we haven't been able to discover the cause of his death, more than one source suggests he was never really well again after the crash.

Two men who are often cited as Scotland's first aviators are Frank and Harold Barnwell (R.H. Barnwell, sometimes referred to as Harold, sometimes as Robert). The Barnwells worked in Stirling and built the first plane in Scotland, but they were born in Kent, England. In January of 1911, Harold Barnwell won the Scottish Aeronautical Society £50 prize for the first flight in a Scots-built airplane, which was a monoplane and his fourth flying machine. Their first machine, a very large canard-style biplane, was completed in 1909 but crashed on its first test. Harold went on to teach flying and test designs for the Vickers company, Frank to serve as a flight commander in the Royal Flying Corps.

SINGAPORE
(GREAT BRITAIN)

Date: November 6, 1913

2nd Lieutenant John Douglas Harvey (1891–?)

2nd Lt. John Douglas Harvey, November 6, 1913. Royal Air Force Museum, Hendon, London; Royal Aero Club of the United Kingdom certificates, Rac 681.

British Second Lieutenant John Douglas Harvey earned his brevet, number 681, on November 6, 1913, and the information contained in his certificate is all we know about him. Harvey was born in Singapore on October 10, 1891. We don't know if he fought during World War I, but his name does not appear in the post-war casualty lists.

SLOVENIA
(AUSTRIA-HUNGARY)

Date: January, 1910
Location: Vienna, Austria
Plane: Rusjan monoplane
Length of flight: 600 meters (1,969 ft.)

Edvard Rusjan (?–1911)

Edvard Rusjan was born in Gorica on the southwestern edge of Austria-Hungary, just a few miles north of the Adriatic Sea and the Gulf of Trieste. After World War I, that area became part of the Kingdom of Serbs, Croats and Slovenes, later to become Yugoslavia. World War II's partitioning cut Gorica in half, giving the western, urban portion to Italy and the eastern, more rural portion to Yugoslavia. In 1910, the year that Rusjan first flew, the large region between Greece and the Baltic Sea was dominated by three imperial powers: Prussia, Austria-Hungary and the Ottoman Empire. Another great empire, Russia, controlled everything to the north and east. At the turn of the current century, no less than 13 countries occupy the same region, not counting any of seven formerly Soviet republics in the east. Each of these nations was formed at a different time, during different independence struggles, and many of the political redrawings have been based on ethnic background, language and religion. For the sake of simplicity, we have tried to use as first fliers those born within the modern political boundaries of each country, no matter to which nation the pilot would have owed citizenship at the time. However, Slovenia and Edvard Rusjan are an exception to that rule.

Rusjan was probably born in what is now the Italian town of Gorizia. Yet, his ancestry was undoubtedly Slovene, and it is possible that he was born east of the urban center in the area of Nova Gorica, the town

Edvard Rusjan. Technical Reports & Standards Unit, Library of Congress, L'Aérophile Collection.

that grew on the Yugoslav side of the border after World War II. Because of his ancestry, because he is recognized as the country's first flier, and because no one else makes a claim for that distinction, we have chosen Rusjan as the first pilot from Slovenia despite doubts about his exact birthplace.

Rusjan was not only the Balkans' first aviator but also the first in the region to design and build his own plane. Like Henry Farman and Baron Pierre de Caters, Rusjan raced cars before he got started in aviation.[85] Sometime in 1909 he began with his brother, Josip, to build an airplane they dubbed *EDA-1*. By the end of November, Edvard had tested the machine with some small success (60 m.). The brothers continued to refine and practice. On the 22nd of January 1910, an English-language periodical reported that the brothers had flown their plane as far as 600 meters (1,969 ft.) and as high as 12 meters. Although the dispatch doesn't say which brother flew, by all other accounts Edvard seems to have been the one who did their piloting. The early 1910 machine was a tractor biplane powered by a 25-horsepower Anzani engine. Rusjan's early work seems to have resembled the Farman and Curtiss designs. One photograph shows a Farman-type pusher biplane with ailerons on the wings, while the plane that flew 600 meters had its ailerons between the wings like an early Curtiss, but with the propeller in front. A later photograph taken with Mihajlo Merčep, the first pilot from Croatia, shows Edvard in a machine that strongly resembles a Blériot monoplane.

The Rusjans apparently teamed up with Merčep sometime in 1910. At the time, no one from the Balkan region had flown in Belgrade. The builders worked on their last plane at Merčep's workshop in Zagreb. Although he probably flew throughout 1910, Edvard Rusjan's next recorded flight wasn't until January 9, 1911, in Belgrade. Rusjan's objective on that day was to fly over the confluence of the Save and Danube Rivers in the middle of the city, which he did successfully. No one knows what happened when he turned and headed back for the airfield. Perhaps there was an overwhelming tailwind on the return trip, or a particularly nasty air pocket over the river. For some reason, Rusjan's plane suddenly lost altitude and crashed into a bridge over the Save. He was killed instantly.

Merčep kept their work alive, however, piloting the Rusjan plane himself that autumn and later building another machine he had designed with Edvard. Merčep stayed in aviation for several years, manufacturing several different designs. Although aerial combat wouldn't evolve for several years, airplanes played an important part in surveillance during the Balkan wars of 1913 and 1914.

SOUTH AFRICA (GREAT BRITAIN)

Date: February 3, 1911
Location: France
Plane: Weston-Farman, pusher biplane

Maximilian John Ludwick Weston (1873–1950)

Even in the annals of early aviation, there are few characters as colorful as John Weston. Mechanic, ship's cook, hunter, cyclist, diver, aeronaut and motorcaravaner, when his British countrymen went to war against the Boers in 1901, Weston fought for the other side. Stories of his exploits and adventures abound, but almost all of these stories come originally from Weston, who himself embodied a rare combination of reticence and mendacity. Because he was generally quiet and didn't give the impression of a braggart, people tended to believe even Weston's most unlikely tales.

The mystery begins with his birth. Weston claimed most of the time to be of Scottish descent, but sometimes he claimed Scots-American heritage. There is little doubt that his father was Scottish, ostensibly a geologist. His mother was probably English but may have been American. It has become generally accepted that he was born near Fort Marshall, in the South African province of Natal, though he told one of his daughters he'd been born in Scotland. (The other daughter believed he was born in South Africa.) According to legend, Weston was born in an oxcart in Natal sometime between 1870 and 1875, probably in 1873. Weston claimed later to be named after his father's friend, the Mexican emperor Maximilian (1863–67), but all contemporary sources refer to him only as "John Weston." He was the oldest of three children, and his younger brother was reportedly killed at the age of three "by a stray bullet."[86] The histories don't say what the family would be doing in a place where bullets accidentally strike small children, but by the time Weston was seven, his father, the "geologist," was training natives in Somaliland to resist the slave trader known as Tippoo Tib. This is when young Weston first learned to handle a gun. Indeed, if his father had been a friend of Maximilian during that man's turbulent reign in Mexico, chances are slim he was really a geologist.

When John was ten, the family moved to the United States, where his father died of undisclosed causes two years later. During this period, John became interested in electricity and may have built a small generator by himself. After his father's death, Weston disappeared for several years. He was only 12 at the time, but a South African historian has confirmed that Weston spent this time mainly aboard ships, as a coxswain, a cook, a mechanic, a whaler, a cod fisherman and a diver. Later, he is also reputed to have done some big game hunting, spliced hawsers in California and hired himself out as a mercenary in South America. In the 1890s he seems to have studied engineering, probably in both the United States and Belgium. Weston later claimed to have a doctorate in engineering, but no one has been able to find a record of this degree in England, Belgium or the United States. When he had become an accomplished pilot many years later, Weston also told people that he had started gliding from hot air balloons with J. J. Montgomery in California in 1892, and that he had worked with American pioneer Octave Chanute on the groundbreaking Chanute-Herring glider design of 1896. Both claims are undoubtedly false. Octave Chanute had three assistants in 1896, none of them named Weston, and Montgomery didn't launch his gliders from balloons until 1906.

In 1901 Weston returned to South Africa to fight with the Boers, helping to hand Britain its most questionable military "victory" of the century. Then he seems to have gone to Belgium for a couple of years, perhaps also working on the lighting system at a new opera house in Paris. He spent an indefinite amount of time working on a Russian railway. Weston was living in Liège, Belgium, when he was accepted as a fellow in the British Royal Geographical Society on December 12, 1904. By 1906 Weston was back in South Africa. He began farming at Bultfontein and married a friend's sister, Elizabeth (Lilly) Maria Jacoba Roux, on August 10, 1906. Legend has it that he cycled 240 kilometers (150 mi.) to propose to Lilly, and that the two of them then rode an additional 160 kilometers (100 mi.) to the magistrate's office in Bloemfontein, to be married in clothes that had gotten wet in the winter rain. Weston continued farming and purchased a wheeled threshing machine that he would drive around to adjacent farms for hire.

Here Weston took a brief hiatus from his travels, staying on his farm for two years. He later said that he began building his first flying machine during this time and that he based his design on a machine by Henry Farman.[87] Since there were no Farman machines for two more years, however, it's probably safe to assume Weston didn't get started until at least 1909. By this time, he and Lilly and their first child, Anna, had moved to the town of Brandfort, still in the central region of South Africa. After Weston had no luck flying his airplane with the 30-horsepower automobile engine he had installed, he shipped the machine to the Farman school in France, where he received flying lessons and some design help. That plane is not listed in any of three published lists of planes flying before the fall of 1909, but according to several sources this plane had flown with its progenitor at the wheel sometime before 1911. He made his first official solo, for French brevet number 357, on February 3, 1911. Weston bought a Farman plane to go with his own "Weston-Farman" and shipped these machines to South Africa that spring.

Weston helped to found the Aeronautical Society of South Africa and started his own venture, the John Weston Aviation Company, Ltd. He purchased three more planes, all Bristol biplanes, and began raising money to start the first South African flight school. Under the patronage of prime minister General Louis Botha, Weston toured the country that winter and spring, giving exhibition flights in Bloemfontein, East London, King William's Town, Queenstown and Johannesburg. He would charge a shilling to view his flying machines before the show, charge admission to the demonstrations, then auction off several passenger flights afterward. Despite all this potential commerce, he was constantly in financial straits. He even sued a prominent member of the Johannesburg stock exchange who failed to pay the agreed upon £11 for his flight. Weston managed to raise £8,000 for an aviation school, but he needed £1,000 more and could never get that last bit together. He took it very personally when another company opened a flying school nearby in Kimberley.

Early in 1913 disaster struck Weston's

shop in Brandfort. In February, someone set fire to the building, destroying all five planes inside. Weston publicly surmised that the blaze was the work of saboteurs from the neighboring German colony of Namibia. The workshop and its contents seem to have been insured for £9,000, more than enough to purchase two Farman and three Bristol biplanes, but Weston never replaced these machines. He traveled to England, where a year later he earned British Aeronaut's Certificate number 38 and Airship Pilot's Certificate number 23. He seems to have become affiliated with the British military sometime before the war, and when the war began 2nd Lieutenant Weston became the ground officer in charge of airfields for the South African Forces. He was officially listed as a member of the Royal Naval Volunteer Reserve, though friends reported seeing him in the uniform of the Royal Naval Air Service during this time. In 1916 he received an official transfer to the R.N.A.S., and he flew surveillance in balloons and planes for No. 3 Wing and No. 2 Wing in the eastern Mediterranean. Weston was promoted to major at the beginning of 1918 and received another transfer, this time to the Royal Air Force, on April 1.

This is when his military service takes a strange turn. He seems to have been stationed in or around Greece from mid–1918. No specific reason was ever given, but for "services rendered" the Royal Hellenic Navy made Weston an honorary rear admiral and awarded him the Cross of Officer of the Royal Hellenic Order of the Redeemer. After the war he stayed with the British Naval Mission in Athens as a commander in the Royal Naval Air Service, though he often wore an unofficial white admiral's uniform he had assembled for himself.

Weston's military career only seems to have enhanced his peripatetic lifestyle. In 1920, while in the United States on a mission, he purchased a 1918 Commerce truck and had it shipped to England, where it was converted into a "motorcaravan," or what we would call a motorhome. The next year, Weston was back in Greece as a member of King Constantine's personal staff and seems to have traveled to the Soviet Union, where he reputedly struck up a friendship with V. I. Lenin. Not long after, Weston loaded his family in the caravan and made his first tour, driving from Belgium through Eastern Europe to Asia Minor. He was there when the Turks drove out Greek troops, and the family barely escaped in the rout. His next adventure was in Bulgaria, where he was driving when that country's communist revolution began. From the mercenary and Boer fighter of the early days, Weston had become an avowed peacenik—at least publicly. He painted one-world slogans on the side of the truck and told the press he was making this trip to educate his children in the ways of the world. Several historians have questioned his motivations, however, as Weston seems unerringly to have turned up in the middle of conflict after conflict. No one has ever discovered how he managed to finance the purchase of an expensive truck, its conversion into a recreational vehicle and his subsequent globe-trotting. Several of his acquaintances later said Weston was a British spy, and perhaps the fact that Weston never said so himself lends credibility to that theory. However, no one has ever been able to confirm that he was a spy.

After his mother and sister died of cholera in 1928, Weston sold his Brandfort home for £775. His children stayed in school in England while he and Lilly drove through Palestine, Iraq, Iran, Turkey, France and Spain. He began the next big caravan in 1931 in Johannesburg, planning to drive all the way to Cairo. By now, the family was so trained in the ways of the road that they could take down the whole van in ten minutes. For the African trip, Weston mounted a machine gun on top. This trip was never completed, however, and Weston returned to South Africa to purchase three farms in the northeast of the country near scenic Bergville. He paid the hefty price of £5,500 ($326,000 today) in the middle of a worldwide depression, and dubbed the parcels "Admiralty's Estate." He was known as a gruff, unfriendly neighbor, and the natives were afraid of him. During this time it was rumored that he was a communist spy with a high rank in the Soviet army.

A friend of Weston's claimed years later that Weston was one of three British master spies and that he had seen photographs of Weston with Winston Churchill, Franklin Delano Roosevelt, Joseph Stalin and Chiang K'ai-Shek. Weston served at least briefly in Britain during World War II, supposedly as an aviation advisor, and returned to his estate in Natal either during or after the war. He died in his home in 1950, killed during a robbery. A local butcher and a police constable were hanged for his murder, and another man was put in prison for life. Weston's estate was valued at £73,785 ($2.5 million today). His wife was also injured during the incident. Though her injuries plagued her for years, Lilly Weston recovered and lived until 1967.

SOUTH KOREA *see* KOREA

SPAIN

Date: November 5, 1909
Location: Nice, France
Plane: Fernández biplane

Antonio Fernández (1876–1909)

Antonio Fernández was born in Aranjuez, Spain, near Madrid, on February 2, 1876. Like so many early aviators, the first Spanish pilot did most of his flying in France. His three brothers worked in the bull ring as picadors, but Antonio was a women's tailor. He left Spain to set up shop in the fashionable Mediterranean town of Nice. We don't know how long he had followed the new developments in aviation, but in 1909 Fernández enlisted the help of one of his fabric cutters in the building of a small, Curtiss-like pusher biplane. The pilot sat in front of the wings, with an elevator protruding in front of him and the Antoinette engine and the propeller mounted behind him. Fernán-

dez showed this lightweight design at the Reims meet that August, at the Paris Salon a couple of weeks later, and at another aviation week in Blackpool, England. By all accounts, he didn't manage to fly much at these meets, but back in Nice by early November, he got the plane and its new, 50-horsepower engine into the air for a full circuit around the Antibes Aerodrome.

After his untimely death, the press called Fernández's machine shabby and crudely built, though this critique may qualify only as perfect hindsight. Whatever the state of his plane, Fernández does seem to have been an impulsive person without a lot of patience for details. A writer for the French journal *L'Aérophile* called the pilot "an excellent little man, full of energy and ambition," but said he was always in a hurry and without the time to do things properly.[88] The remarkable fact is that, living in the south of France and having little traffic with engineers, scientists or aviators in the Paris aviation community, Fernández managed to build a flyable airplane in his tailoring shop. During a time when most new aviators, especially successful businessmen like himself, were buying up factory-made planes, the Nice dressmaker managed to construct his own, in less than a year, and pilot it to success.

A success all too brief, unfortunately. In the early morning of December 6, 1909, Fernández prepared to fly the machine again at Antibes. In the crowd were his wife and two small children, the youngest less than a month old. About the time the pilot was ready to go, his mechanic noticed a broken elevator cable that had been tied together with a simple knot. When confronted, Fernández brushed off the mechanic and got ready for take-off. He had been in the air for almost a half-mile when he swerved suddenly to avoid crossing a set of railroad tracks. In a banked turn, an airplane tends to slide downward toward the inside of the corner, and a pilot must pull up on his elevator

Opposite: Fernández biplane at the inaugural Exposition Internationale Aéronautique (Salon d'Aviation) in Paris, September and October 1909. National Air and Space Museum, Smithsonian Institution (SI Neg. No. 2001-6609).

Antonio Fernández in his 1909 biplane with what appears to be a weaving shuttle for a control stick. Technical Reports & Standards Unit, Library of Congress, L'Aérophile Collection.

to maintain altitude. The sharper the turn, the more pressure on the elevator cables. As soon as Fernández righted his machine, he saw himself approaching a road and made another hard turn. Suddenly the plane dove into the ground from 24 meters up. The knot in the elevator cable had failed and, the elevators being in front of the wings, this immediately dropped the plane's nose. The engine crushed the hapless aviator on impact.

This accident prompted a cry for government regulation of pilots and their craft, and a youth organization in Nice began a subscription for the family, since Fernández had tied up much of his savings in the demolished airplane. At the time of his death, Fernández was 34 years old.

Almost until the First World War began, spectators still came to aviation meets to see for themselves whether it was true that a machine could fly. Though they had heard for years that it was being done, though they lived near cities where flying was common, many sat in the stands dumbfounded, shook their heads and murmured to themselves as pilots soared overhead. Even in this climate, however, Spain deserves special mention, for it's there that the new technology sparked a religious riot. Ironically, Spain's first pilot had already flown, almost a year earlier, when a group of peasants attacked an aviator and destroyed his plane. The Spanish military had also experimented in secret with its own airplane, and King Alphonse XIII had sat in the *Flyer* next to Wilbur Wright two years earlier. But at the turn of the twentieth century, Spain was a profoundly divided society. The economy was still feudal, and the gap cannot be underestimated that separated the educated and wealthy nobility from the uneducated and fundamentally religious peasantry. The country's monarch may have been interested in aviation, but his subjects showed them-

Last photograph of Antonio Fernández before his fatal crash in Nice, December 1909. Technical Reports & Standards Unit, Library of Congress, L'Aérophile Collection.

selves deeply suspicious of anyone who claimed he could imitate the angels.

In 1910, it had been nearly a century since a crowd of spectators did bodily harm to an aeronautical experimenter. Italian inventor Jacob Degen had been beaten unmercifully in 1812 by a mob that expected him to fly his clack-valve, double-umbrella machine. The crowd lost its temper and attacked Degen when it realized he was using a hydrogen balloon to aid his lift-off. In the new century, with wild tales circulating the countryside about men riding machines into the air, frustrated onlookers had sometimes jeered and heckled when the wind blew too hard for flying, or when an unlucky pilot suffered a crash before take-off. But the violence had remained mostly verbal until Englishman Launcelot Gibbs took his flying machine to Spain for an exhibition.

When Gibbs arrived in Durango, his plane was not with him. It didn't arrive, in fact, until nearly midnight on the evening before the show, so that the pilot and his crew had to work around the clock to get the machine ready. Early the next morning, long before the reassembly would be complete, a crowd estimated at 30,000 gathered to see this improbable thing. As Gibbs's mechanics worked into the afternoon inside their makeshift hangar, the spectators began to clamor for something to see, and someone convinced the Englishman to bring his machine outside so they could watch while he worked. No sooner was it outside, however, than the crowd began examining the plane, leaning on it, pushing and shoving, so that it looked as if the biplane would be squashed before it was ready to fly. Meanwhile, another pilot had finished putting his Blériot monoplane together, and he wheeled it out of its hangar for a take-off attempt. Gibbs took advantage of the distraction to get his machine back inside, but when the Blériot's owner failed to get into the air (his elevator broke on take-off), the crowd recoiled on Gibbs's team in fury, throwing stones and yelling. The Spanish Civil Guard tried to help but only succeeded in further infuriating the crowd, which tore a hole in the side of the hangar and stoned the plane and its me-chanics. Knowing no Spanish, Gibbs attempted to explain himself in English, then in French, whereupon a man pulled a knife and told him in broken French, "Flying is impossible. There is no such thing as aviation! Down with Science, long live Religion!"[89] The Civil Guard evacuated the aviators, and the mob burned the hangar and its contents to the ground.

SRI LANKA (GREAT BRITAIN)

Date: February 27, 1912
Location: Brooklands, England
Plane: Bristol biplane

Lieutenant Stephen Christopher Winfield-Smith (1893–?)

Lieutenant Stephen Winfield-Smith got an earlier start in military flying than most of his colonial counterparts. While serving with the 3rd East Surrey Regiment, he earned his brevet, number 187, on the 27th of February, 1912, well before the start of the First World War. Winfield-Smith flew a Bristol biplane for his license trials. He would have been 18 years old at the time, having been born March 8, 1893. We do not know if he fought in World War I, but his name does not appear in the post-war casualty rolls.

SWEDEN

Date: October 13, 1909
Location: Norville, France
Plane: *Jaune et Bleu*, tractor monoplane
Length of flight: 800 meters (2,624 ft.)

Georg Unné (1877–1960)

The man generally celebrated as the first airborne Swede was a very public figure, wealthy and of noble birth, who spent most of his life and did most of his flying in his homeland. While most Swedish writers recognize this man, Baron Carl Cederstrom, as

Above: Canton-Unné 1909 *Jaune et Bleu.* Courtesy of the Library of Congress. *Below:* Salmson airplane and motor car, 1930s. The radiators of the Salmson cars carried the inscription, "Système Canton-Unné," referring to the designers of the early Salmson engines. Technical Reports & Standards Unit, Library of Congress, L'Aérophile Collection.

their first aviator, evidence from the French press suggests Kristianstad-native Georg Unné flew some six months before Cederstrom. As with our first English flier, our pick for pioneer Swedish aviator worked and spent most of his life in France, which is why neither man is widely recognized by his countrymen as their first pilot.

Unlike our English flier, however, Unné at least lived in his native land until adulthood. He grew up in southern Sweden, and received his engineering degree from the Royal College of Technology in Stockholm. After his graduation, Unné began working for Westinghouse in Le Havre, France, also doing work for that company in Italy and Russia. While very little is known about him during this time, we can guess from the dates he got started in aviation that Unné may have been inspired by the work going on around him in France. From the time he arrived there in 1899, aeronautical news, from Santos-Dumont's airships to Henry Farman's cross-country flights, filled the pages of the French newspapers.

When Unné began to work in aviation himself, he teamed with a Frenchman named Georges Canton, and at a field in Norville outside Le Havre they produced their first machine, which the records refer to as a "tandem triplane." Since a triplane is a machine with three sets of wings stacked atop each other, and a tandem has its wings spaced lengthwise down the body, a "tandem triplane" should have six pairs of wings, a set of three in the back and three in front. But such an unwieldy design seems farfetched, even in 1908. Maybe this first Canton-Unné had three wings stacked in front like a triplane and one behind in a tandem arrangement? Or two in front and one behind, for a total of three wings? Or three wings, one in front of the other down the fuselage? From the terminology used, we simply can't tell. Perhaps because they worked so far outside Paris, almost nothing has been recorded about this machine or their next one, a biplane. One historian states that a Canton-Unné machine had flown by the end of 1908. This is possible, but we have no evidence to back up that claim. By mid–1909, however, the duo had

moved to the now-popular monoplane design and had begun to receive coverage in the local newspapers. Their latest machine, the *Jaune et Bleu*, probably named after the colors of the Swedish flag, managed hops of a couple of hundred yards on September 23 before it nosed in and required repairs. On October 13, 1909, *Jaune et Bleu* made several short flights and, following engine adjustments, flew 800 meters (2,624 ft.) at Norville.

The plane apparently flew several more times, since a Swedish army officer later described seeing Unné himself make "some beautiful flights" the next spring in Paris.[90] *Jaune et Bleu* was damaged in a crash on Easter Day of 1910, and the pair never built another plane. At this point, Unné and Canton seem to have narrowed their focus to their machine's most promising feature, its engine. For several years, they had used a radial engine of their own design, light, powerful and water-cooled. The first Danish pilot, Jacob Ellehammer, had used a similar engine in 1905, but he had used an air-cooled, or evaporative, design. When the Canton-Unné hit the market in 1910, perhaps the most popular aircraft motor was the Gnome rotary, a design that looked a lot like the Canton-Unné but had one important difference: the cylinders actually spun with the propeller. This may have improved the Gnome's air-cooling, but it had a marked disadvantage. In the early days of motors, castor oil was used for lubrication, and the centrifugal force of a rotary engine tended to spray lubricant everywhere. If the pilot happened to be sitting behind the engine, he ended up with a face full of cast-off castor oil. Anyone who has experienced the laxative properties of this lubricant can imagine how urgent some of those early landings must have been.

The Canton-Unné engine, on the other hand, kept its seven cylinders stationary like the radials on conventional prop planes today. In 1910, the engine gave 60 horsepower, and it eventually became the choice of several large manufacturers like the Bristol company in England. Sometime during World War I, the Canton-Unné apparently grew to 200 horsepower, one of the most powerful aircraft engines available, and was used in several British and Russian warplanes.

The Canton-Unné radials were produced at La Société des Moteurs Salmson, under director Emile Salmson. When Salmson died in 1917, Unné became the company's director. His aviation work seems to have ended after World War I when Unné returned to electrical engineering. He founded and directed his own company, Le Transformateur, in Rouen, and some sources claim he also owned a cotton plantation in Guadaloupe and a textile works at Pas de Calais. The Salmson planes and automobiles of the 1920s and 30s continued to use engines of the "Système Canton-Unné," and this legend was stamped on their radiators. Further details of Unné's life are lacking. Georg Unné died in 1960 and is buried in the Pere Lachaise cemetery in Paris.

SWITZERLAND

Date: December 20, 1909
Location: Pau, France
Plane: *Blériot XI* monoplane

Maurice Perret (1885–?)

Even as the era of the pioneer aviator-inventor drew to a close, a good many new fliers, inventive or not, began their aeronautical careers building a flying machine. Some started with existing designs and worked toward an original machine, striving not to leave out the essentials. Others worked from magazine pictures or air show exhibits, shamelessly parroting the most popular designs. Looking at a 1909 flying machine made of ash, muslin and wire, it must have been tempting for an erstwhile aviator to think it would be an easy thing to copy. Certainly, the prices for a factory-built machine were enough to give even the ensconced bourgeois heartburn. At the International Aero and Motor-Boat Exhibition in March, a Wright *Flyer* was displayed at a selling price of $7,000.[91] In June, the British Wright franchise, Short Brothers, was charging $5,000 for a plane, the rough equivalent

of $90,000 today.[92] As more competitors entered the market and more planes sold, the price tags fell, but even the Short model was more than prohibitive for most buyers.

In the early days, builders had mimicked Wright *Flyers*. In 1908 they began to copy the successful Voisins, Farmans and Curtisses. After Louis Blériot's English Channel crossing in 1909, they would begin copying Blériots.[93] It was for this reason that in the early days the Wrights had kept the fine points of their machine well hidden from the public eye. They had even coated their control cables with a dull silver paint so the details would wash out of photographs. By late 1909, however, manufacturers were far too busy developing their fast-evolving machines and defending their patents from each other to worry about individual copycats.

Not unlike Antonio Fernández in Nice or Feng Yu in San Francisco, who both worked from the Curtiss design, Maurice Perret got his start working on a Wright-type in Geneva. Perret evidently spent a good part of his time in France, for he had seen the Brazilian Santos-Dumont make the first flight in Europe in the autumn of 1906 and had seen Wilbur Wright demonstrate the *Flyer* in 1908. What little has been written about Perret says only that he worked with two Swiss brothers named Picker beginning in 1908. Considering the fates of both Fernández and Feng, perhaps it was good that Perret eventually stopped working on his own flying machine. He left Geneva before the plane was finished, and no record remains of what happened to the Pickers' plane. Perret had inherited some 70,000 Swiss francs, a good third of which he must have spent in buying himself a *Blériot XI*, the famed Channel-crosser. He tried to fly the machine himself and even entered a September competition in Juvisy, at which he apparently had little luck. Sometime that fall, Perret finally quit the do-it-yourself approach and enrolled in the Blériot school at Pau. According to a Swiss source, he made his first solo flight on December 20, 1909, though this is hard to confirm because he never earned his brevet.

Perret entered several aerial competitions in the next couple of years and worked

Henri Dufaux in the Dufaux brothers' 1909 biplane, Geneva. National Air and Space Museum, Smithsonian Institution (SI Neg. No. 2001-6607).

Dorab Framroze Adenwalla, August 14, 1948. Royal Air Force Museum, Hendon, London; Royal Aero Club of the United Kingdom certificates, Rac 24876.

with another experimenter on an original design called *Himmelslaus Mignet*. Details are scarce, however. He seems to have abandoned aviation for journalism after his inheritance petered out. If he did indeed fly on December 20, 1909, Perret was one of the elite, one of less than 120, who flew before the end of the first decade.[94] In the next year, several hundred would follow.

The first men to complete an airplane in Switzerland were the Dufaux brothers, Armand and Henri. On August 29, 1910, Armand flew their biplane for the first aerial crossing of Lake Geneva, a trip of 66 kilometers (41 mi.) in 56 minutes.

TANZANIA

Date: August 14, 1948
Location: England
Plane: de Havilland *Tiger Moth*

Dorab Framroze Adenwalla
(1926–?)

As might be guessed by his name, Dorab Framroze Adenwalla was of Indian descent. He was born in Zanzibar on Octo-

Phraya Chalerm Akas, front, with one of Siam's Breguet 14s and General William "Billy" Mitchell of the United States on Mitchell's 1924 Asian tour. Courtesy of the Library of Congress.

ber 17, 1926, and earned his pilot's license, number 24,876, flying a de Havilland *Tiger Moth* at Air Service Training Ltd. in England on August 14, 1948. His license information is all we know of Adenwalla.

THAILAND (SIAM)

Date: October 22, 1912
Location: France
Plane: Breguet biplane

Luang Sakdi Sanlayawut (Phraya Chalerm Akas) (1887–?)

Prince Vajiravudh, Rama VI, inherited the Thai throne during the first blossoming of aviation and continued the push toward modernization that his grandfather had begun decades before. The last Ramas of the Kingdom of Siam were the sort of rulers to inspire disciples, and the first Thai aviator tread the paths of his kings so closely that it has become hard to distinguish the man's character from that of his long government career. For nearly two decades Phraya Chalerm Akas, beginning from nothing, built Thai military aviation along the lines laid out by his progressive kings.[95] Judging from his achievements, Chalerm must have been a man of vision, perseverance and ability. While King Vajiravudh built a modern country that commanded the respect of western Europe and preserved the traditions of the Thai people, Chalerm built independent military and commercial aviation services that were the envy of the Orient.

When the publisher of London's *Daily Mail*, Britain's most enthusiastic aviation booster, visited Siam in 1921, he was quick to notice the quality of the country's aeronautical facilities:

The Times correspondent states that Lord Northcliffe was surprised to find the air station equal to most of those in Europe. Siam, he states, has 25 landing places and five aerodromes. At Don Muaung [sic] there are 115 planes, including school machines, and a staff of 650 men. It looks as if there should be a good opening for British development in this land of promise.[96]

While the reporter's numbers may be correct, the conclusion that England would be able to capitalize on Thai aviation facilities was a bit presumptuous. The British and French empires had competed for control of this kingdom, halfway between Bombay and Peking, since the 1850s. Each had annexed large portions of historical Siam, but each also appreciated the presence of a buffer between Burma and French Indochina. As long as the Siamese monarchs remained in power, none of the colonial powers of Europe would gain control of that much-coveted air space. In its approach to aviation, and to the colonial pressures of the 19th and 20th centuries, Thailand was unique among non–European countries.

Beginning with the rule of King Mongkut (Rama IV) in the mid–1800s and continuing through the reigns of his son, Chulalongkorn (Rama V), and two grandsons, Siam's monarchs used a mix of cooperation, concession and defiance to keep the country independent. Siam's policy combined westernization, industrial and military modernization, and territorial, political and economic concessions. The kings sent their sons to Europe for a Western education to augment their traditional Thai education. They expanded industry and opened trade. Chulalongkorn even brought in Westerners to organize his administration, and, while using Western technologies, the monarchs appealed to the national pride by keeping foreign advisors away from the country's military. The object of this approach was to moderate territorial losses while convincing the colonial powers that Siam was a modern and self-sufficient country that could cooperate in international trade and didn't need to be "civilized" by colonial armies and missionaries. By the end of Chulalongkorn's reign in 1910, the nation had lost nearly half its traditional land area to European annexation yet, unlike most of the Orient, retained control of its government, ports, trade routes and military.

Before he received the honorary name of Phraya Chalerm Akas for his aviation exploits, Major Luang Sakdi Sanlayawut of the Royal Engineers had been chosen by his government to learn to fly at a school in France. He was sent to Europe in early 1912 with two fellow officers. While his compatriots attended the Nieuport monoplane school, Sakdi learned nearby on Breguet biplanes, earning his brevet on October 22. He continued his studies for a brevet militaire, the full French certification that required, among other tests, a knowledge of aerodynamic theory, engine and plane construction, navigation and meteorology, as well as the ability to perform dead-motor descents and long cross-country flights. Sakdi, who was promoted in the interim to lieutenant colonel, earned his advanced certificate in August of 1913. Before returning home, he and his fellow trainees tested a batch of eight new planes for a fledgling Thai air service.

In Siam, as in Japan, the name of the first man to fly became synonymous with national aviation. Chalerm had been the only one of the three officers to earn his full military license, and he was accordingly placed, on March 23, 1914, at the head of the new Siamese Royal Flying Corps, a position he would occupy for 18 years until a coup forced his retirement. Under Chalerm's direction, the corps immediately began to build and promote Thai aviation, beginning with a series of exhibition flights in the provinces and a new aerodrome and flying school at Don Muang. In 1915 the school took on its first class of cadets, and aviation had become such a national enthusiasm that on a trip to the southern provinces the king was able to collect a citizens' gift of 24,183 baht ($170,000 today) for aviation. Public subscriptions for the purchase of airplanes continued, and by 1925 the country had received 1,201,995 baht ($8.4 million today) in citizen contributions. This in a country where a schoolteacher, one of the better paid positions in the provinces, would have earned less than $175 a month in today's money.

For most of World War I, Siam remained cautiously neutral, until in 1917 the Allies appeared to be marching toward victory. At that point, King Vajiravudh volunteered an air unit, which eventually traveled to France to help the Allies. This canny maneuver seems to have benefited Thailand in its future negotiations with Western powers, particularly in discussions of open trade and commercial air service in southeast Asia.

By 1920, Phraya Chalerm Akas had become a full colonel reporting directly to the commander in chief of the army. He reorganized the Flying Division into pursuit, reconnaissance and bombing wings, and also had under him the flight school and the aeronautical workshops. During this time Chalerm formulated the approach that would define the Thai military air service for the next decade. The colonel knew that Thailand couldn't put a force in the air large enough to attack its neighboring French and British colonies, but he hoped for just enough of a presence to deter aggression, figuring that 200 planes would be enough. Although Chalerm was in reality never able to keep more than about 150 trained pilots available, his efforts seem to have been sufficient. Chalerm would establish air mails and supply lines to the country's remote northeast, oversee the design and building of the first Siamese airplanes, and develop the country's first commercial air service. In 1922 the Aerial Transport Company of Siam, which reported to the military, made its first commercial flight from Nong Khai to Udon on the northeast frontier carrying one passenger and 23 parcels, including 16 bags of mail.

In 1931, a bloodless coup put a military leadership in place and replaced the King's absolute powers with constitutional ones. Because the air service was considered royalist and had not collaborated in the coup, Chalerm and most of his fellow officers were

2nd Lieutenant Frank Graham McIntosh, May 30, 1916. Royal Air Force Museum, Hendon, London; Royal Aero Club of the United Kingdom certificates, Rac 3021.

forcibly retired. He was, however, entrusted a few years later with the supervision of the Civil Aviation Division under the Ministry of Economics and was made an honorary group captain of the new Royal Siamese Air Force in 1937. Past this point we have no more details of the life of Phraya Chalerm Akas.

TRINIDAD & TOBAGO

Date: May 30, 1916
Location: England

2nd Lieutenant Frank Graham McIntosh (1894–?)

Frank McIntosh was already serving in the King's Royal Rifle Corps before he received his brevet, number 3021, on May 30,

John Maxwell Buckler, July 8, 1936. Royal Air Force Museum, Hendon, London; Royal Aero Club of the United Kingdom certificates, Rac 14043.

1916. His license lists him as a second lieutenant, but it's hard to know whether that was a rank awarded him upon completion of his Royal Flying Corps license, or whether he had already been an officer in the rifle corps. McIntosh does not appear in the postwar casualty rolls, so it is presumed he lived through World War I.

TURKEY

Date: December 23, 1910
Plane: Blériot monoplane

J. Sismanglou

The first Turkish aviator we know only by his last name. Some sources spell it "Sis-manglou," some "Sismanoglou." He was born at Samsun, but we do not know when. We do know that he earned a British license, number 336, on a Blériot monoplane on the 23rd of December, 1910. He must have kept flying for at least a couple of years. Early plane indices list him as owning a machine in 1912 and as flying with the Ottoman military in 1913, but that is all we know of him.

UGANDA

Date: July 8, 1936
Location: Liverpool, England
Plane: Avian *Gypsy I*

John Maxwell Buckler

John Maxwell Buckler earned his brevet on July 8, 1936 at the District Aero Club in Liverpool. His license, number 14,043, says he was born in Entebbe, though it does not say when. At the time, he was a cadet in the Royal Naval Reserve. He soloed an Avian *Gypsy I*.

UKRAINE (RUSSIAN EMPIRE)

Date: March 15, 1910
Location: Odessa
Plane: *Farman IV* biplane

Sergei Isaevich Utochkin (1876–1916)

Long before the differences between communists and capitalists erected the "Iron Curtain," a religious curtain separated Eastern Europe from the West. Whether it was, practically speaking, the Catholic-Orthodox schism or simply the differences in Roman and Cyrillic text that kept these areas isolated, at the turn of the twentieth century these two worlds seemed to orbit their own individual stars.

In Eastern Europe in late 1910 there were dozens of men practicing for their brevets, making exhibition flights, even setting up aircraft factories. Yet the only ones who are recorded in the western flight literature are those who did much of their flying in France or Germany. Based on the scant testimony of the Western press, it becomes almost impossible to determine who flew and when. There are numerous Ukrainian men flying by the end of 1910. At the beginning of the year, as far as we can tell, there are none. Although we were unable to scan the Ukrainian and Russian press for references, we have consulted general Russian-language histories and found the first positive mention of a Ukrainian aviator to be in March of 1910.

Sergei Isaevich Utochkin, the son of an Odessa merchant, was already famous in the Russian Empire for his athletic prowess. One source calls him "the most noted all-round sportsman in Russia." Already 34 years old in 1910, he was a world champion cyclist, a skater, boxer, swimmer, balloonist and swordsman. Of course, Utochkin also participated in that compulsory sport for the fin-de-siècle wealthy, motoring. He was said to be an unparalleled driver. Utochkin reportedly made his first airplane flight on the 15th of March, 1910, in Odessa, one month after his Russian counterpart, Mikhail Efimov, had earned his license in France. Efimov, though born in Smolensk, had spent much of his adult life in Odessa, and he and Utochkin together had flown one of the empire's first gliders for the Odessa Aero Club. Efimov may also have taken balloon flights with Utochkin. Utochkin kept himself busy with aviation for the rest of 1910, practicing on the *Farman IV* biplane he first flew (which may have belonged to the Odessa Aero Club) and building his own Farman-type biplane and a small monoplane along the lines of the Santos-Dumont *Demoiselle*.[97] In August he became a test pilot for the new Duks plant in Moscow, and he gave the first flight demonstrations in that city. In the fall, Utochkin performed for crowds in Nishniy Novgorod, in the Povolzhye region on the Volga River, and in the Caucasus. One source

refers to him as a "populizer of aviation in Russia," while another credits his demonstrations with increasing the number of Russian aviators from zero to 50 by year's end.[98,99] His flights were the first seen by numerous future Russian aviators and designers.

Utochkin had a reputation as a somewhat eccentric personality. He refused to dress in the heavy suits and special hats that aviation made popular in Western Europe. He flew in his business suit, sitting erect with his bowler on his head. After a particularly nasty wreck in St. Petersburg, the crowd, expecting him dead or at least unconscious, instead found him sifting through the wreckage looking for his hat. Though we have no details of his injury, Utochkin apparently suffered a bad crash in a St. Petersburg–Moscow flight that at least one source suggests affected his reason. He continued to make exhibition flights all over the empire until he was committed to an asylum in 1913 after spending three days living on the streets and sleeping under bridges, completely broke. He returned to flying upon his release and was given a military commission on Russia's entry into World War I. He was committed again, however, and died in an asylum on January 13, 1916, at the age of 39. He is buried in the Nikol'skoe Cemetery at the Holy Trinity Alexander Nevsky Laura monastery in St. Petersburg.

United States of America

Date: December 17, 1903
Location: Kitty Hawk, North Carolina, U.S.A.
Plane: Wright *Flyer I*, pusher biplane
Length of flight: 12 seconds, 120 feet (36.6 m.)

Wilbur & Orville Wright
(1867–1912, 1871–1948)

The first sustained flight was a remarkable feat of science, technology and athletics. The problem required a solid foundation in physics, a mechanical genius and an intuitive

Wilbur Wright, a portrait signed to Léon Bollé on December 18, 1908. National Air and Space Museum, Smithsonian Institution (SI Neg. No. 76-1280).

made an efficient propeller. No one had piloted a motorized flying machine using levers to steer. In four short years the Wrights would solve each of these problems, then build their own engine. Their preeminence in aerodynamics is illustrated by the fact that in 1903 there were much more powerful engines for the weight than the Wrights'. Samuel Pierpont Langley of the Smithsonian Institution, for one, used an engine the same size and roughly four times as powerful. Even years later in 1908, the Wright *Flyer* could carry a pilot and passenger with a motor of 25–30 horsepower, while many experimenters had difficulty leaving the ground with a 50-horsepower engine. What set the Wrights apart from other inventors was their staunch independence of mind and their rigorous scientific approach to the problem.

Wilbur Wright was born April 16, 1867, in Millville, Indiana, the third son of Milton and Susan Wright. The Wrights' next surviving child, Orville, came four years later, on August 19, in the family's new home at 7 Hawthorne Street, Dayton, Ohio. Their father was a frontier preacher and a bishop of the Church of the United Brethren in Christ. At different times during his clerical career, Milton Wright taught theology, edited the church's national newsletter and rode Midwest and West Coast preaching circuits. Never one in danger of moral confusion or self-doubt, Bishop Wright's stubbornness and conservatism caused a permanent schism in the church's national congregation. This painful experience confirmed the bishop's innate distrust of society and helped foster the same attitude in his children.

feel for what it would be like to fly. The conceptual leap that set the Wright brothers on the path to first flight was Wilbur's instinctive understanding that an airplane would have to be controlled, not just up and down, right and left, but also in a bank, like a bicycle leaning into a turn. No other 19th century inventor, as far as we know, fully understood the problem of lateral control in flight. From this auspicious start, the Wrights proceeded to solve the problems, one by one, that had stymied the world's most funded aeronautical scientists for a decade.

At the time the brothers were getting started, no one had defined a proper airplane wing: How long should it be? How deep? What sort of camber should it have? No one had studied what length and curve and pitch

Of the Wright brood, Orville was the businessman and Wilbur the academic. Orville traveled their neighborhood as a young-

Orville Wright. National Air and Space Museum, Smithsonian Institution (SI Neg. No. 86-3016).

avid reader with a nearly photographic memory and a love of history, literature and science. Wilbur was also a talented athlete. But when he was just out of high school, an unfortunate hockey accident, coupled with a family illness, ended Wilbur's university ambitions. His mother had had tuberculosis for years, but by 1886 the disease had made her an invalid. In a neighborhood hockey game that winter, Wilbur was hit in the head when someone released a stick by accident. Details of the injury are scarce. His father didn't think there was cause for alarm at first, but several weeks later the 19-year-old Wilbur developed heart palpitations and digestive problems. These lasted several months and convinced Wilbur he was not healthy enough to attend college. Not long out of high school and without a definite purpose, Wilbur took over the care of his mother, his younger brother, then 15, and his sister Katharine, 12.

Wilbur had spent a good bit of his youth with his older brothers, Reuchlin and Lorin. However, situated as he was four years after his older siblings and four years before Orville and Katharine, he was often isolated in the middle. He was probably closer to his father than the other children, and during the troubles that led up to the schism in Milton's church, Wilbur published several articles in defense of his father's strict religious beliefs. But it was in partnership with Orville that both boys' talents for invention seemed to blossom. Their first joint construction project was a 6-foot lathe for turning wood and was completed well before Orville had reached high school. About the time Wilbur took over the household, Orville put together his

ster collecting bones to sell to the fertilizer plant or scrap to sell to the junkyard. Although he was shy in public, Orville was considered the family dandy, wit and practical joker. He was also the natural builder, always making things with cast-off metal, wood and cloth. Although his grades weren't bad, Orville often got into mischief in school. College was never one of his ambitions.

Wilbur, on the other hand, wanted to go to Yale. When he was in high school, his parents planned to use the extra money they had earned on rents and real estate to pay for Wilbur's college education. He was an first printing press using a discarded tombstone and some metal scrap. He and a school friend started doing contract printing, and when business got to be too much for his partner, Orville bought him out. In 1889 he built a larger press that could turn out a thousand sheets an hour and started publishing a local newspaper, of which Wilbur shortly became the editor.

The troubles in the Wright family came to a head in 1889. The United Brethren in Christ church, in which Milton had worked for 38 years, split over the church's historical condemnation of freemasonry. Milton Wright led the walkout of the conservative faction. Two months after this cataclysm, his wife died of tuberculosis. As the leader of a new denomination, Milton had his work cut out for him. He would spend many of his remaining years traveling the country and piecing his church back together. The Wright siblings stayed in their father's home and kept their own company, rarely venturing into society. The brothers' isolation, their father's mistrust of society, which he constantly reinforced in his letters home, and their choice not to attend college would all contribute to the independent personalities required for them to work in a field with as much potential for ridicule as aeronautics.

In 1892, the Wrights, who were still running a commercial printing press, bought their first bicycles and were swept up in the popular craze. They would go cycling for hours on end and became known in West Dayton as skilled repairmen. They promptly started their own bicycle shop. The business did well enough, and when they had become bored four years later with selling and fixing other people's designs, they decided to begin building their own. This is the business that would sustain them until the sale of their first airplanes more than ten years later.

As the century drew to a close, Wilbur had the sense that aeronautics might be the place for him to make his mark on history. He was 32 years old in 1899, and he felt that he had never found a niche for himself. He knew he was too independent and opinionated for a business career. For several years, he and Orville had casually followed the trials of glider pioneers Otto Lilienthal in Germany and Percy Pilcher in Scotland. Lilienthal had died in a crash in 1896 after making more than two thousand glides on different machines. Pilcher died similarly in 1899. That year, Wilbur wrote the Smithsonian Institution asking for all the literature they had on heavier-than-air flying. In his aeronautical reading, he was surprised to find that the aviation experimenters of the preceding century had left very little empirical evidence for their successors to work from.

Wilbur was also surprised to find that no one had addressed the problem of steering in three dimensions. It seemed obvious to the inventors of the day that they would have to steer left and right, like on a cart or a boat. It was also obvious that a machine had to steer upward to leave the ground and downward to return to it. Few of the 19th-century pioneers, and none of the Wrights' contemporaries, had considered the third dimension. To make a safe, effective turn, a plane must also be able to lean, so that the lift of its wings can support the turn. Wilbur had a flash of inspiration one day while fiddling with an inner-tube box in the bike shop. If he could rig the wings of a biplane so that he could put a helical twist in them, like the open box he twisted between his fingers, he might be able to make an airplane lean at will, or recover from an unexpected lean. He would build wings so that the front edge of one tip could be raised at the same time that the front edge on the other tip was lowered. This would increase lift on one side, decrease it on the other, and bank the airplane. Wilbur built a kite that fall incorporating this principle and found that it worked quite well. After that, things began to happen quickly.

In 1900, the brothers built a full-sized glider with what they now called "wing-warping." They tested it on the dunes of Kitty Hawk that fall, choosing the barrier islands of North Carolina for their steady winds and sandy landings. The Wrights flew this first machine as both a kite and a glider. In both cases they were disappointed with the lift they got from the wings. Using Lilienthal's lift and drag calculations, they had designed the glider to fly with Wilbur aboard in a 15-m.p.h. headwind (they had, however, used a different wing camber than Lilienthal). The 1900 glider required a wind of nearly 25 miles per hour. This complicated things, and they did most of their tests with the elevator and wing-warping controls tied in place, even when Wilbur was aboard. For their next machine in 1901, the Wrights decided to be more conservative, and they used the deeper wing camber preferred by Lilienthal. This met with all sorts of confusing results. The new glider was hardly controllable, and it still didn't provide the lift they had expected. It wasn't until they went back to a shallower camber that Wilbur was able to glide safely. Working directly as they did from Lilienthal's calculations, they could only conclude that his numbers were somehow flawed. This time, Wilbur tried the warping controls. They seemed to work, but this test introduced a new com-

Engineer Octave Chanute, who compiled all the available flight literature for his 1894 book, *Progress in Flying Machines*, designed a breakthrough glider in 1896, and consulted with the Wrights on their experiments. National Air and Space Museum, Smithsonian Institution (SI Neg. No. A-21147-B).

plication. The drag induced by warping one wingtip upward tended to make the glider skid sideways, a frightening sensation which prompted Wilbur to put the machine into the sand every time it happened.

In his frustration, Wilbur told his brother on the train home that men wouldn't fly for a thousand years. However, the nagging feeling that something was wrong with their numbers kept them plugging away at the problem. The formulas for lift and drag were well known. Using the standard coefficient of air pressure arrived at some years before, Lilienthal had calculated the lift of his glider wings and recorded

those calculations for posterity. How could they be wrong?

Here the Wrights did what nobody else in aviation would do for years. They built a wind tunnel and proceeded to find out just what was wrong with the numbers. They found that Lilienthal's calculations were correct but that the standard coefficient of air pressure, on which his tables had been based, was way too high. No one had tested it for decades, and the Wrights found the standard to be in error by more than 50 percent. They didn't stop there. Now having an apparatus to test airfoils, Orville built two balances out of bicycle spokes, hacksaw

First success of the Wright *Flyer*, December 17, 1903, Orville piloting, Wilbur at right. National Air and Space Museum, Smithsonian Institution (SI Neg. No. A-26767-B).

blades and other scrap metal. The brothers could clip a small airfoil to one balance, put it in the wind tunnel and measure the lift of a wing with that particular shape. The other balance measured drag. It may seem a given that an inventor would start with the basics and work his way to a solution in this manner, but the average person who was attracted to flying in the 19th century had perhaps too much of the dreamer and not enough of the scientist. The Wrights had adopted what little science had been left behind, only to find out that it was flawed. But as they tested some 150 potential wing sections with different widths and cambers, the excitement of that first summer returned. This was exactly the kind of theoretical and mechanical detective work that most suited Wilbur and Orville Wright.

By the fall of 1902, the brothers had a modern-looking glider that could stay off the dunes for more than 600 feet. They had found that they needed very long, narrow wings, that their camber had to be quite different from Lilienthal's and that their

wings needed more surface area than they had thought. This new configuration performed according to their calculations. The only thing that remained was for Orville to propose a solution to the skidding caused by warping the wings. They had already added a pair of vertical stabilizers to the rear of the glider to counteract this tendency. Probably due to their more efficient wings, however, the problem seemed worse than the year before. At breakfast one morning, Orville mentioned that the vertical stabilizers might be replaced by a hinged rudder, with which the pilot could actively compensate for the one-sided drag induced by wing-warping. They talked it over for a while, and Wilbur suggested that instead of adding another control to worry the pilot, they should link the action of the rudder to the wing-warping. This was the breakthrough that allowed them to get a powered machine into the air the next year.

By the time they left for home in the autumn of 1902, Wilbur and Orville had already calculated how much their engine could weigh and what size wings they would need to carry the extra weight. Two problems remained, however, that they didn't foresee. No one had yet done any testing on efficient propeller designs, and no manufacturer would make an engine as light as they needed.

They were too excited at this point to let another scientific problem stand in their way, and if no manufacturer would make a 200-pound, 12-horsepower motor, they would do it themselves. The Wrights designed the engine and put their long-time mechanic Charlie Taylor to work machining the parts. The propeller was the most complicated physics problem they had yet encountered. Orville realized that a good propeller was just another type of airfoil, a wing that rotated. But it seemed impossible to calculate the proper camber and pitch when they didn't know how fast their engine would run, how long to make the propeller or what sort of airspeed to expect once their machine had left the ground. Since any of these factors would affect the propeller's efficiency, they had to make educated guesses. By the summer of 1903, Taylor had finished one engine, cracked the block in testing and built another. The brothers tested the engine and propeller and stockpiled all the materials they would need to put their airplane together in Kitty Hawk.

The *Flyer*, as the machine was called, was constructed of spruce, linen and wire cable and had a wingspan of more than 40 feet. Like the 1902 glider, the *Flyer* had its elevator in front and its rudder behind. The engine spun twin propellers, located behind the wings in a "pusher" configuration and twirling in opposite directions to avoid torquing the machine sideways. Wilbur Wright guessed the whole endeavor had cost them $1,000, in constant dollars about the cost of a mid-priced car today ($18,700).

A series of mishaps with their propeller shafts kept the Wrights from trying a flight until December 14. They had suffered a serious scare in early November when they had finished putting the machine together. It weighed 70 pounds more than they had calculated, and with the thrust they expected

from their propeller, the machine wouldn't fly with an extra 70 pounds. After one set of propeller shafts had been replaced, however, they had tested the machine on the ground and found to their great relief that the propeller provided about 50 percent more thrust than expected. When yet another propeller shaft had cracked, Orville had gone all the way back to Dayton to machine a new pair out of spring steel.

Finally everything was reassembled on December 14. Wilbur won the coin toss for the first try. Anxious to get off the ground, the brothers set up their launching rail on a dune, facing downhill. When Wilbur released the catch holding the *Flyer* in place, things happened much too quickly. The plane sped off, shot into the air at too steep an angle, stalled and fell back to the sand with a crunch. Wilbur had covered 60 feet before he knew what had happened. One of the elevator supports was broken.

Repairs and bad weather kept them from trying again until three days later. This time it was Orville's turn. The brothers decided to trust their calculations and make a true take-off this time. They placed the launching rail on the flats near their hangar and, with the help of several Kitty Hawk lifesavers who had come to help, placed the *Flyer* at one end of the rail. Then they started the engine and stepped away for a brief conference. A camera had been set up to the right side of the rail, and one of the lifesavers had instructions to release the shutter if the machine left the ground.

Orville climbed aboard and lay on his belly. His hips rested in the cradle that controlled the wing-warping and rudder. His left hand held the elevator stick. Orville tested the controls. With his right hand, he released the lever that held the machine in place. The *Flyer* started slowly down the wooden rail on its two bicycle hubs. The wind was blowing 27 miles per hour in his face. Wilbur walked alongside supporting the right wing, then he ran alongside. Finally, Wilbur released the wing and watched in amazement as the *Flyer* rose from the rail. The cameraman released the shutter at that moment, 10:35 a.m. on December 17, 1903.

Wright 1905 *Flyer*, Wilbur piloting. Courtesy of the Library of Congress.

Their first flight lasted 12 seconds and covered 120 feet. The next try was 195 feet, then 200. On the last flight of the day, Wilbur piloting, the *Flyer* stayed in the air for 59 seconds and 859 feet (262 m.). Adjusting for the headwind, Wilbur had flown the equivalent of a half mile, proving their machine could make sustained flight. There would have been more flying that day, but after this last trial, a gust of wind lifted the machine and rolled it sideways, throwing the engine off and crushing the wings. The brothers telegraphed Dayton with news of their success. The carefully prepared press release they had left with their brother Lorin was ignored by the *Dayton Journal* and the Associated Press. A bastardized version of the brothers' telegram home, intercepted in Norfolk and passed on to the local *Virginian-Pilot*, appeared in five newspapers nationwide. It claimed the brothers had flown three miles at an altitude of 60 feet and featured a fabricated illustration of something that looked like a hovercraft. Future efforts at publicity would fare little better.

With the exhilaration of the first flight behind them, the Wrights began the laborious work of transforming their machine into a practical transport. They worked on a farm outside Dayton, at first making take-offs from a rail, then using a derrick to accelerate the machine into the air. In 1904 they made adjustments to their wing camber again, but with bad results. They had more, and more dangerous, accidents during this period than during their thousand previous tests. Their breakthrough came in 1905 when they lengthened the machine for better stability and added a separate control lever for the rear rudder, unlinking the wing-warping and rudder mechanisms. Suddenly, the machine that couldn't stay in the air much longer than five minutes was making 20-minute flights without a hitch. Soon, they could fly until their gas ran out. The best flight of that fall lasted 39 minutes and covered more than 24 miles. They finally had an airplane they could teach someone else to fly, an airplane they could sell. And until they had been awarded a patent, until someone bought their machine, they would fly it no more.

Perfectly suited to the invention of a highly technical and complex machine, the Wright brothers were hardly suited to public relations work. If ever there was a product that would have sold itself, the Wright *Flyer* was it. If only the public could have seen it fly. At the time, the Wright family was passing through another difficult period in the United Brethren in Christ church. Bishop Wright had been involved in constant lawsuits with the old church since the split of 1889. Another schism was narrowly averted when his fellow bishops took Milton Wright's side in another policy dispute, but Milton was gradually relieved of his responsibilities after that. The misanthropy that Milton had nurtured in his family for several decades reached a peak. Wilbur and Orville, fearing that outsiders would steal their invention, would not demonstrate the *Flyer*. This attitude may have been understandable before their patents were granted in mid–1906, but once that obstacle had been surmounted, nothing stood between them and wild commercial success. Either Orville had lost the business

Le Mans, France: a monument to Wilbur Wright's 1908 demonstration flights, including a list of early piloting casualties over the heading, "Les Victimes." National and Air and Space Museum, Smithsonian Institution (SI Neg. No. A-31290).

Wright pilot Eugene Lefebvre in a Wright *Flyer* at the first international air meet, Reims, France, August 24, 1909. National Air and Space Museum, Smithsonian Institution (SI Neg. No. 89-16905).

acumen he had possessed as a young man, or Wilbur's business instincts, which he had been correct to doubt a decade earlier, were given too much sway in the partnership. Considering all the work that had gone into wing cambers and propellers and subtle control systems, the brothers really had little to fear from copycats as long as they could keep people from taking measurements, but they wouldn't even show the machine in the air to potential government buyers. Their reluctance to demonstrate didn't inspire confidence in the bureaucrats with whom they corresponded, and the Wrights wouldn't do business with anyone who wouldn't take their word that they could fly. They required a signed contract before demonstrating the machine.

For anyone who admires the Wrights and their work, this is a frustrating period to recount. It was as if they didn't want to sell their invention. Certainly, they were in no

hurry. They didn't really need money. They lived in their father's house and spent almost nothing. The bicycle building had been more than adequate to feed them and pay for the development of the world's first flying machine. So, they would only sell the *Flyer* to a government, and they would only sell it at a premium. Had they demonstrated the *Flyer* in 1906, they would have saved themselves a lot of difficulty later on. Instead, they kept it under wraps throughout 1906 and 1907, as Parisian fliers began to leave the ground in unsafe but overpowered machines. Although the Europeans could only fly in a relatively straight line and had to make wide, awkward and unsafe turns, the Wrights had lost something substantial when they failed to make the first public demonstrations. At one point they turned down a deal for a half million dollars plus royalties, and the offers only came down as more people got planes into the air. However, they gradually began to

Wilbur Wright over the Hudson River, 1909. National Air and Space Museum, Smithsonian Institution (SI Neg. No. A-43148-B).

meet with bureaucrats in higher positions, and as people got to know them, government interest increased. The Wrights were obviously honest men, and meeting them face to face made the difference. In late 1907 and early 1908, they finally won contracts with the French and American governments.

Wilbur began demonstration flights in France in August of 1908. His flights provoked astonishment and wild enthusiasm. It was obvious to anyone who had watched recent European flights that the Wrights were in a class all their own. Crowds flocked to a military parade ground near Le Mans to see the "birdman" carve turns and figure-eights in the sky. Wilbur made exhibition flights and record attempts through December, logging a total of 129 flights and nine world records, including an endurance mark of 2 hours, 18 minutes. He was the toast of Europe, but even this period was marred by trouble. Orville had begun demonstrations for the U.S. military in September. The first few flights had gone well, but a cracked propeller had resulted in a crash, on September 17, 1908, that injured Orville and killed his passenger, Lieutenant Thomas E. Selfridge. It took many months for Orville, nursed by Katharine, to recover from a broken femur and several broken ribs. When he was well enough to travel, Orville joined

Wilbur in France, taking Katharine along with him. Wilbur was now training cadets for the French army, and the three siblings attended state banquets all over Europe. Honor and glory were theirs, but the stoic Wright brothers seemed to enjoy the acclaim a lot less than their sister.

By the spring of 1909, every aircraft designer except the Voisin brothers had added lateral control to their machines. These devices infringed on the Wright patents, and a new era of court battles began. The European designers quickly caught up with the Wright technology. Louis Blériot crossed the English Channel in July. The world's first international air meet at Reims the next month saw all the Wrights' records surpassed. Orville, now fully recovered, renewed the demonstration flights that had been postponed by his crash the year before. During these trials, he recaptured a number of Wilbur's records.

In November, the brothers signed a contract with a group of investors to start the Wright Company. The company took over the patents and their legal defense. The brothers retained one-third ownership, received $100,000 in cash ($1.8 million today) and would earn a 10-percent royalty on all planes sold. Orville and Wilbur hoped to return to developing their airplane, but Wilbur

Wright Brothers National Memorial, Kitty Hawk, North Carolina, c. 1932. National Air and Space Museum, Smithsonian Institution (SI Neg. No. A-52719).

would spend most of his time for the next several years working on the patent infringement cases. While European builders came up with more stable designs that could also be controlled laterally, the *Flyer* languished. The machine retained its unstable wing configuration and the wing-warping that was clearly inferior to the new aileron for lateral control. The Wrights would finally put wheels on certain Wright models in 1910, though others had been adding wheels to *Flyers* for two years. As their machines fell behind and their patent suits piled up, the brothers faced harsh criticism from those who thought the glory of invention and the advancement of mankind should be enough remuneration. In this atmosphere of litigation and public struggle, Wilbur succumbed to typhoid fever on May 30, 1912. Orville car-

ried on the patent fights, eventually winning the biggest case in 1914 against American manufacturer Glenn H. Curtiss. Not long afterward, Orville bought out the shareholders of the Wright Company and sold the whole concern, netting himself an estimated $1.5 million ($24.2 million today) and leaving the aircraft business entirely after his one-year contract as a consultant.[100]

Orville died of a heart attack 32 years later, January 27, 1948, at his laboratory in Dayton, having served as the grand old man of aviation through its golden age in the 1920s and 30s. He had won the Collier Trophy in 1913 for an auto-pilot system. He invented the split-flap, a wing innovation used on dive bombers, and his home was filled with practical inventions in a Jeffersonian vein. He also took out patents on several of his own toy designs. Orville received visits from Charles Lindbergh and President Franklin Delano Roosevelt. In 1932, the U.S. government dedicated a National Monument to the brothers at the site of their 1903 flight on Kill Devil Hill on the Outer Banks of North Carolina. The United States celebrates National Aviation Day each year on Orville Wright's birthday, August 19.

URUGUAY

Date: November 8, 1910
Location: France
Plane: Blériot monoplane

Mario García Cames (1883–?)

Mario García Cames may have flown his new Blériot monoplane in late 1909, or it may have been almost a year later before he left the ground. In early February of 1910, Cames took a Blériot to the air meet in Barcelona with a French aviator and Blériot mechanic named Julien Mamet. There is no evidence of Cames flying at the meet, but Mamet competed with the monoplane, making two short flights of six and 11 minutes on the 17th in a very heavy wind. On the 19th the weather improved, and Mamet made a longer flight. Unfortunately, a photographer got into his landing path on his first flight of the day, and Mamet was forced to bring the plane down too fast, shattering the propeller.

A 1911 index of fliers lists Cames as Uruguayan, though we have no way to confirm that the "San José" listed as his birthplace is actually San José in Uruguay. We do not know when he purchased the Blériot, whether it was 1909 or early 1910, nor whether he was working in France or only visiting at the time. He may have attended the meet in Barcelona to compete himself but thought better of it after the nasty winds of the 17th. Wealthy plane owners often hired a mechanic to travel with them, and Cames may have begun flying some time previous. Or he may have still been learning.

However, we have no definitive proof of a flight by Cames until he earned his brevet,

number 287 of the Aéro-Club de France, on November 8, 1910. An airplane index lists him as the only Uruguayan flier through 1913, and this is all we know of him.

VENEZUELA

Date: September 4, 1912
Location: France
Plane: Blériot monoplane

Lt. Colonel Luis Camilo Ramírez-Rivas (1886–?)

Lt. Colonel Luis Ramírez-Rivas of Caracas appears in a Spanish aviation history in the year 1912, receiving his brevet from French inventor and pilot Louis Blériot on September 4. There is no license number mentioned, and Ramírez-Rivas is not listed in the French license rolls. The reference to "Professor Blériot" may be only figurative, and Ramírez-Rivas may have simply learned to fly at one of the Blériot schools without actually earning a certificate. At any rate, this is all the information we have on Ramirez-Rivas.

The next Venezuelan pilot seems to have been Lieutenant Carlos Meyer Baldo, who moved from Maracaibo to Germany in 1908 and fought with the Germans in World War I. He learned to fly Gotha planes in early 1917 and reportedly flew with Baron von Richthofen at some point.

VIETNAM (FRANCE)

Date: October 6, 1911
Location: Étampes, France
Plane: Blériot

Lieutenant Tay Do Huu (1879–?)

The French aviation press in 1911 referred to Lieutenant Tay Do Huu as "the first genuine Oriental to win his certificate." Do Huu, a native of Saigon in what was then French Indochina, had been serving with the French army for some time when he earned

Lt. Tay Do Huu, right, in the student's seat of a Maurice Farman biplane, May 25, 1911, with a Lt. Menard as instructor. Technical Reports & Standards Unit, Library of Congress, L'Aérophile Collection.

his brevet, number 649, on October 6, 1911. We have few details of his service, though we know he was with the French forces in Morocco at some point. He may have flown well before he actually received his license, as there are photographs of him training on various planes in the spring of 1911. We know nothing of him past this point.

YUGOSLAVIA
(AUSTRIA-HUNGARY)

Date: Spring 1910
Location: Subotica
Plane: Sarić monoplane

Ivan Sarić

Ivan Sarić built a plane of his own design starting near the end of 1909. According to a Yugoslav historian, Sarić had made a flight in one of his machines by the spring of 1910, though we have no details of that flight or the plane that made it. A replica of one of his monoplanes, *Sarić II*, hangs in the Yugoslav Air Museum in Belgrade. Unfortunately, this is all we know of Saric''s aviation career.

The choice of the first Yugoslav aviator presents a real geographical and political challenge. The breakup of communist Yugoslavia has left the country roughly within the borders of the old nations of Serbia and Montenegro. Although this designation has not been recognized by the rest of the world, many Yugoslavs call their country "Serbia and Montenegro." Depending on birthplace, language and religion, the residents of present-day Yugoslavia may consider themselves Serb, Croat, Albanian, Montenegrin, Vojvodenar, etc. Ivan Sarić was born in Subotica, in what is now the far north of Yugoslavia. At the time of his experiments, Subotica was part of Austria-Hungary, and in western Europe Sarić would have been considered

2nd Lt. Norman Vivian de Beer, June 18, 1916. Royal Air Force Museum, Hendon, London; Royal Aero Club of the United Kingdom certificates, Rac 3075.

Hungarian. He spoke the Serbian language (as well as Hungarian), but he worshipped as a Catholic, which makes him, to his fellow Yugoslavians, a member of the Bunjevci ethnic group.

The same historian who confirmed his early flights argued against recognizing Sarić as the first Yugoslav, precisely because he was not "pure Serb." The first person of Serbian descent (and Serbian citizenship) to fly was Zagreb native Mihajlo Merčep, on November 13, 1911. He is listed as our first Croatian aviator.

ZIMBABWE

Date: June 18, 1916
Location: Hendon, England
Plane: Grahame-White biplane

2nd Lieutenant Norman Vivian de Beer (1897–?)

Norman Vivian de Beer had by far the shortest, and perhaps the saddest, career of any of our first fliers. Not only did he die the month after earning his brevet and his officer's commission, but he never had the honor of flying a mission. De Beer came from Bulawayo, in what was then Rhodesia, to serve his country in World War I. He passed his license test on June 18, 1916, at the military school at Hendon, outside London. Still in Hendon the next month, he died in a car crash. De Beer was 18 years old.

The Chronology

Even in the twenty-first century, the date of a pilot's first true flight can easily become a topic for debate. Which flight was fully controlled by the student and which may have been assisted by an instructor can be hard enough for a student pilot to remember, let alone an historian who later wishes to document his career. Go back in time a hundred years: The condition of the flying machines, the isolation of most experimenters and the lack of any public knowledge about the characteristics of flight can make this determination very difficult. Even some fliers' nationalities can be impossible to decide without a pre-arranged set of criteria.

We have tried to choose criteria that could be most easily researched and consistently enforced. Consequently, we favor birthplace above other considerations of nationality, such as ethnic origin, religion or peerage. Ancestry takes a strong second to and even sometimes beats out birthplace. In order to avoid temporal questions of statehood, we have used today's map to determine in which country a pilot was born.

True flight, in our definition, requires an engine powerful enough and wings efficient enough to keep a machine in the air, as well as control systems effective enough to do the same. To qualify, a flight must be manned and powered, and it must be sustained beyond the point where a machine's initial momentum would have carried it without the guiding hand of the pilot. That is, the flight's length and direction must be controlled to some degree. Qualifying flights must also be solos. For this reason, we have usually used the licensing date for later fliers, though in some instances we can document earlier solo flights.

Here, then, are the fliers and their countries in the order of their first flights:

Pioneer Aviators of the World

timeline

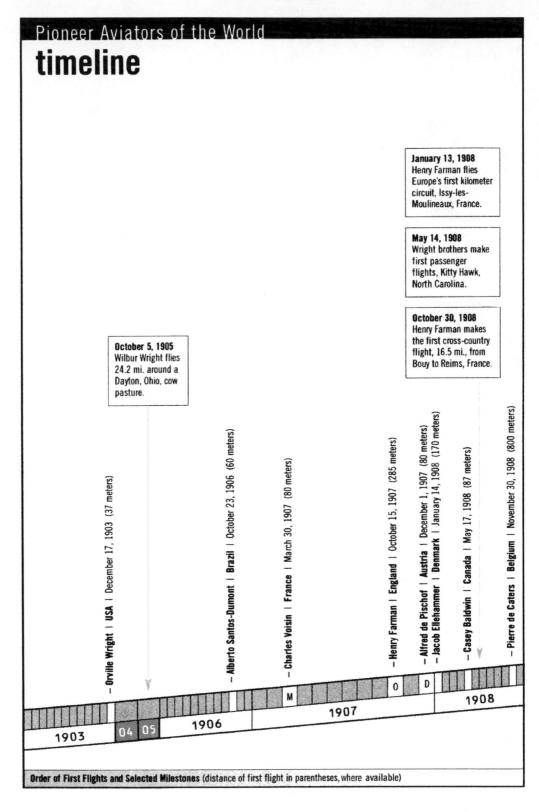

January 13, 1908
Henry Farman flies Europe's first kilometer circuit, Issy-les-Moulineaux, France.

May 14, 1908
Wright brothers make first passenger flights, Kitty Hawk, North Carolina.

October 30, 1908
Henry Farman makes the first cross-country flight, 16.5 mi., from Bouy to Reims, France.

October 5, 1905
Wilbur Wright flies 24.2 mi. around a Dayton, Ohio, cow pasture.

– Orville Wright | USA | December 17, 1903 (37 meters)

– Alberto Santos-Dumont | Brazil | October 23, 1906 (60 meters)

– Charles Voisin | France | March 30, 1907 (80 meters)

– Henry Farman | England | October 15, 1907 (285 meters)

– Alfred de Pischof | Austria | December 1, 1907 (80 meters)

– Jacob Ellehammer | Denmark | January 14, 1908 (170 meters)

– Casey Baldwin | Canada | May 17, 1908 (87 meters)

– Pierre de Caters | Belgium | November 30, 1908 (800 meters)

1903　04　05　1906　M　1907　O　D　1908

Order of First Flights and Selected Milestones (distance of first flight in parentheses, where available)

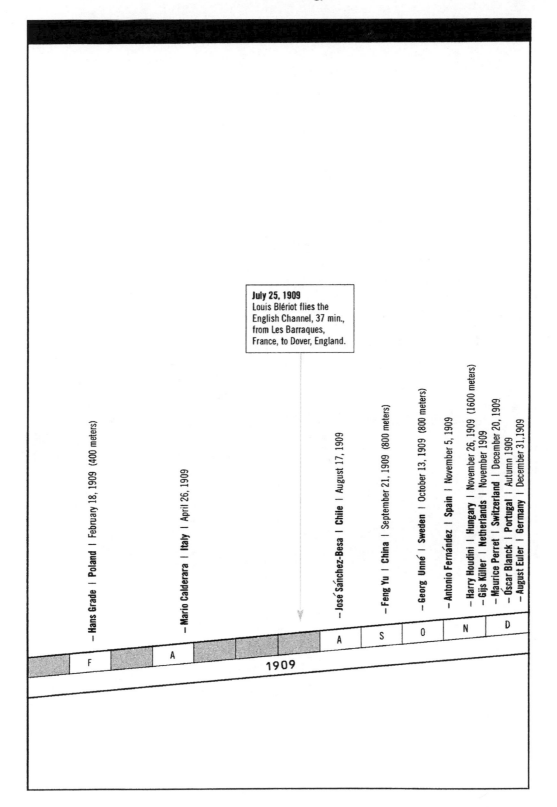

July 25, 1909
Louis Blériot flies the
English Channel, 37 min.,
from Les Barraques,
France, to Dover, England.

Hans Grade | Poland | February 18, 1909 (400 meters)

Mario Calderara | Italy | April 26, 1909

José Sánchez-Besa | Chile | August 17, 1909

Feng Yu | China | September 21, 1909 (800 meters)

Georg Unné | Sweden | October 13, 1909 (800 meters)

Antonio Fernández | Spain | November 5, 1909

Harry Houdini | Hungary | November 26, 1909 (1600 meters)

Gijs Küller | Netherlands | November 1909

Maurice Perret | Switzerland | December 20, 1909

Óscar Blanck | Portugal | Autumn 1909

August Euler | Germany | December 31, 1909

F A A S O N D

1909

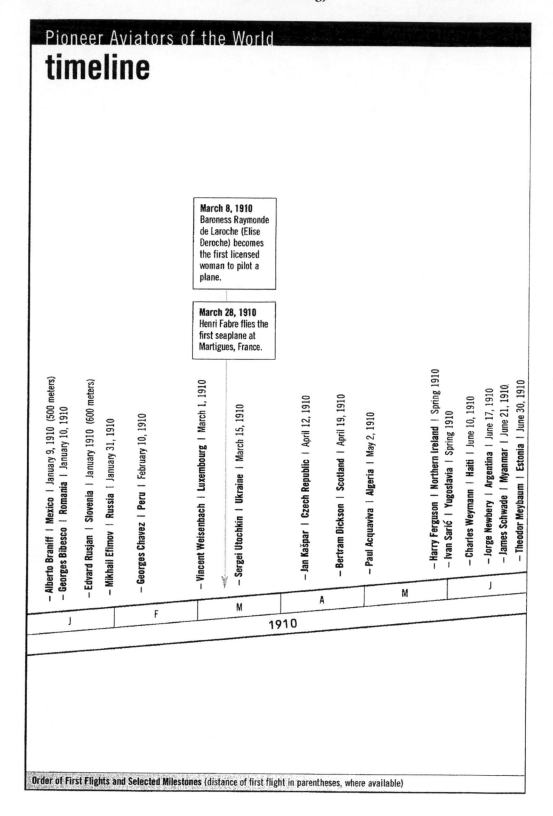

Pioneer Aviators of the World

timeline

March 8, 1910
Baroness Raymonde de Laroche (Elise Deroche) becomes the first licensed woman to pilot a plane.

March 28, 1910
Henri Fabre flies the first seaplane at Martigues, France.

— Alberto Braniff | Mexico | January 9, 1910 (500 meters)
— Georges Bibesco | Romania | January 10, 1910
— Edvard Rusjan | Slovenia | January 1910 (600 meters)
— Mikhail Efimov | Russia | January 31, 1910
— Georges Chavez | Peru | February 10, 1910
— Vincent Weisenbach | Luxembourg | March 1, 1910
— Sergei Utochkin | Ukraine | March 15, 1910
— Jan Kašpar | Czech Republic | April 12, 1910
— Bertram Dickson | Scotland | April 19, 1910
— Paul Acquaviva | Algeria | May 2, 1910
— Harry Ferguson | Northern Ireland | Spring 1910
— Ivan Sarić | Yugoslavia | Spring 1910
— Charles Weymann | Haiti | June 10, 1910
— Jorge Newbery | Argentina | June 17, 1910
— James Schwade | Myanmar | June 21, 1910.
— Theodor Meybaum | Estonia | June 30, 1910

J   F   M   A   M   J

1910

Order of First Flights and Selected Milestones (distance of first flight in parentheses, where available)

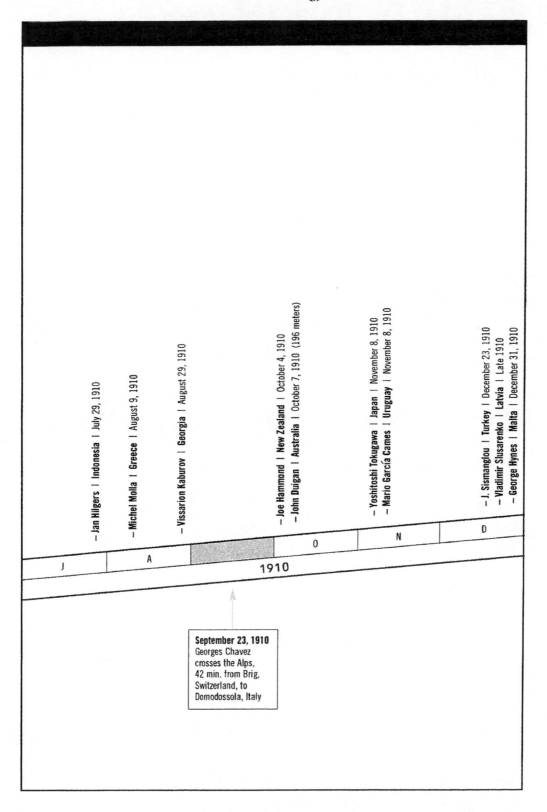

– Jan Hilgers | Indonesia | July 29, 1910

– Michel Molla | Greece | August 9, 1910

– Vissarion Kaburov | Georgia | August 29, 1910

– Joe Hammond | New Zealand | October 4, 1910

– John Duigan | Australia | October 7, 1910 (196 meters)

– Yoshitoshi Tokugawa | Japan | November 8, 1910

– Mario García Cames | Uruguay | November 8, 1910

– J. Sismanglou | Turkey | December 23, 1910

– Vladimir Slusarenko | Latvia | Late 1910

– George Hynes | Malta | December 31, 1910

J   A   O   N   D

1910

September 23, 1910
Georges Chavez
crosses the Alps,
42 min. from Brig,
Switzerland, to
Domodossola, Italy

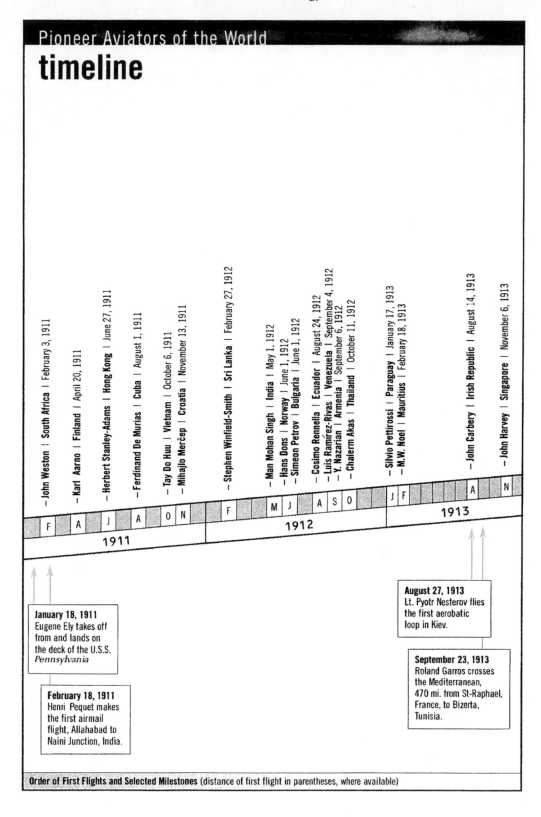

Pioneer Aviators of the World
timeline

– John Weston | South Africa | February 3, 1911

– Karl Aarno | Finland | April 20, 1911

– Herbert Stanley-Adams | Hong Kong | June 27, 1911

– Ferdinand De Murias | Cuba | August 1, 1911

– Tay Do Huu | Vietnam | October 6, 1911

– Mihajlo Merčep | Croatia | November 13, 1911

– Stephen Winfield-Smith | Sri Lanka | February 27, 1912

– Man Mohan Singh | India | May 1, 1912

– Hans Dons | Norway | June 1, 1912

– Simeon Petrov | Bulgaria | June 1, 1912

– Cosimo Rennella | Ecuador | August 24, 1912

– Luis Ramírez-Rivas | Venezuela | September 4, 1912

– Y. Nazarian | Armenia | September 6, 1912

– Chalerm Akas | Thailand | October 11, 1912

– Silvio Pettirossi | Paraguay | January 17, 1913

– M.W. Noel | Mauritius | February 18, 1913

– John Carbery | Irish Republic | August 14, 1913

– John Harvey | Singapore | November 6, 1913

| F | A | J | A | O | N | | F | | M | J | A | S | O | | J | F | | A | N |

1911   **1912**   **1913**

January 18, 1911
Eugene Ely takes off
from and lands on
the deck of the U.S.S.
Pennsylvania

February 18, 1911
Henri Pequet makes
the first airmail
flight, Allahabad to
Naini Junction, India.

August 27, 1913
Lt. Pyotr Nesterov flies
the first aerobatic
loop in Kiev.

September 23, 1913
Roland Garros crosses
the Mediterranean,
470 mi. from St-Raphael,
France, to Bizerta,
Tunisia.

Order of First Flights and Selected Milestones (distance of first flight in parentheses, where available)

- Julio Yudice | El Salvador | Spring 1914
- Ali Verdiev | Azerbaijan | Late 1914
- Avenir Kostenchik | Belarus | Late 1914

- Yin Leong | Malaysia | May 5, 1915
- Frederick Stent | Cyprus | August 31, 1915
- Henry Worrall | Fiji | September 30, 1915

- Richard Shepherd | Antigua & Barbuda | December 20, 1915

- Clive Logan | Belize | January 18, 1916
- William da Costa | Barbados | January 29, 1916

- Frank McIntosh | Trinidad & Tobago | May 30, 1916
- Ernest Floyer | Egypt | June 2, 1916
- Oscar Torres | Angola | June 2, 1916
- Albert Kartham | Jamaica | June 9, 1916
- Norman de Beer | Zimbabwe | June 18, 1916

- Ernst Leman | Lithuania | June 1916

- Luis Quimson | Phillipines | October 15, 1916
- José Alarcón | Bolivia | October 1916

1914   1915   J   M   J   O   1916

Pioneer Aviators of the World
timeline

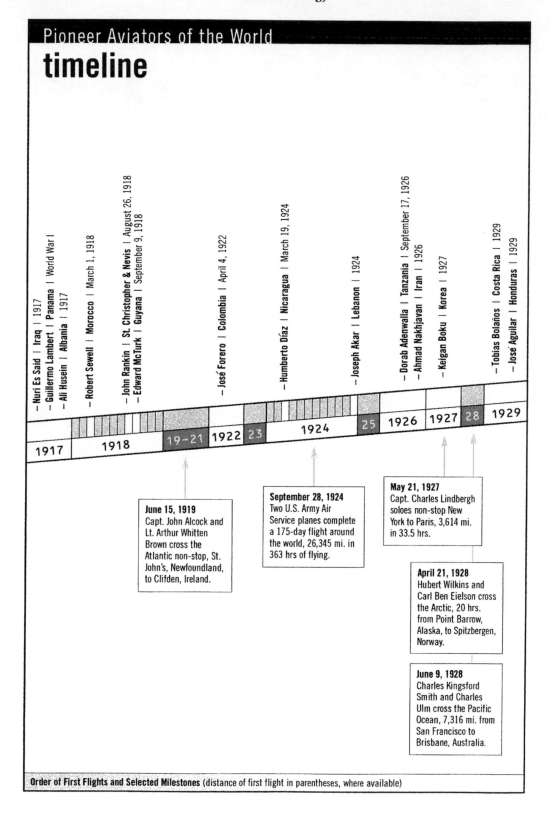

— Nuri Es Said | Iraq | 1917
— Guillermo Lambert | Panama | World War I
— Ali Husein | Albania | 1917
— Robert Sewell | Morocco | March 1, 1918
— John Rankin | St. Christopher & Nevis | August 26, 1918
— Edward McTurk | Guyana | September 9, 1918
— José Forero | Colombia | April 4, 1922
— Humberto Díaz | Nicaragua | March 19, 1924
— Joseph Akar | Lebanon | 1924
— Dorab Adenwalla | Tanzania | September 17, 1926
— Ahmad Nakhjavan | Iran | 1926
— Keigan Boku | Korea | 1927
— Tobias Bolaños | Costa Rica | 1929
— José Aguilar | Honduras | 1929

1917   1918   19–21   1922   23   1924   25   1926   1927   28   1929

June 15, 1919
Capt. John Alcock and Lt. Arthur Whitten Brown cross the Atlantic non-stop, St. John's, Newfoundland, to Clifden, Ireland.

September 28, 1924
Two U.S. Army Air Service planes complete a 175-day flight around the world, 26,345 mi. in 363 hrs of flying.

May 21, 1927
Capt. Charles Lindbergh soloes non-stop New York to Paris, 3,614 mi. in 33.5 hrs.

April 21, 1928
Hubert Wilkins and Carl Ben Eielson cross the Arctic, 20 hrs. from Point Barrow, Alaska, to Spitzbergen, Norway.

June 9, 1928
Charles Kingsford Smith and Charles Ulm cross the Pacific Ocean, 7,316 mi. from San Francisco to Brisbane, Australia.

Order of First Flights and Selected Milestones (distance of first flight in parentheses, where available)

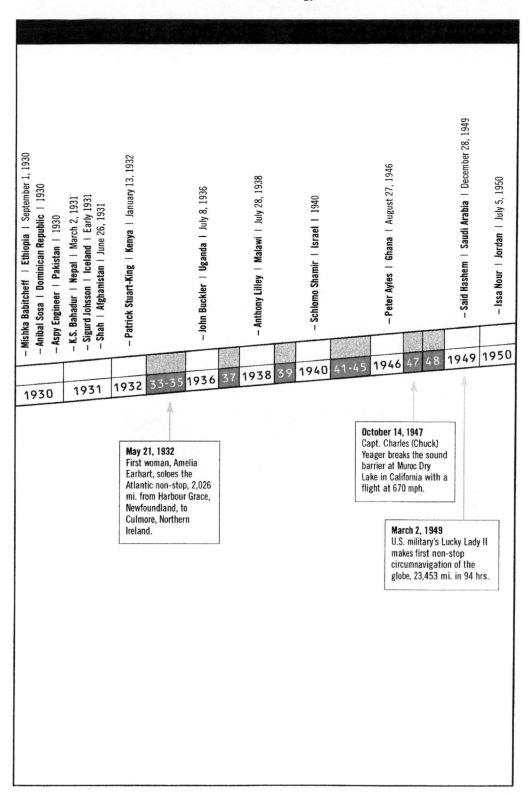

— Mishka Babitcheff | **Ethiopia** | September 1, 1930
— Anibal Sosa | **Dominican Republic** | 1930
— Aspy Engineer | **Pakistan** | 1930
— K.S. Bahadur | **Nepal** | March 2, 1931
— Sigurd Johsson | **Iceland** | Early 1931
— Shah | **Afghanistan** | June 26, 1931
— Patrick Stuart-King | **Kenya** | January 13, 1932
— John Buckler | **Uganda** | July 8, 1936
— Anthony Lilley | **Malawi** | July 28, 1938
— Schlomo Shamir | **Israel** | 1940
— Peter Ayles | **Ghana** | August 27, 1946
— Said Hashem | **Saudi Arabia** | December 28, 1949
— Issa Nour | **Jordan** | July 5, 1950

1930 | 1931 | 1932 | 33-35 | 1936 | 37 | 1938 | 39 | 1940 | 41-45 | 1946 | 47 | 48 | 1949 | 1950

May 21, 1932
First woman, Amelia Earhart, soloes the Atlantic non-stop, 2,026 mi. from Harbour Grace, Newfoundland, to Culmore, Northern Ireland.

October 14, 1947
Capt. Charles (Chuck) Yeager breaks the sound barrier at Muroc Dry Lake in California with a flight at 670 mph.

March 2, 1949
U.S. military's Lucky Lady II makes first non-stop circumnavigation of the globe, 23,453 mi. in 94 hrs.

Glossary

Ader, Clement (1841–1925)—French electrical engineer who made the world's first unassisted, powered take-off, in 1890, in his steam-powered craft, *Eole*. This machine covered approximately 50 meters with Ader aboard, but a later and larger craft, *Avion III*, failed to leave the ground when it was tested in 1897.

aeronaut—one who pilots a lighter-than-air craft.

aeronautics—the science of flight, whether in lighter-than-air or heavier-than-air craft.

aileron—a control surface that changes the lateral attitude of an aircraft, i.e., changes its bank; a "wing flap"; usually located on the rear edge of an airplane's wing, alters the lift of the wing to affect or correct a bank; used in opposition to an aileron on the opposite wing for faster response. Non-linked ailerons are called elevons.

airfoil—any structure designed to create a reaction in moving air.

airship—a lighter-than-air craft with means of propulsion and steering

angle of attack—the angle of an airfoil as it meets the wind.

Archdeacon, Ernest (1863–1957)—wealthy Paris lawyer in the early 1900s who experimented with gliders and financed some of Europe's earliest aviation prizes. Served as an early chairman of the Aéro-Club de France, was the first to fly as a passenger in Europe, and helped organize the world's first international air meet at Reims in 1909.

Auvours (Camp d'Auvours)—a military training ground east of Paris on which Wilbur Wright gave demonstrations of the *Flyer* from August 21 through December 31, 1908, setting and re-setting every existing flight record.

aviation—manned, heavier-than-air flight, i.e., in gliders and airplanes.

bank—(n.) the sideways tilt of an airplane, i.e., the movement of its lateral (wing) axis in relation to the horizontal, or movement around its longitudinal (lengthwise) axis; an airplane in a right bank has the right wing lower than the left. (v.) to tilt an airplane to one side or another.

Bell, Dr. Alexander Graham (1847–1922)—Scottish telephone pioneer who experimented with motorized kites and in 1907 convened the Aerial Experiment Association at his home in Nova Scotia. The A.E.A. made the first official public flights in North America, gave Glenn Curtis a start designing aircraft and actually produced the first Curtiss June Bug.

Bétheny—see Reims.

biplane—an airplane with two sets of wings, one over the other.

Blériot, Louis Charles-Joseph (1872–1936)—French engineer and successful manufacturer of auto headlamps who began experimenting with airplanes in 1905. Through four years and 50 crashes, Blériot developed one of the earliest monoplane designs. In 1909 he was the first to cross the English Channel.

boxkite—originally a form of kite pioneered by Australian inventor Lawrence Hargrave, who used rectangular kites to lift himself from the ground; many early European airplanes, such as the Voisin, used boxkite-type wings or tail units.

brevet—a pilot's license or certification.

brevet civil—the simpler, or "A" form of the pilot's license, for use in civil aviation.

brevet militaire—the more difficult, or "B" form of the early pilot's license developed by the French military; required more extensive flying and a thorough knowledge of the mechanics of various machines.

Buoy—see Camp-de-Châlons

camber—the rise of an airfoil's curve, expressed as a ratio of its length to its highest point from the center line.

Camp-de-Châlons—an area east of Paris and southeast of Reims, on the Plain of Châlons, where Englishman Henry Farman established an aircraft factory in 1908 and where numerous manufacturers later set up factories and schools; called variously by the names of the surrounding towns: Buoy, Louvercy, Mourmelon-le-Petit, Mourmelon-le-Grand, or just Mourmelon.

canard—an airplane in which the control surfaces come in front of the main wings; to modern eyes a canard seems to be flying tail first.

Cayley, Sir George (1773–1857)—The Father of Aviation; versatile English inventor who first surmised that a successful flying machine would require lifting surfaces separate from the source of power, rather than flapping wings (1799); also created the first successful model airplane (1804) and man-carrying gliders (1849 and 1953).

Chanute, Octave (1832–1910)—engineer and glider experimenter who in 1894 published all the available literature on aviation in his seminal *Progress in Flying Machines*; later advised the Wright brothers in their experiments and introduced European ex-

perimenters to the gliding advances made by the Wrights.

Cody, Samuel F. (c. 1861–1913)—expatriate American showman who made the first sustained flights in England; worked with the British military on man-carrying kites and early government airplanes.

control surface—an airfoil that can be manipulated by the pilot of an aircraft to change its direction of travel.

Curtiss, Glenn (1878–1930)—American bicycle, motorcycle and engine manufacturer who joined the Aerial Experiment Association in 1907 as the Fastest Man on Earth, having set a record of 136.3 m.p.h. on a motorcycle earlier that year. Designed the A.E.A.'s third plane, *June Bug*, won the first Gordon-Bennett competition in 1909, and made the first flight from Albany to New York City in 1910. Curtiss' company produced many successful airplanes and seaplanes, including the famed World War I trainer, the *J.N.4* "Jennie."

Delagrange, Léon (1873–1910)—French sculptor who in 1907 purchased the first Voisin biplane to fly; he required that the Voisins fly it first, by way of proof, and thereby lost his chance to become the first French pilot; learned to fly the machine in 1908, becoming the sixth man to fly, and toured Europe giving exhibitions; killed flying a Blériot on January 4, 1910, the sixth pilot to die flying.

Deutsch de la Meurthe, Henri (1845–1919)—Paris engineer and oil magnate who financed many of the aviation prizes that gave European pioneers a start manufacturing airplanes.

dihedral—the downward angle of the two halves of a wing as they approach an airplane's center line or fuselage (making a shallow "V"); often used by early designers to impart a measure of stability to a flying machine. Wings that rise from the center line have dihedral; wings that fall from the center line, like on the first Wright Flyer, have "anhedral" or "cathedral."

dirigible—a rigid lighter-than-air craft, an airship.

elevator—a control surface that alters an aircraft's climbing angle (pitch).

elevons—a pair of control surfaces on either side of an aircraft which can be used as elevators or ailerons simultaneously; ailerons, or "wing flaps," that can be worked in opposition for lateral (roll) control or together for climb (pitch) control.

Étampes—a town south of Paris where several manufacturers, including Henry Farman and Louis Blériot, set up piloting schools around 1910.

flying boat—a seaplane whose hull provides both floatation and a landing/taking-off surface.

fuselage—the center body of an aircraft to which the wings and tail unit are attached.

Goupy, Ambroise (1876–1951)—French pioneer who worked with Frenchman Gabriel Voisin, Belgian Baron Pierre de Caters and Italian Mario Calderara on very early European triplanes and biplanes; produced perhaps the most modern pre–1910 design.

La Grande Semaine de l'Aviation de la Champagne (Reims Aviation Week)—the first international air meet, held northeast of Paris on the Plain of Bétheny, near the town of Reims, in August of 1909.

Hargrave, Lawrence (1850–1915)—Australian engineer, astronomer and explorer whose early work in aerodynamics was tremendously influential on early European designers; in the 1890s developed a rectangular man-lifting kite, the boxkite, that later became the basis for early European wing and tail-unit designs.

Harmsworth, Alfred (Lord Northcliffe) (1865–1922)—flamboyant English newspaper publisher who in 1906 hired the world's first aviation correspondent (Harry Harper) and who financed many of aviation's early prizes, including the cross Channel race won by Louis Blériot in 1909, the London-Manchester race of 1910, and the first non-stop Atlantic crossing in 1919.

heavier-than-air flight—manned flight that uses the aerodynamic characteristics of a wing for lift, as opposed to using lighter-than-air gasses (hydrogen, helium, or heated air).

Hendon—an early English airfield in north London.

Hunaudières—a race course east of Paris, near Le Mans, where Wilbur Wright gave the first official public demonstrations of the Wright *Flyer*, August 8–13, 1908.

hydroplane—an airplane designed for landing on water; usually with floats for landing gear; also called a seaplane; when a full hull is employed, called a flying boat.

Issy-les-Moulineaux—military parade ground in a south Paris suburb where Parisian inventors did most of their testing from 1906 into 1909; the center of European aviation for a number of years, it had to be shared with the army; during certain times of the year experimenters could only work on the field very early in the morning or late in the evening.

Juvisy (Port d'Aviation)—the first dedicated aerodrome, located in southeast Paris, it opened with one of the world's first air meets in July of 1909, though attendance was limited to a couple of French aviators.

Langley, Samuel Pierpont (1834–1906)—American astronomer who in the 1890s built several tandem-winged flying machines, including a man-carrying design tested unsuccessfully in 1903.

lighter-than-air flight—manned flight that uses the lighter-than-air qualities of certain gasses (e.g., hydrogen or heated air) for lift.

Lilienthal, Otto (1848–1896)—German engineer who pioneered the practical glider, making more than 2,000 glides from 1891 to his death in an 1896 crash.

monoplane—an airplane with one set of wings.

Mourmelon—see Camp-de-Châlons.

multiplane—an airplane having more than two sets of wings arranged vertically.

Pau—a town in the southwest of France where the Wrights began teaching the first French military pilots in 1909 and where Louis Blériot later established a school.

Pénaud, Alphonse (1850–1880)—French inventor who created an inherently stable model airplane incorporating a propeller, cambered wings and a cruciform tail unit; discovered the proper relationship between the angle of attack of the wings and that of the horizontal stabilizer, such that his model, rather than crash, would tend to right itself from too steep a climb or dive; discovered the benefits of high aspect-ratio wings (long and narrow).

pitch—the movement of an object about its lateral axis; in an airplane, ascending and descending are the result of changes in pitch; controlled by elevators or elevons. Also having to do with the angle of a propeller to the air it acts upon.

Port d'Aviation—see Juvisy.

pusher—an airplane with its propeller located behind the wings.

radial engine—an internal combustion engine in which the cylinders are arranged radially around the driveshaft like the spokes of a wheel.

raid—a cross-country flight (from the French).

Reims—a town northeast of Paris on the Plain of Bétheny near which the world's first international air meet was held, August 22–29, 1909; see La Grande Semaine de l'Aviation de la Champagne.

roll—the movement of an object about its lengthwise, or longitudinal, axis; in an airplane, a bank is the result of a change in roll; controlled in early airplanes by wing warping or ailerons, in later airplanes by ailerons; also, an aerobatic maneuver.

rotary engine—an internal combustion engine in which the cylinders rotate with the drive shaft; commonly used in early airplanes to improve the circulation of air around the cylinders and allow them to be air cooled, and therefore lighter than if they had to be water cooled.

seaplane—an airplane designed for landing on water; usually with floats for landing gear; also called a hydroplane; when a full hull is employed, called a flying boat.

semi-radial engine—an internal combustion engine in which the cylinders are arranged radially around the driveshaft, but only in a semi-circle; sometimes called a "fan engine."

sesquiplane (semi-biplane)—a biplane in which the lower wing is less than one-and-a-half times the length of the upper.

side curtains—the vertical wing components of a boxkite-type flying machine.

tandem—an airplane having more than one set of wings arranged lengthwise down its fuselage; not a common arrangement, even in early experiments.

tractor—an airplane with its propeller located in front of the wings.

triplane—an airplane having three sets of wings arranged vertically atop each other.

vol plané—a gliding descent in an airplane with the engine either shut off or not working, a required skill for some early pilot licenses.

wing-warping—a method of lateral (roll) control whereby the tip of one wing flexes upward, increasing lift, while the tip of the opposite wing flexes downward, decreasing lift, thereby causing or correcting a "bank"; the Wrights' method of lateral control; eventually superceded by ailerons.

yaw—the movement of an object about its vertical axis; in a car, yaw is controlled by the steering wheel, in a boat, by rudder; in an airplane, yaw is also controlled by rudder.

Notes

1. Gibbs-Smith, *Aeroplane,* p. 35.
2. *Flight,* June 26, 1931, p. 576.
3. Faroux, Ch., and G. Bonnet. *Aéro-Manuel: Réperetoire Sportif, Technique et Commercial de l'Aéronautique.* H. Dunod et E. Pinat, Paris (1914), p. 845.
4. *The Aero,* Aug. 3, 1910, p. 96.
5. See Canada.
6. Brodgen, pp. 14-16.
7. *The Aero,* March 8, 1911, p. 191.
8. Uncited news article, property of R.A.A.F. Museum, Point Cook, Victoria, Australia.
9. For Santos-Dumont, see Brazil; for Wilbur Wright, see United States of America.
10. Cole, *Royal Flying Corps,* p. 241.
11. *The Barbados Advocate,* Nov. 16, 1932.
12. Angelucci, *Civil Aircraft,* pp. 79–81.
13. See page 24 for a picture of the Voisin-Goupy–type triplane.
14. Wohl, *Passion,* pp. 100–3.
15. *New York Herald.* Undated article, 1906. Bell scrapbooks, NASM.
16. Crouch, *Bishop's Boys,* p. 326.
17. Wykeham, p. 24.
18. *Ibid.,* pp. 236–38.
19. Winchester, vol. 1, p. 486.
20. Scott, pp. 185–88.
21. Crouch, *Bishop's Boys,* pp. 486–87.
22. Gibbs-Smith, *Directory and Nomenclature,* p. 77.
23. For Farman, see England.
24. In Chinese custom, the family name comes first, so Sun Yat-sen's surname would have been Sun, just as Feng Yu's family name is Feng.
25. All information and quotes taken from Forero, *Historia de la Aviación en Colombia,* 1964.
26. *Aero Digest,* 1930, p. 214.
27. Hagedorn, *Central American and Caribbean Air Forces,* p. 123.
28. For the Rusjans, see Slovenia.
29. *Troy Times,* Aug. 1, 1911.
30. For McCurdy and the Aerial Experiment Association, see Canada.
31. For Santos-Dumont, see Brazil.
32. Ellehammer, *Jeg floj.*
33. *Ibid.*
34. For details on Bell's aeronautical work, see Canada; for Cody, England.
35. Gibbs-Smith, *Directory and Nomenclature,* pp. 51–52.
36. *Opening Tomorrow's Airways,* Foltmann, p. 7.
37. Ellehammer, *Jeg floj.*
38. Franks, Norman, *Above the War Fronts* … pp. 124, 155.
39. *London Gazette,* 9/1909.
40. For Santos-Dumont, see Brazil.
41. Angelucci, *Civil Aircraft,* p. 72.
42. *Chronicle of Aviation,* p. 80.
43. Gibbs-Smith, *Directory and Nomenclature,* p. 34.
44. See Introduction for a discussion of "hops" versus "flights."
45. For Grade, see Poland.
46. Voisin, p. 69.
47. Crouch, *Bishop's Boys,* p. 321.
48. For Farman, see England.
49. For Houdini, see Hungary.
50. Silverman, p. 6.
51. For a discussion of Fred Custance, see Australia.
52. *Flight,* May 1, 1931.
53. Postma, Thijs.
54. Carbery, pp. 139–40.
55. Lovell, *Straight on Till Morning,* p. 161.

56. For de Pischof, see Austria.

57. See page 24 for a photograph of this plane.

58. For the Voisins, see France.

59. Cobianchi, pp. 16–19.

60. McFarland, no page available.

61. *Flight*, Feb. 17, 1927.

62. For the Wrights, see USA; for the Voisins, see France; for the Farmans, see England.

63. Taylor & Munson, pp. 76–79.

64. Supf, p. 338.

65. For more on Farman, see England; for Sanchez-Besa, see Chile.

66. Aponte, no page available.

67. *Ibid.*

68. Prada Effio, p. 26.

69. Villard, p. 100.

70. *Ibid.*, p. 99.

71. Taylor & Munson, p. 75.

72. Whitehouse, p. 153.

73. For Weymann, see Haiti.

74. For the Wrights, see USA; for Santos-Dumont, Brazil; for Ellehammer, Denmark.

75. Supf, p. 260.

76. For de Pischof, see Austria.

77. Supf, p. 504.

78. *Ibid.*, p. 264.

79. *Chronicle of Aviation*, p. 66.

80. For Santos-Dumont, see Brazil; for Grade, see Poland; for de Pischof, see Austria.

81. Obviously not his first flight, but the earliest record found.

82. For Farman, see England; for Chavez, see Peru.

83. *Flight*, 3/5/1910, p. 165.

84. Mellor, pp. 21, 23.

85. For Farman, see England; for de Caters, Belgium.

86. Oberholzer, p. 61.

87. For Farman, see England.

88. *L'Aérophile*, 1/1910, p. 11.

89. Brett, pp. 45–46.

90. *Svensk Motortidning*, Aug. 15, 1910.

91. *Chronicle of Aviation*, p. 66.

92. *Ibid.*, p. 69.

93. For the Voisins, see France; for Farman, England; for more on Curtiss, see Canada.

94. The Swiss historian who compiled most of the available details about Perret, Dr. Erich Tilgenkamp (see Bibliography), claims he was the 100th person to fly.

95. *Luang* and *Phraya* are honorary titles. As in the rest of Oriental custom, what we would call a "surname," or a family name, comes before the given name. Hence, Luang Sakdi Sanlayawut is referred to as Sakdi; after he earns the honorary name, Phraya Chalerm Akas, we refer to him as Chalerm.

96. *Flight*, Jan. 5, 1922, p. 14.

97. For Santos-Dumont, see Brazil.

98. *Great Russian Encyclopedia*, vol. 27, p. 705.

99. Keldysh, p. 229.

100. Crouch, *Bishop's Boys*, pp. 465–66.

Bibliography

Adler, Cyrus. "Samuel Pierpont Langley." Annual Report of the Board of Regents of the Smithsonian Institution, year ending June 30, 1906. Washington: U.S. Government Printing Office, 1907; pp. 515–33.

Aero Blue Book and Directory. New York: Century, 1918.

Aéro-Club de France Annuaire. Vols. 1909–1910. Siège Social, Paris.

The Aero Manual. Vols. 1909–1910. Compiled by the Staff of "The Motor." London: Temple Press.

Aircraft Illustrated. Thinesen, Johannes. "First Danish Aviator." November, 1976, pp. 445–51.

The Airman's Year Book and Light Aeroplane Manual, 1935. The Royal Aero Club of the United Kingdom. London: Sir Isaac Pitman & Sons, 1935.

Alexander, Ronald Trevor. *High Adventure; From Balloons to Boeings in New Zealand.* New Zealand National Airways Corporation, Wellington, 1968.

Allen, Peter. *The 91 Before Lindbergh.* England: Airlife, 1984.

American Heritage History of Flight. New York: Simon and Schuster, 1962.

Angelucci, Enzo. *The Rand McNally Encyclopedia of Military Aircraft: 1914 to the Present.* New York: Gallery Books, 1990.

_____. *World Encyclopedia of Civil Aircraft from Leonardo da Vinci to the Present.* New York: Crown Publishers, 1982.

Anwar, Mustafa, Captain. *Civil Aviation in India.* Calcutta: Thacker, Spink and Co., 1954.

Apold, Raul Alejandro. "La vida ejemplar de Jorge Newbery." Homenje del Aero Club Argentino al Fundador Inolvidable de la Aeronautica Argentina con Motivo de la Inauguracion de su Monumento. April 25, 1937.

Aponte, Leandro. *Cincuenta Años de Aeronautica en el Paraguay.* Asunción, Paraguay: El Arte S.A., 1957.

_____. *Pettirossi: Un sud americano insuperable.* Asunción, 1966.

Aviation in Siam. Royal Aeronautical Service, Thailand, 1923 (1927).

Aymar, Brandt. *Men in the Air: The Best Flight Stories of All Time from Greek Mythology to the Space Age.* New York: Crown Publishers, 1990.

Bain, Gordon. *De Havilland: A Pictorial Tribute.* St. Catherines, Ontario: Vanwel Publishing 1992.

Baldwin, N.C. *Abyssinia, 1929–1931: An Aero Philatelic Guide and Price Check List of Abyssina and French Somaliland.* The Aero Field Handbook No. 1., Sutton Coldfield, England: Francis J. Field, n.d.

Balotescu, Nicolae, et al., redactor Carmen Zgavardicil. *Istoria aviatiei române.* Bucuresti: Editura Stiintifică si Enciclopedică, 1984.

Barclay, K.M. *Civil Aviation Report Malaya/Borneo Territories 1961.* Printed at the Government Printing Office, Singapore, 1962.

Becker, Beril. *Dreams and Realities of the Conquest of the Skies.* New York: Atheneum, 1968.

Bernhard, Leopold, Consort of Julian, Queen of the Netherlands. "The Netherlands People, Their Country and Their Civil Aviation, Today and in the Future." *1976 Wings Club "Sight" Lecture.* New York City: Wings Club, Dec. 2, 1976.

Biddle, Wayne. *Barons of the Sky.* New York: Simon and Schuster, 1991.

Biedma Recalde, Antonio M. *Crónica Histórica de la Aeronáutica Argentina.* Volumen 1, Colección Aeroespacial Argentina: Direccion de Publicaciones, 1969.

Blakeney, Stepney. *How an Aeroplane Is Built.* London: "Aeroplane" & General Publishing, 1918.

Böhme, Adolf. *Wir flogen für Iran: deutsche Flieger für ein neues Persien.* Steinebach-Wörthsee: Luftfahrt-Berlag Walter Zuerl, 1976.

Borovan, Václav. *Historický let ing. Jana Kašpara.* Praha: Ministerstvo obrany ČR—AVIS, 2001.
_____. *Historický let Prvního Českého Aviatika.* Praha: Květen, 1991.
Brancker, Sir W. Sefton. *A Commercial and Historical Atlas of the World's Airways.* Birmingham, England: Francis J. Field, 1925.
Brescia. Circuito Aero Internazionale Italian, 1909. *Guida Ufficial del Primo Circuito Aero Internazionale Italiano Organizzato dalla Citt di Brescia.* Milano: Uffici della Guida, Settembre, 1909.
Brett, R. Dallas. *History of British Aviation 1908–1914.* Vols. 1–2. London: The Aviation Book Club, c. 1930.
Brogden, Stanley. *The History of Australian Aviation.* Melbourne: The Hawthorn Press, 1960.
Brown, C.L.M. *The Conquest of the Air: An Historical Survey.* London: Oxford University Press, 1927.
Bruno, Harry. *Wings Over America.* New York: Robert M. McBride, 1942.
Buist, Hugo Massac. *Aircraft in the German War.* London: Methuen, 1914.
Burge, Cyril Gordon. *Encyclopedia of Aviation.* London: Isaac Pitman, 1935.
Burnett-Rae, D.W. *Civil Aviation Report on Development in the Colony.* Vols. 1955–1960. Government of Cyprus, printed at the Cyprus Government Printing Office, Nicosia.
Burney, Sir Charles Dennistoun. *The World, the Air and the Future.* London: Alfred A. Knopf, 1929.
Calderara, Lodovico, and Attilio Marchetti. *Mario Calderara: Aviatore e Inventore.* Rome: LoGisma editore, 1999.
Carbery, Mary. *Mary Carbery's West Cork Journal 1898–1901.* Jeremy Sandford, ed. Dublin: The Lilliput Press, 1998.
Cardoso, Edgar. *História da Força Aéreo Portuguesa.* Amadora Gratelo SARL, 1981.
Chambre, René. *Histoire de l'aviation.* France: Flammarion, 1972.
Chanute, Octave. *Progress in Flying Machines.* Mineola, N.Y.: Dover, 1997. (Originally published in installments by *American Engineer and Railroad Journal*; New York, 1894.)
Charfardet Urbina, Luis María. *Trayectoria de la Aviación en Venezuela.* Prólogo del Doctor Diógenes Escalante, Caracus: Taller Offset, 1941.
The Chilton Aero Directory. Philadelphia: The Chilton Company, 1911.
China Today: Aviation Industry. Beijing: The China Aviation Industry Press, 1989.
Chronicle of Aviation. Mark S. Pyle, editor. UK: Chronicle Communications, 1992. In USA by JL International Publishing, Liberty, Missouri.

Cinquante Quatre. *Flying Corps Songs.* Cambridge: Bowes & Bowes, 1918.
Il Circuito Aero di Brescia. Guida Ufficiale. Milano: Uffici della Guida, Settembre, 1909.
Civil Aviation Department. *Jamaica Annual Report of the Civil Aviation Department for the Year 1952.*
Civil Aviation Report Malaya/Borneo Territories. Vols. 1953–1954. Printed at the Government Printing Office, Singapore by F.S. Horslin, Government Printer.
Cobham, Sir Alan. *Twenty Thousand Miles in a Flying Boat.* London: Long Rider's Guild Press, (c. 1928).
Cobianchi, Mario. *Pionieri dell' aviazione in Italia, con rare e storiche illustrazioni.* Rome: Editoriale Aeronautico, 1943.
Cole, Christopher. *Royal Flying Corps, 1915–1916.* London: Wm. Kimber, 1969.
Cole, Martin. *Their Eyes on the Skies.* Glendale, Calif.: Aviation Book Company, 1979.
Coonts, Stephen. *War in the Air. True Accounts of the 20th Century's Most Dramatic Air Battles-by the Men Who Fought Them.* New York: Pocket Books, 1996.
Corlett, John. *Aviation in Ulster.* Belfast: Blackstaff Press, 1981.
Crosara, Leonardo. *Cronologia Aeronautica Vol. II.* Milano, Roma: Lvigi Alfieri, 1932.
Crouch, Tom D. *The Bishop's Boys: A Life of Wilbur and Orville Wright.* New York: W.W. Norton, 1989.
_____. *Blériot XI: The Story of a Classic Aircraft.* Washington: NASM, Smithsonian Institute Press, 1982.
Cynk, Jerzy B. *Polish Aircraft 1893–1939.* London: Putnam, 1971.
Dalwick, R.E.R., and C.H.C. Harmer. *Newfoundland Air Mails 1919–1939 with Additional Notes on Subsequent Flights and Air Mail Stamps.* London: D.F. Hodgson and Son, 1953.
Davis, Peter. *East African: An Airline Story.* Fontwell, Sussex, UK: Runnymeade Malthouse Publishing, 1993.
de Caters, Guy. "Baron Pierre de Caters, 1908: naissance de l'Aviation belge il y a 70 ans." *Amis du Musée de l'Air et de l'Espace.* April, 1978.
DéPagniat, Roger Leon. *Les Martyrs de l'Aviation.* Paris: Les hommes Préface de Paul Painlevé, n.d.
Department of Civil Aviation. *1948 Annual Report, Colony of Trinidad and Tobago.*
De Seversky, Major Alexander P. *Victory Through Air Power.* New York: Simon & Schuster, 1942.
Dollfus, Charles, and Henry Bouché. *Histoire de l'aéronautique.* Paris: Société Nationale des Enterprises de Presse, 1932.
Donald, David. *The Complete Encyclopedia of*

World Aircraft: The Development and Specifications of over 2500 Civil and Military Aircraft from 1903 to the Present Day. New York: Barnes and Noble, 1997.

The Dorling Kindersley World Reference Atlas. London: Dorling Kindersley, 1996, 1998.

Draper, Chris. *The Salmson Story.* London: David & Charles, n.d.

Dumont-Villares, Henrique. *Santos-Dumont, the Father of Aviation.* São Paulo: Comp. Melhoramentos de São Paulo, 1956.

The East Africa Civil Aviation Report for 1948–1960. Published by the Directorate of Civil Aviation under the Authority of the Commissioner for Transport, East Africa High Commission.

Eisendrath, Joseph L. *Crash Covers: An Aerophilatelic Challenge.* Cinnaminson, N.J.: American Air Mail Society, 1979.

Ellehammer. *Jeg Fløj—nogle erindringer fra en uforglemmelig tid.* København: Udgivetaf Drenglbladet, 1931.

Ellis, Frank H. *Canada's Flying Heritage.* Toronto: University of Toronto Press, 1954.

Emde, Heiner. *Conquerors of the Air. The Evolution of Aircraft 1903–1945.* New York: The Viking Press, 1968.

Enciclopedia de Aviación y Astronautica. Vols. 1–8. Barcelona: Ediciones Garriga, 1972.

Encyclopedia Lituanica. Volumes 1–6. Boston, Mass.: Juozas Kapocius, 1975.

Ewing, Ross, and Ross Macpherson. *The History of New Zealand Aviation.* Auckland, New Zealand: Heinemann Publishers, 1986.

Eyermann, Karl-Heinz. *Die Luftfahrt der USSR 1917–1977.* Berlin: Transpress, 1977.

Fales, Elisha Noel. *Learning to Fly in the U.S. Army: A Manual of Aviation Practice.* New York: McGraw-Hill Book Company, 1917.

Farman, Henry, Dick Farman, et al. *The Aviator's Companion.* London: Mills and Boon, 1910.

Faroux, Ch., and Et. Bernard. *Aéro-Manuel: Repertoire Sportif, Technique et Commercial de l'Aéronautique.* Paris: H. Dunod et E. Pinat, 1911.

_____, and G. Bonnet. *Aéro-Manuel: Repertoire Sportif, Technique et Commercial de l'Aéronautique.* Paris: H. Dunod et E. Pinat, 1914.

Federation of Nigeria Annual Report on Civil Aviation. Vols. 1953–1959. Printed and Published by the Federal Government Printer, Lagos 1955.

Federation of Rhodesia and Nyasaland. *Report of the Controller of Customs and Excise for the Period 1st April, 1954–30th June, 1959.* Presented to the Federal Assembly, 1960.

"Flying Around Barbados." *The Bajan.* Vol. 12, No. 3, November 1964, pp. 9–13.

The Flying Book. 1914 Edition. Richmond Hill: The Aviation World Publishing, 1914.

Fokker, Anthony Herman Gerard, and Bruce Gould. *Flying Dutchman.* New York: Arno Press, 1972.

Foltmann, John, Captain. "Who Was Jacob Christian Ellehammer?" *Opening Tomorrow's Airways,* pp. 5–7.

Forero, José Ignacio F. *Historia de la Aviación en Colombia con la colaboración y Colofón de Uriel Ospina Londoño,* Aedita, Editores Ltda. 1964.

Forsdyke, D.K. *Civil Aviation Report on Development in the Colony.* Vols. 1953–1954. Government of Cyprus, printed at the Cyprus Government Printing Office, Nicosia, 1954.

Fox, James. *White Mischief.* London: Penguin Books, 1982.

Franks, Norman L. R., Frank W. Bailey and Russell Guest. *Above the Lines: The Aces and Fighter Units of the German Air Service, Naval Air Service and Flanders Marine Corps 1914–1918.* London: Grub Street, 1993.

_____, Russell Guest, and Gregory Alegi. *Above the War Fronts: The British Two-Seater Bomber Pilot and Observer Aces, the British Two-Seater Fighter Observer Aces, and the Belgian, Italian, Austro-Hungarian and Russian Fighter Aces 1914–1918.* London: Grubb Street, 1997.

Friedelander, Mark P., Jr., and Gene Gurney. *Higher, Faster, and Farther.* New York: William Morrow, 1973.

Fuller, G.A., J.A. Griffin, and K.M. Molson. *125 Years of Canadian Aeronautics: A Chronology 1840–1965.* Willowdale, Ontario: The Canadian Aviation Historical Society, 1983.

Fyfe, George. *From Box-Kites to Bombers.* London: John Long, 1936.

Gebauer, Eugenio. *The Air Post Stamps of Colombia.* Caracas, Venezuela: Editorial Sucre, 1963.

_____, and Jairo Londono Tamayo. *Los Primeros 50 Anos de Dorreo Aereo en Colombia.* Bogota: Italgraf S.A., 1975.

Gibbs-Smith, Sir Charles. *The Aeroplane: An Historical Survey.* London: Her Majesty's Stationery Office, 1960.

_____. *Clement Ader: His Flight-Claims and His Place in History.* London: Her Majesty's Stationery Office, 1968.

_____. *A Directory and Nomenclature of the First Aeroplanes, 1809 to 1909.* London: Her Majesty's Stationery Office, 1966.

_____. *Early Flying Machines 1799–1909.* London: Eyre Methuen, 1975.

_____. *A History of Flying.* London: B.T. Batsford, 1953.

_____. *The Invention of the Aeroplane 1799–1909.* New York: Taplinger Publishing, 1966.

_____. *Sir George Cayley's Aeronautics, 1796–1855.* London: Her Majesty's Stationery Office, 1962.

Giebert, Ron, and Tucker Malishenko. Ed. *Early Flight 1900–1911.* Dayton, Ohio: Landfall Press, 1984.

Glass, Andrze. *Polish Wings.* Translated by Emma Harris. Warsaw: Interpress Publishers, 1985.

Glines, Carroll V. *Airmail: How It All Began.* Blue Ridge Summit, Pa.: Tab Aero, 1990.

Glubb, Sir John Bagot, Lt. Gen. *A Soldier with the Arabs.* London: Hodder and Stoughton, 1957.

Goode, John. *Wood Wire and Fabric: A Saga of Australian Flying.* Melbournes: Lansdowne Press, 1968.

Grahame-White, Claude, and Harry Harper. *Aircraft in the Great War: A Record and Study.* London: T. Fisher Unwin, 1915.

Grandes Vuelos de la Aviación Española. Madrid: Espasa-Calpe, S.A., 1983.

Great Soviet Encyclopedia. Moscow: Sovetskaia Entsiklopediia Publishing House, 1970. In the U.S., Macmillan, New York. Vols. 6, 7, 9, 22, 26, 27.

Green, William, and John Fricker. *The Air Forces of the World: Their History, Development and Present Strength.* New York: Hanover House, 1958.

Greer, Louise, and Anthony Harold. *Flying Clothing: The Story of Its Development.* Shrewsbury, England: Airlife Publishers, 1979.

Gunston, Bill, editor in chief. *Chronicle of Aviation.* English Edition. Liberty, Mo.: J.L. International Publishers, 1992.

Hackenberger, Willi. *Die Alten Adler Pioniere der deutschen Luftfahrt.* Munchen: J.F.Lehmanns Verlag, 1960.

Hagedorn, Daniel P. *Central American and Caribbean Air Forces.* Air-Britain Publication, 1993.

_____, and Antonio Luis Sapienza. *Aircraft of the Chaco War 1928–1935.* Atglen, Pa.: Schiffer Military/Aviation History, 1997.

Hager, Alice Rogers. *Frontier by Air: Brazil Takes the Sky Road.* New York: McMillan Press, 1942.

Halpern, John. *Early Birds: An Informal Account of the Beginnings of Aviation.* New York: E.P. Dutton, 1981.

Hardesty, Von, and Dominick Pisano. *Black Wings: The American Black in Aviation.* Washington, DC: National Air and Space Museum, Smithsonian Institution, 1983.

Hare, Dan. *The Airmails of New Guinea 1922–42.* Melbourne: The Hawthorne Press, 1978.

Harper, Harry. *The Evolution of the Flying Machine, Balloon: Airship: Aeroplane.* Philadelphia: David McKay Company, 1930.

Harris, Harold R., Gen. *Twenty-First Wings Club "Sight" Lecture.* New York: The Wings Club, 1984.

Harris, Sherwood. *The First to Fly: Aviation's Pioneer Days.* New York: Simon and Schuster, 1970.

Haskins, Jim. *Black Eagles: African Americans in Aviation.* New York: Scholastic, 1995.

Hébrard, Jean André Leon. *L'Aviation des Origines à Nos Jours.* Robert Laffont: Paris, France, 1954.

Hegener, Henri. *Fokker— The Man and the Aircraft.* Letchworth, England: Harleyford Publications, 1961.

Herrera, Juan Peña. *Historia de la Aviación Ecuatoriana.* Published under the Auspices of the Minister of National Defense. Quito, Ecuador. [n.d.]

Higham, Robin, John T. Greenwood, and Von Hardesty, eds. *Russian Aviation and Air Power in the Twentieth Century.* London: Frank Cass Publishers, 1998.

Hildreth, C.H., and Bernard C. Nalty. *1001 Questions Answered About Aviation History.* New York: Dodd, Mead, 1969.

Hill, Wing Commander Roderic. *The Baghdad Air Mail.* New York: Longmans, Green, 1929.

Hodgeman, Ann, and Rudy Djabbaroff. *Sky Stars: The History of Women in Aviation.* New York: Atheneum, 1981.

Horvat, William J. *Above the Pacific.* Fallbrook, Calif.: Aero Publishers, 1966.

Howard, Frank, and Bill Gunston. *The Conquest of the Air.* New York: Random House, 1972.

Hubbard, Thomas O'Brien. *The Essays of an Aviator.* London: Aeronautics, 1914.

Hurren, B.J. *Fellowship of the Air: Jubilee Book of the Royal Aero Club 1901–1951.* London: Iliffe and Sons, 1951.

Hussain, Syed Shabbir. *History of the Pakistan Air Force 1947–1982.* Karachi, Pakistan: PAF Press, 1982.

Institut National de la Propriété Industrielle. *Brevet d'Invention, 16 January 1904–22 September 1906.* Paris, France: Aérostation, 1904–1906.

Iriarte, David R. *Historia de la Aviación Civil en Venezuela.* Seguda Edición, Obra del Ano Jubilar de la Aviacion Venezolana, 1971.

Jablonski, Edward. *Man with Wings: A Pictorial History of Aviation.* New York: Doubleday, 1980.

Jane, Fred T., ed. *Jane's All the World's Airships.* Vols. 1909–1914. Devon, England: David & Charles (Publishers), 1969. Originally published by Sampson Low Marston, 1909.

Jane's Fighting Aircraft of World War I. London: Jane's Publishing, 1919.

Janus, Allan. "Dog Is My Copilot." *Air and Space Smithsonian* (May 1996). Vol. 32.

Jarvis, S. D., and D. B. Jarvis. *The Cross of Sacrifice, Vol I. Officers Who Died in the Service of British, Indian and East African Regiments and Corps, 1914–1919.* Reading: Roberts Medals, 1993.

_____. *The Cross of Sacrifice, Vol IV. Non-commissioned Officers, Men and Women of the United Kingdom, Commonwealth and Empire who Died in the Service of the Royal Navy, Royal Marines, Royal Naval Air Service, Royal Flying*

Corp and the Royal Air Force, 1914–1921. Reading: Roberts, 1996.

"J.C.H. Ellehammer, the First Flight in Europe," courtesy of the Royal Danish Embassy.

Jefford, C. G. *Royal Air Force Squadrons.* Shrewsbury, England: Airlife Publishing, 1990.

Jerwan, S.S. *Flying as It Was.* New York: Sportsman Pilot, 1938.

Jiménez, Don Ignacio, Capitan. *Ligera historia de la aviación española.* Conferencia dada por el Capitan Jiménez, en los Salones del Patronato Escolar Español el dia 13 de Abril de 1953. Manila: Manila Grafica, April 1935.

Jiménez G., Carlos Ma. *Historia de la aviación en Costa Rica.* San José, Costa Rica, 1962.

Johnston, H. M., Director of Civil Aviation. *Nyasaland Protectorate Annual Report of the Civil Aviation Department 1950.* Printed and published by the Government Printer, Zomba, Nyasaland, 1951.

Jordanoff, Assen. *Jordanoff's Illustrated Aviation Dictionary.* New York: Harper and Brothers, 1942.

Jorgensen, Erik. "Another Way to the Stars." *Opening Tomorrow's Airways,* pp. 17–18, 31.

Josefovič, Miloš, and Jan Hozák. *Československé Letectví.* Národní Technické Muzeum, 1988.

Keimel, Reinhard. *Österreichs Lurftfahrzeuge Geschichte ob Luftfahrt von dem Anfanger bis Ende 1918,* Graz, Austria, 1981.

Keldysh, M.V., G.P. Svishchev, S.A. Xristianovich et al. *Aviation in Russia.* Moscow: Mashinostroenie, 1998.

Kelly, Fred C. *Miracle at Kitty Hawk.* New York: De Capo Press, 1996.

Kohri, Katsu, Ikuo Komori, and Ichiro Naito. *Aireview's The Fifty Years of Japanese Aviation, 1910–1960.* Vols. I–II. Tokyo: Kantosha, 1961.

König von und zu Warthausen, Baron Friedrich Karl. *Wings Around the World.* New York: G.P. Putnam's Sons, 1930.

Kronstein, Dr. Max. *Pioneer Airpost Flights of the World 1830–1935.* Washington, D.C.: American Air Mail Society, 1978.

Kurutz, Gary. *The Only Safe and Sane Method.* Alexandria, Va.: Time Life Books.

Kwiecínski, Bogdan Jósef. *L'aéronautique en Pologne.* Varsovie: Edition de L'Aeroklub Rzeczypospolitej Polskiej, 1935.

Lanchberry, Edward. *A.V. Roe: A Biography of Sir Alliott Verdon-Roe, O.B.E.* London: The Bodley Head, 1956.

Lassalle, E.J. *Les 100 Premiers Aviateurs Brevetés au Monde et la Naissance de l'Aviation.* Paris: Nauticaero Editions Nautiques et Aérospatiales, n.d.

Lewis, Peter M.H. *British Aircraft 1809–1914.* London: Putnam, 1962.

Lieberg, Owen S. *The First Air Race. The International Competition at Reims, 1909.* Garden City, N.Y.: Doubleday, 1974.

Light, Richard Upjohn. *Focus on Africa.* New York: American Geographical Society Special Publication No. 25, 1941.

Linney, A.G., and T. Stanhope Sprigg, eds. *Who's Who in Aviation.* London: Airways Publications, 1928.

Lloyd Aereo Boliviano. *Primera Memoria Anual.* Presentada por el Directorio a los Señores accionistas, en Junta General Ordinaria del 31 de Marzo de 1927. La Paz. Cochambamba, Bolivia, 1926.

Loeblein, John M. *Memoirs of Kelly Field, 1917–1918.* Manhattan, Kans: Aerospace Historian for the Air Force Historical Foundation, 1974.

Lomax, Judy. *Women of the Air.* New York: Dodd, Mead, 1987.

Longyard, William H. *Who's Who in Aviation History: 500 Biographies.* Novato, Calif.: Presidio, 1994.

Lopez, Donald. *Smithsonian Guides: Aviation.* New York: Macmillan Press, 1995.

Lovell, Mary S. *Straight on Till Morning: The Biography of Beryl Markham.* New York: St. Martin's, 1987.

Lüning, Orjan. *Luftpostens historia i Norden (The History of Airmail in Scandinavia).* Stockholm: Sveriges Filatelist-Förbund, 1978.

Mackworth-Praed, Ben. *Aviation: The Pioneer Years.* London Studio Editions, 1990.

MacMillan, Norman. *Great Flights and Air Adventures.* London: G. Bell and Sons, 1964.

Markham, Beryl. *The Illustrated West with the Night.* Abridged by Elizabeth Claridge, Camden Town, London: Virago, 1989.

Mateu i Pi, Meritxell. *Les années 1930 en Andorre. Incidence sur les mentalités 1930–1935.*

Matthias, Joachim. *Unsere Flièger Erzählen.* Berlin: C.T.E Voldmann Hadsf., Gmbh.

May, Charles. *Women in Aeronautics.* New York: Thomas, Nelson and Sons, 1962.

McFarland, Marvin W. *The Papers of Wilbur and Orville Wright.* New York: McGraw-Hill Book Company, 1953.

McMinnies, William Gordon. *Practical Flying: Complete Course of Flying Instruction.* New York: George H. Doran Company, c. 1918.

Mellor, Capt. C. *The Airman: Experiences While Obtaining a Brevet in France.* London: John Lane, The Bodley Head, 1913.

Melner, Samuel. FAA Historical Staff. "Wiley Post's First Around the World Flight: An Appreciation of the Flight and of Post on its 50th Anniversary."

Meregalli, Jaime, and Carlos L. Bernasconi. *Aportes para la Historia de la Fuerza Aérea Uruguaya.* Montevideo: Imprenta Nacional, 1974.

Miller, Francis Trevelyan. *The World in the Air*. New York: GP Putnam's Sons, 1930.

The Modern Encyclopedia of Russian, Soviet and Eurasian History. Formerly *The Modern Encyclopedia of Russian and Soviet History*. Volumes 12, 14, 15, 16, 17, 18, 20, 60. Gulf Breeze, FL: Academic International, 2000.

Mondey, David. *The International Encyclopedia of Aviation*. New York: Crown Publishers, 1977.

Moolman, Valerie. *The Road to Kitty Hawk*. Alexandria, Va.: Time Life Books, 1980.

_____. *Women Aloft*. Alexandria, Va.: Time Life Books, 1981.

Mormino, Giuseppe. *Storia dell'Aeronautica*. 2nd edition. Milan: Casa Editrice A. Corticelli, 1940.

Morton, Fred. *Aussie Air Stories*. Vols. I–IV. Victoria: West Web Printers, 1985.

Mulgan, David. *The Kiwi's First Wings: The Story of the Walsh Brothers and the New Zealand Flying School 1910–1924*. Wellington: The Wingfield Press, 1960.

Napoleao, Aluizio. *Santos-Dumont and the Conquest of the Air*. Translated by Luiz Victor le Cocq d'Oliviera. Vols. I & II. Ministry of State for Foreign Affairs of Brazil, Division of Intellectual Co-operation; Brazilian Studies Collection. Rio de Janeiro: National Printing Office, 1945.

Nedialkov, Dimitar. *Air Power of the Kingdom of Bulgaria*. Parts I–IV. Sofia, Bulgaria: Fark Ood, n.d.

Negro, Piero Dott. *Nidi d'Aquila*. Torino: Tip. Cesare Valentino, 1927.

Nevin, David. *The Pathfinders*. Alexandria, Va.: Time Life Books, 1980.

Nigeria Annual Report on Civil Aviation. Vols. 1948–1953. Printed and Published by the Government Printer, Lagos.

Notable Flying Men. Compiled by the staff of *The Motor*. London: Temple Press, 1910.

Novo, Salvado. *Historia de la Aviación en Mexico*. Mexico: Publicado por la Compania Mexicana de Aviacion en le 50°. Aniversario de su fundación. 1974.

Nowarra, Heinz J., and G.R. Duval, A.F.M. Alan Myers, trans. *Russian Civil and Military Aircraft 1884–1969*. London: Fountain Press, 1970.

Oakes, Claudia M. *United States Women in Aviation through World War I*. Smithsonian Studies in Air and Space, number 2, Smithsonian Institution, Washington, D.C., 1978.

Oberholzer, Hannes. *Pioneers of Early Aviation in South Africa*. Bloemfontein, Republiek Van Suid-Afrika, 1974.

Orbay, Hasmet Kazim. *Original Guide of Turkish Aviation Museum Republic of Turkey*. Istanbul,Turkey: Turkish Aviation Museum, 1987.

Ovington, Adelaide. *An Aviator's Wife*. New York: Dodd, Mead, 1920.

Park, Edwards. "Langley's Feat and Folly. The Smithsonian Secretary Assembled a Devoted Team, a Remarkable Engine and a Plane That Wouldn't Fly." *Smithsonian* (November 1997) Vol. 28, No. 8, 30–34.

Parramore, Thomas C. *Triumph at Kitty Hawk*. Raleigh, N.C.: Division of Archives and History, 1993.

Payne, Lionel G.S., Air Commodore. *Air Dates*. New York: Frederick A. Praeger, 1957.

Peña Herrera, Juan. *Historia de la Aviación Ecuatoriana: 1842–1943*. Quito, Ecuador: Editorial Quito, c. 1947.

Penrose, Harald. *British Aviation: The Great War and Armistice*. London: Putnam, 1969.

_____. *British Aviation: The Pioneer Years*. London: Putnam, 1967.

Petit, Edmond. *Histoire mondiale de l'Aviation*. Hachette, 1967.

Peyrey, François. *Les Premiers Hommes-Oiseaux, Wilbur et Orville Wright*. Paris: H. Guiton, Imprimeur-Editeur, 35 rue de Trevise, 1909.

Pisano, Dominik A., and Cathleen S. Lewis. Ed. *Air and Space History: Annotated Bibliography*. New York and London: Garland, 1988.

Planck, Charles E. *Women with Wings*. New York and London: Harper and Bros., 1942.

Potgieter, Herman, photographer, various authors. *Aviation in South Africa*. London: Jane's Publishing Company, 1986.

Prada E., Capitán E. P. Alberto Fernández. *La Aviación en el Perú*.

Prendergast, Curtis. *The First Aviators*. Alexandria, Va.: Time Life Books, 1986.

Prytz, Leif. "An Engine and Its Descendants." *Opening Tomorrow's Airways*. pp. 14–16.

Pyragius, J. *Pauksciu Keliais*. Kaunas: Lietuvos Aero Klubo Leidinys, 1933.

Radosavljevic, Radoslav, and Niko Milosević. *Pedeset Pet Godina Juyoslovenskog Vazdahoplovstva*. (*55 Years of Yugoslav Aviation*.) Beograd, 1973.

Rafael del Pino Amanecer en Girón. La Habana: Editorial de Arte y Literatura, 1974.

Render, Shirley. *No Place for a Lady*. Winnipeg, Manitoba, Canada: Portage and Main Press, 1992.

Rennie, Neil. *Conquering Isolation. The First 50 Years of Air New Zealand*. Auckland: Heinemann Reed, 1990.

Report of the Director of Civil Aviation for the Year 1951. British Guiana.

Report on the Opportunities for Civil Air Transport in the West Indies. London: His Majesty's Stationery Office, 1927.

Report on the West African Airways Corporation for the Period Ending 31st March, 1947. Printed and published by the Government Printer, Lagos, 1948.

La République Tchécoslovaque et Son Aviation. Aeroklub R. C. S., Praha (1925).

Rimell, Raymond Lawrence. *WWI Survivors.* Bourne End, Buckinghamshire, England: Aston Publications, 1990.

Roberts, E.G. *Box Kites & Beyond.* Melbourne: The Hawthorne Press, 1979.

Robertson, Bruce, ed. *Air Aces of the 1914–1918 War.* Letchworth: Harleyford Publications, 1959.

Robie, Bill. *For the Greatest Achievement.* Washington and London: Smithsonian Institute Press, 1993.

Rocamora, Manuel. *Historia de la Navegación Aérea en Barcelona. Sequida del Catálogo de la sección española de la colección del autor, desde los precursores hasta 1914.* José Porter, ed. Barcelona: Royal Annam de La Gelidense, 1948.

Rosholt, Malcolm. *Flight in the China Air Space 1910–1950.* Rosholt, Wisc.: Rosholt House, 1984.

Roustam-Bek, Lt. Col. *Aerial Russia: The Romance of the Giant Aeroplane.* London: John Lane, the Bodley Head, 1916.

Royal Aero Club of the United Kingdom. *Royal Aero Club Yearbook.* London: 1914.

_____. *Year Book 1915–1916.* London: Ed. J. Burrow, 1916.

_____. *The Airman's Year Book and Light Aeroplane Manual 1935.* London: Sir Isaac Pitman and Sons, 1935.

Rubenstein, Murray, and Richard Goldman. *Shield of David: An Illustrated History of the Israeli Air Force.* Englewood Cliffs, N.J.: Prentice-Hall, 1978.

Saladin, Raymond. *Les Temps Héroïques de l'Aviation.* Paris: Editions Arcadiennes, 1949.

San, Tan Beng. *Civil Aviation Report Malaya/Borneo Territories.* Vols. 1962–1965. Printed at the Government Printing Office, Singapore, 1963.

Santos, Enrique B. *Trails in Philippine Skies: A History of Aviation in the Philippines from 1909 to 1941.* Manila: Philippine Airlines, 1981.

Sazerac de Forge, Capitaine. "L'Aéroplane Ellehammer." *L'Aérophile.* March 1, 1908, pp. 85, 86.

Schmidt, Dr. F.H., acting director. *Meteorological Data of Indonesian Aerodromes.* Djarkarta, Indonesia: Ministry of Communications Meterological and Geophysical Service, 1949–1952.

Schoenmaker, Wim, and Thijs Postma. *Aviateurs van het Eerste Uur: De Nederlandse Luchtvaart Tut de Eerste Wereldoorlog.* Romen Luchtvarrt, 1984.

Scott, Phil. *The Shoulders of Giants: A History of Human Flight to 1919.* New York: Addison-Wesley, 1995.

Shavrov, V.B. *History of Aircraft Construction in the USSR.* 1994.

Shell Aviation Department. *Air Route Schedule for Cairo, Damascus, Aleppo, Baghdad, Jask, Karachi, Calcutta.* London: Shell Aviation Department, September, 1934.

Shores, Christopher F., Norman Franks and Russell Guest. *Above the Trenches: A Complete Record of the Fighter Aces and Units of the British Empire Air Forces, 1915–1920.* Stoney Creek, Ontario: Fortress Publications, 1990.

Siegrist, Martin E. "Bolivian Air Power—Seventy Years On." *Air International.* October 1987, pp. 170–176, 194.

Silverman, Kenneth. *Houdini!!! The Career of Ehrich Weiss.* New York: HarperCollins, 1996.

Simms, Frederick R. "The Possibilities of Aerial Flight." A paper read before the Society of Literary Twaddlers. London: Adams Brothers, 1902.

Southern Rhodesia Department of Civil Aviation Annual Report. Salisbury, England: Defence Headquarters, March 1935–1936.

Spick, Mike. *Milestones of Manned Flight.* New York: Smithmark Books, 1994.

The Sportsman Pilot. September 1932. Planck, Charles E. "Santos-Dumont—Sportsman," pp. 32–33, 44–45.

Stewart, Oliver. *Aviation: The Creative Ideas.* New York: Frederick A. Praeger, 1966.

_____. *First Flights.* London: Routledge & Kegan Paul, 1957.

The Story of the Pakistan Air Force: A Saga of Courage and Honour. Islamabad, Pakistan: Shaheen Foundation, 1988.

Sunderman, James F., Major, U.S.A.F. *Early Air Pioneers.* New York: Franklin Watts, 1961.

Supf, Peter. *Das Buch der deutschen Fluggeschichte.* Vols. 1–2. Berlin-Grunewald: Verlagsanstalt Hermann Klemm AG, 1956.

Talbot-Booth, E.C., Paymr. Lt. Commandr, R.N.R. *Rank and Badges in the Navy, Army, R.A.F. and Auxiliaries.* London: George Philip and Son, 1940.

Tanner, J.H., Chief Aviation Officer. *Annual Report of the Aviation Department for the Year 1947.* Tanganyika Territory Aviation Department. Printed by the Government Printer, Dar es Salaam, 1948.

Taylor, John W.R., ed. *Combat Aircraft of the World from 1909 to the Present.* New York: G.P. Putnam's Sons, 1969.

_____, Michael J.H. Taylor, and David Mondey. *Air Facts and Feats.* New York: Two Continents Publishing Group, 1973.

_____, and Kenneth Munson. *History of Aviation.* New York: Crown, 1977.

Taylor, Michael J.H. *The Aerospace Chronology.* London: Triservice, 1989.

_____, and David Mondey. *Milestones of Flight.* Janes, 1983.

Thinesen, Johannes. "First Danish Aviator." *Aircraft Illustrated.* November 1976, pp. 445–451.

Thomas, Lowell, and Lowell Thomas, Jr. *Famous*

First Flights That Changed History. Garden City, N.Y.: Doubleday, 1968.

Thornton, A. P. *The Imperial Idea and Its Enemies: A Study in British Power.* London: The Macmillan Press, 1959.

Tilgenkamp, Dr. Erich. *Die Geschicte der Schweizerischen Lufthart.* Vols. 1–3. Zurich: Aero-Verlag, 1941.

Tuchman, Barbara W. *Practicing History: Selected Essays by Barbara W. Tuchman.* New York: Alfred A. Knopf, 1981.

_____. *Stilwell and the American Experience in China, 1911–45.* New York: Macmillan Company, 1970.

Turkish Air Force. Nurol Printing and Trading Co.

Ulanoff, Stanley M., Brig. Gen. and Lt. Col. David Eschel. *The Fighting Israeli Air Force.* New York: Arco Publishing, 1985.

United Kingdom of Great Britain, War Office. *Training Manual, Royal Flying Corps.* London: Her Majesty's Stationery Office, 1914.

Vanthomme, N. "Le premier avion du Baron Pierre de Caters." *Amis du Musée de l'Air et de l'Espace.* Vol. 21 (April 1978), pp. 7–9.

Vazin, F. *The Soviet Airforce.* Moscow: Novosti Press Agency Publishing House, 1975.

Vella, Walter F. *Chaiyo! King Vajiravudh and the Development of Thai Nationalism.* Honolulu: The University Press of Hawaii, 1978.

Villa de la Tapia, Amalia. *Alas de Bolivia. Síntesis Histórica de la Aviación Nacional.* La Paz, Bolivia, 1976.

Villard, Henry Serrano. *Contact! The Story of the Early Birds.* New York: Bonanza Books, 1968.

Villela, Ing José, Jr. *Pioneros de la Aviación Mexicana.* Ixtapalapa, Mexico: Ediciones Colofon, S.A., 1964.

Voisin, Gabriel. *Men, Women and 10,000 Kites.* Translated from the French, *Mes dix mille cerfs volants* (1961), by Oliver Stewart. London: Putnam, 1963.

Wade, W. L. *The Flying Book: The Aviation World Who's Who and Industrial Directory.* London and New York: Longmans, Green, 1914.

Webster, Jack. *The Flying Scots: A Century of Aviation in Scotland.* Glasgow: The Glasgow Royal Concert Hall, n.d.

Weishaupt, Per. "Success Brought Only Honour." *Opening Tomorrow's Airways.* pp. 11–13.

West African Airways Corporation Report and Statements of Account for 1954–55. Printed by the Nigerian Printing and Publishing Company, Airways House, Lagos Airport, Ikeja, 1955.

White, Leo. *Wingspread: The Pioneering of Aviation in New Zealand.* Auckland, New Zealand: White's Aviation, 1945.

Whitehouse, Arch. *The Early Birds: The Wonders and Heroics of the First Decades of Flight.* Garden City, N.Y.: Doubleday, 1965.

Who's Who in World Aviation. Vol 2. Washington, DC: American Aviation Publications, 1958.

Winchester, Clarence, ed. *Wonders of World Aviation.* Vols.1–2. London: The Amalgamated Press, n.d.

Wings for a Nation: A Chronology of Philippine Aviation Development Before World War II 1909–1941. Philippine Air Lines.

Winter, William, William Byshyn, and Hank Clark. *Airplanes of the World, 1490–1976.* New York: Simon and Schuster, 1979.

Wohl, Robert. *The Generation of 1914.* Cambridge, MA: Harvard University Press, 1979.

_____. *A Passion for Wings: Aviation and the Western Imagination, 1908–1918.* New Haven, Conn., and London: Yale University Press, 1994.

Wooldridge, E.T., Jr., *A Directory of Sources for Air and Space History: Primary Historical Collections in United States Repositories.* Washington D.C.: National Air and Space Museum Smithsonian Institution, 1989.

Wrigley, Henry Neilson. *The Battle Below, Being the History of No. 3 Squadron, Australian Flying Corps.* Sydney: Errol G. Knox, 1935.

Wykeham, Peter. *Santos-Dumont: A Study in Obsession.* New York: Harcourt Brace and World, 1962.

Wyndham, L.A. *The Airposts of South Africa.* Cape Town: Cape Times, 1936.

Young, Edward M. *Aerial Nationalism: A History of Aviation in Thailand.* Washington and London: Smithsonian Institution Press, 1994.

Zenopoulos, L. *Civil Aviation Report on Development in the Colony.* Vols. 1960–1961. Government of Cyprus. Printed at the Cyprus Government Printing Office, Nicosia, 1961.

Zeuthen, K. G. "A Hop That Made Aviation History." *Opening Tomorrow's Airways,* pp. 7–10.

Zhívković, Radmío P. *L'aéronautique Yougoslave.* Belgrade: Edition de l'Aero-Club Royal de Yougoslavie, 1935.

Periodicals

Aerial Age Weekly. September 1916.

Aerial Year Book. 1920.

The Aero. 1909–11, 1913.

Aero-Club de Portugal, Boletin trimestral publicado peta Commissão Technica. No. 1, March 1911.

Aero Field. 1926–27.

L'Aero Philatelie. Nos. 1–18, 1925–27.

Aerofan. Trimestrale Anno 4 Gennaio, March 1981.

Aeronautica Argentina. 1934.

Aeronautica Venezuela. Vol. 5, 1948.

Aeronautical Digest. 1922, 1924–31.

Aeronautical World News. 1934.
Aeronautics (London). 1907–9, 1915.
L'Aéronautique. Vol. 4, 1922.
L'Aérophile. 1903–09, 1927.
Aero-Pilot. 1934.
The Aeroplane. 1911–17.
L'Air. Revue Bi-Mensuelle Organe de L'Aviation Française, Paris. 1921.
Air BP. Nos. 4–11, 39–52.
Air Mail Magazine. Nos. 10–51, 1939–1943.
Air Power Historian. Vols. 1–4, 1954–57.
Air Progress. 1938–1942, 1943.
Air Transportation. 1927–28.
Aircraft (Australia). 1936–37.
The Airpost Journal. 1929, 1931–32.
Airways. 1924–26.
L'Ala d'Italia. Direttore: Cipriano Diverio, Pubblicazione Mensile della Editoriale Italiana Aerea. 1922–23.
American Aviation Historical Society Journal. 1956.
Avia. GE illustreerd Tijdschrift Gewijdaan de Luchtvaart. Nos. 1–23, 1911–12.
Aviation. 1916–17, 1921, 1929.
Aviation Heritage. Vols. 2–3, 1991–92.
Aviation History. Vols. 4–5, 1994.
Aviation News. 1930, 1943–44.
Avion. Organo oficial del Real Aero Club de España. Vol. 6, 1951.
Boletin del Aero Club de Chile. 1914–15.
Braunbeck's Sport-Lexicon, Automobilismus, Motorbootwesen, Luftfarht. Berlin: Gustav Braunbeck's Sport-Lexicon.
The Call. University of California at Berkeley. 1909, 1916.
Chirp. Nos 1–82.
Far East Aviation. Published monthly by Grimes and Co. Vol. 1, 1920.
Flight. 1909–12, 1914–40, 1945–46.
Fly. 1908–1909
Flyg. 1945.
Foreign Air News Digest. Part 1.
Historic Aviation. Vol. 2, 1968–70.
Historical Aviation Album. Vols. 1–2, 1965.
History of Aviation. Parts 1–72.
International Aviation. Vol 1, 1944.
Journal of the Aero Club of India and Burma, Vol 3, 1931.
London Times. 1906–1922.
National Aeronautic. 1934.
New York Times. 1903–1914.
News Wing. 1927.

Popular Aviation. 1927–29.
Putnam Aeronatical Review. Nos. 1–4, 1989.
Revista de Aeronautica. Publicada por Los Organismos Aeronauticos Oficiales de la Republica Espanola. Nos. 1–9, 1932.
Revista de Aeronautica. Orgao Oficial Do Aero-Club de Portugal, Lisboa. Vol. 3, 1913–14.
La Revue de l'Aviation. 1906–11.
Romania Aeriana. Sub Inaltulpatronaj Al M. S. Regeliu Carol II, Organul Problemelor Aeriene Aviatie-Aerochimie-Radiofonie. 1937.
Schweizer Aero Review. 1916.
Skylady. Vol. 1, 1945–46.
Skyways. 1942.
Speed. 1930.
Sport Aviation and the Experimenter. Vol. 7, 1958.
Wings Royal New Zealand Aeroclub. 1943–1946.

Smithsonian Institution, National Air & Space Museum Archives, Garber Facility:

Aero History of the 20's and 30's.
Aeronautical News 1921–1935.
Aviation Clippings 1910 Scrapbook.
Aviation Headlines.
Aviation History 1784–1931.
Aviation News Scrapbook.
Aviation Newspaper Clippings 1911–1912.
Early Aviation 1910.
Early Aviation Photo Album.
Early Aviation Photographs.
Early Aviation Seaplanes and Landplanes.
Early Bird files.
Glenn Curtiss Scrapbook.
McCauley Collection.
Moisant Scrapbooks.
Morehouse papers.
National Aeronautical Association Records.
New York Times and Tribune Aviation Page 1919.
Paul Weisser Photo Albums.
Rumanian Air Meet.
William H. Leininger World War I Collection.
World War I Aviators Photos and Autographs.
World War I German Aviation Photo Album.
World War I Italian Naval Air Photo Album.
World War I News Clippings.

Index